The Art of NEWS COMMUNICATION

a beginning textbook
for classes in news writing

by

CHILTON R. BUSH

Director, Institute for Journalistic Studies
Stanford University

New York
APPLETON-CENTURY-CROFTS, Inc.

TO
PALMER HOYT

WHO SHOULD BE A PROFESSOR
WHENEVER THERE IS ESTABLISHED
A SCHOOL FOR PUBLISHERS

PREFACE

THIS BOOK is an effort to meet the demand for an elementary textbook that focuses on the *writing* of news. It now seems possible to have a textbook that not only reflects the influence of radio and readability research on news writing, but also one that is based on the recent findings of the researchers in communication.

We now have, to a considerable degree, a new way of writing news. The new way is not necessarily very different from the old way or from the way that the perceptive elder editors used to teach. Instead, however, of having its basis in the accumulated dicta of professors and editors, news writing today has its rationale in the writer's conscious recognition of his audience. The main difference, therefore, is in the attitude of the news writer, namely, that he is a communicator as well as an artist.

This book tries to develop that attitude in the beginning student. Yet the text is in the tradition of the 1913 edition of Bleyer's *Newspaper Writing and Editing* to the extent that it is primarily about the techniques of writing news and not very much about the techniques of gathering news. It concentrates almost entirely on helping the beginner to write news because that alone is a sufficient task.

Consequently, much has been omitted here. There are advanced textbooks about reporting the courts and public business and about libel. The student should study such materials—especially the substantive materials—in advanced courses in which there can be a thorough treatment of the subjects. Presentation in an elementary textbook of a smattering of such complex material is disadvantageous to the student at both the elementary and advanced stages of his training.

Most of the techniques of reporting are presented best by the instructor in class and in conference. Some direction and assistance in reporting, however, have been supplied in the Exercises.

The author has tried to avoid the presentation of dicta. As the distinguished editor of the Cleveland *Press* has said, "Too many newspapers are inflexibly anchored to rules." Whenever a rule is stated in this book, we have tried to explain its basis either in the science of communication or in art. We have tried to avoid, for example, pat statements about readability formulas so that the student will understand *why* he should prefer (say) concrete words or short average sentences. He will probably be a better communicator if he learns why he should write a certain way than if he is told merely to follow a formula.

The book is deliberately pitched on the "adult" level. The author assumes that the usual student is a sophomore or junior who has had college courses in English composition and an introductory course in psychology. There seems no good reason for a textbook on news writing that is a primer. As a treatise on the science of communication, however, it scarcely achieves the level of a primer; it is hardly an introduction to that complex subject.

The discussion refers simultaneously to both the newspaper and radio. News writing for these two media requires few distinctions. The differences are mentioned, however, whenever the author is aware of them.

Although all of the reading material will presumably be assigned during the first term, some of the exercises may be assigned for the remainder of the year. In some institutions, this means that during the second term the student will do some of the exercises in the laboratory as well as do outside reporting assignments. In that sense, the book is designed for a one-year course.

A major purpose of the exercises is to elaborate the discussion in the text. The instructor is advised to read in advance all of the exercises that refer to the text because they are designed to assist class discussion of the points in the text. That is true of some of the writing exercises as well as of the problem exercises. A few of the exercises relate to ethics.

The exercises were prepared on the assumption that the student would begin to do news writing in the first week.

The author is especially indebted to Dr. Albert G. Pickerell. His understanding of the English language and his practical experience on newspapers and news agencies made his advice of inestimable value. Although his assistance almost amounted to joint authorship, he is not responsible for any of the faults in the book.

The author is also indebted to several newspapers and all of the news agencies for many of the examples. These have generally been acknowledged in the text. In several instances, the author has drawn examples from the reports of the continuing study committees of the Associated Press Managing Editors Association, and he does not feel he should let the opportunity pass to acknowledge the contributions to effective news communication of Dr. Rudolf Flesch, Alan J. Gould, Victor Hackler, and the various chairmen of those committees.

The author also thanks Professors Roy E. Carter, Jr. and Clifford F. Weigle for their critical reading of portions of the manuscript, and Thomas M. Newell, who devised some of the exercises.

C. R. B.

CONTENTS

CONTENTS

Chapter I ···

THE COMMUNICATION PROCESS

PROBABLY VERY FEW readers of this book have ever heard of the unusual language in which the following message is transcribed:

$$31610\ 92618\ 02402\ 45655$$

Translated into the English language, it means: "Tuesday 6 P.M. From 61 degrees north latitude, 92 degrees 36 minutes west longitude: Breeze blowing from north northeast; cloudy; barometer 945 millibars; moderate visibility; temperature 55 degrees Fahrenheit."

This language is the International Code for Radio Weather Reports from Ships. Its vocabulary is not familiar to lay persons, but it is understood by every meteorologist in the world, no matter in which country he lives. Meteorologists can translate it in about 15 seconds because they are familiar with the code and because they take it down on a form that has four five-verbal-unit boxes.

One way in which this code differs from the English language is that it is *not redundant*. When more symbols than are necessary are used to encode a message we say the code (or language) is redundant. The international weather code is not redundant because the verbal units are not related to each other: each verbal unit has an independent meaning and *only one meaning* (although the sequence in which the encoder sends the verbal units is specified). Since the code is not redundant, it contains *no verbal context*[1]—except that a trained receiver might find some inconsistency in a message (e.g., the barometric reading might not accord with the reported weather) and suspect a mistake had been made in encoding.

This introduction to the subject-matter of this chapter—and to much of the material in this book—is not as far fetched as it may now seem. As the reader continues through the book, he will (we hope) come to think of news writing as communication, and he will come to be more aware that he must encode a message that can be decoded easily. If he does, he can expect as a news writer a larger audience than the news writer who assumes that all of his readers are as familiar as he is with the code that is the English language.

The diagram below (Fig. 1) illustrates the news communication process. It is descriptive of all interpersonal communi-

Fig. 1. A simplified communication system.

cation systems in that it represents the encoding and decoding of a message. It shows how the encoder (news writer for the newspaper or radio) sends a message to the decoder (reader or listener) by the use of written or spoken symbols.

The problem of the encoder is how to manipulate the symbols in the way that maximizes the efficiency of the decoding process. (The encoder also sometimes has the function of using the symbols in a way that maximizes the emotional satisfaction of the reader or listener; that function will be discussed in later sections of this book.)

[1] Verbal context are the parts of a written or spoken discourse that precede or follow a specific expression and are directly related to it.

News in the newspaper and on the radio is a "mediated" communication. The encoder of a news message directs his message to thousands of persons who decode it at the same time. The encoder sometimes forgets (or is unaware) that the individual members of his large audience have varying efficiencies of decoding. If the encoder, therefore, wishes his message to be received by a large audience, he must adapt his message to the decoding efficiency of as many members of his audience as possible.

The encoder's task is made harder because of the factors of "noise." [2] These factors are represented in the diagram by the wavy lines of the message. We describe and illustrate these factors further along in this chapter. The encoder of news messages sometimes forgets about (or is unaware of) the interference of the "noise" factors.

The usual encoder of news messages is highly efficient in the use of the symbols of communication—so much so that he sometimes incorrectly assumes the decoder is equally efficient. The encoder has a large stock of symbols to choose from and sometimes selects those that are hard for the receiver of the message to decode, or he arranges them in a pattern that is not adapted to the decoder's semantic [3] capacities.

The main problem of the encoder is to make certain that his message can be decoded correctly and *with the least effort* by the decoder. The probability of his achieving this objective depends upon (*a*) his selection of symbols, and (*b*) his presentation of the selected symbols in the order which their interdependence requires. The first is mainly a matter of diction, the second a matter of organization and syntax. These points will be discussed at length in later chapters.

[2] This term is used by students of information theory to refer to those disturbances in the channel of communication that change the symbols or permute their sequence. See C. E. Shannon and W. Weaver, *The Mathematical Theory of Communication* (University of Illinois, 1949); also G. A. Miller, *Language and Communication* (New York, 1951).

[3] We use this expression generically to include both the meaning of words and the arrangement and relation of words (syntax).

How we read: Only very inefficient readers read one word at a time. Most of us perceive words in groups. This fact is illustrated by Fig. 2, which is a photograph of the eye movements of a specific reader. The camera has photographed the reflections of a light beam on the reader's eyes as they oscillated over the lines of print.[4] The numbers above the line indicate the order of the successive fixation pauses of the eyes. It will be noted that the order in one line is not 1, 2, 3, and 4, but 1, 2, 4, and 3. Some of these are regressions (i.e., the reader has to go back and reread a part of the line). An inefficient reader will have more fixation pauses per line and will make more regressions (i.e., he will have to go back over a part of a line and start again) than an efficient reader. A very inefficient reader will exhibit a *cluster* of fixation pauses which indicates mental confusion—as if he were trying to decipher a complex code. This is in contrast with the efficient reader whose eyes move in a rhythmic progression with few regressions and with very few clusters of fixation pauses.

The numbers at the bottom of the lines show the duration of the fixation pauses in thirtieths of one second. An inefficient reader will exhibit a longer average duration of fixation pauses than an efficient reader—indicating a slower recognition of the word or group of words. The average reader reads average writing at the rate of about 250 words a minute. This is about four words a second and the duration of his fixation pauses is about one-fourth of a second.

Reading ability, as measured by the eye-camera, is not solely a measure of a reader's intelligence or vocabulary (although these are components of reading ability), but also of certain physiological and psychological factors. One can increase his reading ability by increasing his eye span without regard to his intelligence or vocabulary. That is, he can train

---

[4] For a full discussion of the operation, see G. T. Buswell, "How Adults Read," *Supplementary Educational Monographs, The School Review and Elementary School Journal,* No. 45 (August, 1937).

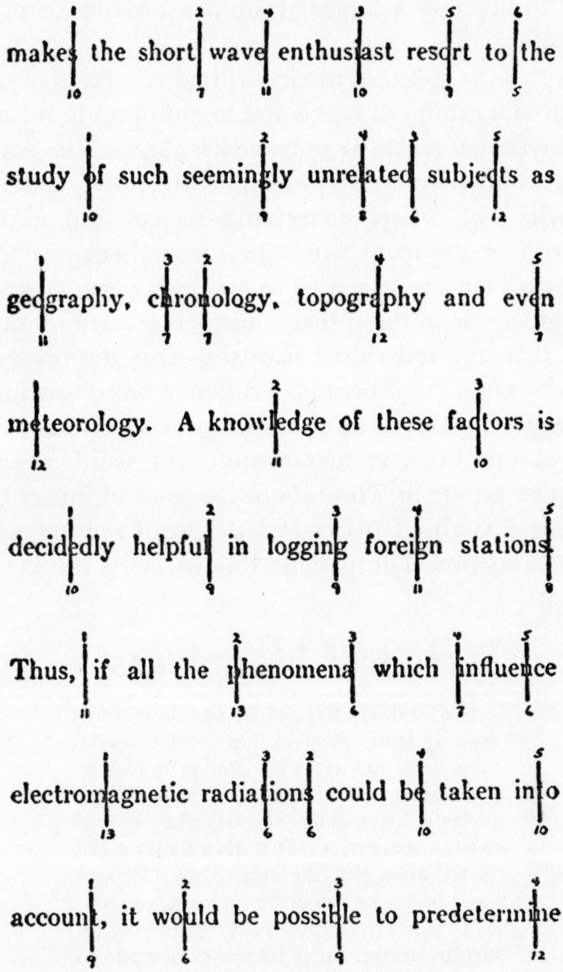

makes the short wave enthusiast resort to the
study of such seemingly unrelated subjects as
geography, chronology, topography and even
meteorology. A knowledge of these factors is
decidedly helpful in logging foreign stations
Thus, if all the phenomena which influence
electromagnetic radiations could be taken into
account, it would be possible to predetermine

Fig. 2. Illustrating the eye movements of a reader [by Professor Guy T. Buswell]. The vertical lines designate the centers of fixation as the eyes move across the lines of type. The numerals above each line show the order in which the fixations occurred; for some lines they show a regression by the reader.

The numerals below the lines indicate the length of time the eyes stopped at each center of fixation. This unit is 1-30 of a second; thus the first fixation lasted 10 one-thirtieths of one second.

himself to perceive a larger group of words in a single fixation.[5]

Whatever the speed of the individual reader, his eyes focus on words and groups of words and he stores up in his memory their provisional meaning until he has reached the end of the sentence. This is an active process in which the reader thinks along with the writer—perceiving images and evaluating. Each word or group of words he comprehends in terms of the context that was presented in previous words or sentences.

The process is so rapid that context is sometimes more important than the individual words—so that the reader sometimes misreads a word because a different word was suggested by the context. Here is an example of how this happens: the author of this book at first misread the word *imports* for *prices* in an article in *Time* about the price of butter because the article was about prices and the word *soaring* preceded the word *imports*. The passage follows, with the key words italicized:[6]

Pursuit of Happiness

Is everybody happy? In the dairy business, at least, the U.S. has tried to make them so. Housewives who had grumbled at the high *price* of butter were made happy as state after state allowed the sale of colored margarine. This didn't please the butter men. But the Agriculture Department had a way to make them happy, too: it promised to support *prices* by buying up surplus butter. An effort was even made to make foreign dairymen happy. They were allowed to ship as much dried milk, cream

[5] The average adult slackens his reading speed after leaving college because he reduces the amount of his reading, especially of books.—N. Lewis, *How to Read Better and Faster,* rev. ed. (New York, 1951), p. 14.

[6] In recognition of this aspect of decoding, some of the news agencies require that the report of a person being acquitted in a criminal trial state that he was found "innocent": too many tape punchers and printers have failed to perceive the "not" in "not guilty" in the original copy.

and buttermilk to the U.S. as they wanted
to send. That seemed to take care of every-
one.

But soon this pursuit of happiness ran
into a detour. Oleo sales boomed and butter *prices* melted. Soaring *imports* of dried
dairy products displaced millions of quarts
of U.S. milk, etc.

Listeners to the radio have the same problem of miscom-
prehension because they have missed some word or expression
and have relied on the context. For example, some person has
mistakenly been reported dead because his name was used in
connection with the name of a person who had actually died:
"Actor John Bradford, whose wife is the glamorous Betty
Bauer, died last night in Hollywood."

It is a common experience of editors to receive inquiries
about the rumored death of some prominent person who has
happened to be in the news in some other connection, as for
example, when Herbert Hoover's birthday anniversary was
observed and Clark Gable was married. This is sometimes
because the listener has tuned in after the broadcast has
begun and has supplied some context that he had in mind.
Shortly after the Lindbergh baby was kidnaped in 1932, the
Associated Press in New York received numerous telephone
messages that the baby's body had been found near Princeton,
New Jersey. Origin of the false reports was this radio broadcast: "New Jersey State Police have just announced that there
is no truth to the report that *the Lindbergh baby's body has
been found near Princeton.*" Listeners who had tuned in late
had heard only the italicized part of the message. It is a safe-
guard, therefore, to place the negative part of a radio message at the end of the sentence; thus: "The New Jersey State
Police have just announced that a rumor about the finding of
the Lindbergh baby's body is not true." [7]

[7] For an account of this episode, see Robert St. John, *This Was My World*
(New York, 1953), pp. 306-307.

Radio listeners have a more passive mental set than readers. They do not use eye movements in decoding, but submit to the pace of the newscaster. One reason that many persons prefer to get their news from the radio is that they are inefficient readers.[8]

The "noise" factors: When one starts to read a book or to view a film he is relaxed and he expects to give his whole and his uninterrupted attention to the medium. He frequently has the same mental set when he starts to read a magazine, a news magazine, or the Sunday newspaper on Sunday. When he reads a daily newspaper or when he listens to the news on the radio, however, he is not always attentive. Much news reading is done while the reader is achieving some other goal; for example, while riding to and from work or while eating. Some reading is done when the reader is weary and the act of reading is a respite. He has to do his daily reading, generally, between alternative kinds of behavior: during breakfast, on the way to and from work, before dinner is ready, after dinner before his favorite television program comes on, and before some folks come in to play bridge. His wife must do her reading after dishes are done or before she goes shopping; she often gets her radio news, however, while she is ironing or dusting.

Any or all of these factors constitute what we have called "noise" because they interfere with the efficient decoding of the news communication. Specifically, they constitute "channel noise" (or, as the information theorists say, "engineering noise") because they are disturbances in the channel of communication that alter the message in some way after it has left the encoder. "Channel noise" can be compensated for to a great extent by the encoder's elimination of "semantic noise." [9] The latter, technically, is a discrepancy between the

---

8 See P. F. Lazarsfeld, *Radio and the Printed Page* (New York, 1940), Chap. 4.

9 See footnote 3 on p. 3.

codes used by the encoder and the decoder. In terms of English diction and syntax, semantic noise may mean, for example, that the encoder is using words that the decoder does not understand or the encoder is using a sentence pattern that is confusing to the decoder or the encoder has organized his facts in a confusing order. A considerable part of this book is a discussion of how to eliminate semantic noise.

Conditions for writing: Newspaper format: Just as the decoder of a news message is handicapped by "noise," the encoder is restricted by certain factors that determine the form and clearness of the communication. We could say that these factors also are imperfections in the "channel" of communication. The writer for the newspaper must generally present the communication in a column which is, on the average, less than two inches wide; in types that are sometimes too small to accommodate readers of poor vision; in a form that permits the copyreader or makeup man to cut the news story from the bottom; in a form that will accommodate insertions of new matter for later editions; and in a space that is often limited by the competition with other reading matter. These mechanical restrictions often force the news writer to adopt conventionalities of style and structure that make the decoding process harder.

Certain other aspects of format, however, assist the decoder. For example, headlines present the gist of a news story and thereby provide a synopsis for the hurried reader so he can select those messages he prefers to read. Subheads within the news story and other typographical devices are calculated to enlist the reader's interest in the later parts of the news story. Art is placed next to some news stories to give the reader a visual image of some of the subject-matter.

Limitations of the decoder: Only a minority of the news writer's audience are his intellectual peers, yet the writer often assumes that all of them are. He assumes too often that all of the members of his audience have the same education that he has had, forgetting that only 15 per cent of the adults in this country have ever attended college and that the average person over 25 years of age has had only 9.3 years of schooling.[10]

He sometimes also overestimates the vocabulary of most of his readers. The average recognition vocabulary of an American is about 10,000 words.[11] How small this actually is will be impressed upon the news writer who makes a cursory examination of the Thorndike-Lorge *Teacher's Word Book of 30,000 Words*.[12] He will be astonished to note that many words that are familiar to him are not listed among the 10,000 most commonly used words. A vocabulary of 9000 words is required for reading the New York *Daily News*, the newspaper of largest circulation in the United States and one with an easy readability.[13]

The following compensating facts about vocabulary should be noted, however. First, the average adult has increased his recognition vocabulary since leaving school; this means that his vocabulary is actually somewhat larger than that of one who has just finished the ninth or tenth grade. Second, many adults—especially males—have some technical vocabulary which is related to their particular occupation. Third, the decoder's lack of a large vocabulary, as will be explained in later chapters, can be largely compensated for by the encoder who is skillful in handling context and in arranging words in a familiar pattern.

Lack of a certain kind of vocabulary, however, is of distinct disadvantage to the decoder when the news communication

10 U. S. Bureau of the Census, *Census of Population, 1950* Series PC-7, No. 6 (May 13, 1952), p. 6. This is a national average; a comparable statistic for San Francisco, for example, is 11.7 years and for Oakland 11.5 years. U. S. Bureau of the Census, *Census of Population, 1950*, "Census Tract Statistics for San Francisco-Oakland," Bull. P-D49, pp. 7 and 14.

11 S. S. Smith, *The Command of Words* (New York, 1949), p. 13.

12 E. L. Thorndike and I. Lorge, *Teacher's Word Book of 30,000 Words* (New York, 1949).

13 Smith, *op. cit.*, p. 12.

contains terms used in government, in the courts, in finance, in medicine, and in other spheres of life that are outside the experience world of the reader or listener.

The writer must understand that the reader and listener are self-selective in what they read or listen to. The reader of a metropolitan daily newspaper, for example, devotes to his reading, on the average, a little more than one minute per page; this means that he skips many items entirely. Such a newspaper contains about the same number of words as the usual novel. If a particular news communication does not immediately yield meaning to the reader, he forsakes it for another news story or for some alternative form of behavior. What determines his selection is sometimes the subject-matter: he rejects a particular news story because the information it contains does not relate to his personal needs or his past experience. Often, however, he rejects a news story because of its form: the facts are poorly organized, the sentence structure is complex, or some of the vocabulary lacks meaning for him.

Equally as important is the fact that, although the reader or listener does attend to the message to the extent that he reads it or listens to it, he may not adequately comprehend it. This is the same as saying that some of the news is not meaningful. A case in point is a study made by the Audience Research Department of the British Broadcasting Corporation of a news commentary program. "Topic for Tonight" is a five-minute-talk broadcast five days a week after the 10 o'clock news program in the "Light Programme" designed "to provide, in an interesting way, succinct background information about some items in the news, and directed to the broad mass of the population." The talk is heard by 30 per cent of the adult population during the course of a week. The study revealed that the average listener understood only 28 per cent of the ideas and facts presented and that some of them were not those that the commentator thought were most important.

The assigned reasons for the incomprehensibility of the talks were: (1) overestimation of the listener's background knowledge; (2) too many difficult words; (3) poor organization of ideas and facts; and (4) absence of repetition (i.e., not enough redundancy).[14]

Redundancy: Redundancy is that part of a message which is unnecessary and therefore is repetitive. Repetition, however, increases the probability that the communication will be understood. If parts of the message are lost—because of "noise"—it can yet be intelligible if the message is sufficiently redundant: the redundancy provides enough contextual clues for the decoder of the message to supply the "missing" parts of the message.

This principle is well recognized in public speaking, but has been ignored somewhat in news writing. The reason is that repetition is monotonous, and news writers, trained in English classes, have often emphasized style at the expense of efficiency of communication. Repetitions of the same symbols, especially when they are fairly adjacent in a message, make for a monotony that is unpleasant to the reader and listener. As one writer has said: "The reader will feel as if he's listening to bagpipes with only the drone working."[15] Just as important in communication, however, is the necessity for the reader or listener to understand the message. Hence, the problem for the news communicator is how to make his message sufficiently redundant without making it offensively monotonous.[16]

In later sections, we shall distinguish redundancy from mere wordiness and shall discuss those devices which reduce

[14] W. A. Belson, "Topic for Tonight," *The B.B.C. Quarterly*, Vol. 7 (1952), pp. 65-70; and W. Allen, "The Question of Intelligibility," *op. cit.*, pp. 147-151.

[15] Smith, *op. cit.*, p. 129.

[16] We are speaking here of *understanding* a news message, not remembering it. Apparently, "repetition of facts in a newscast has no significant effect on an audience memory of these facts." See, T. W. Harrell, D. E. Brown, and W. Schramm, "Memory in Radio News Listening," *Journal of Applied Psychology*, Vol. 33 (1949), pp. 265-274.

monotony and those situations in which redundancy is desirable. At this point it is sufficient to state that news sometimes is not as meaningful as it could be because the writer has an exaggerated fear of redundancy. There is too much emphasis by some editors today on "tight writing" which is achieved at the expense of efficient communication.[17] The postwar demand for tight writing is, in several instances, based on a species of reasoning about the high cost of newsprint: that each line of news "costs 20 cents." Such reasoning neglects to consider how well readers are satisfied with the ways in which news is presented to them. Readers may want "more news in fewer words," but they also want to know what the words mean.

An excellent example of how repetition increases the probability that the communication will be understood is a news story by James Marlow, of the Associated Press Washington bureau, about the expected arrival in the United States on October 30, 1948, of 813 displaced persons from Europe. The following facts were pertinent: (1) there were then in Europe 750,000 persons who had been classified as "DPs"; (2) the special law passed by the United States Congress permitted the admission of a total of 205,000 (these being in addition to those who were admitted under the existing law which regulated admission of aliens by annual quotas from various countries); (3) only 40,000 DPs had previously been admitted under the existing law; and (4) 22 per cent of all DPs are Jews.

The writer repeated fact (1) four times, fact (2) four times, fact (3) five times, fact (4) twice, and the fact that 813 DPs were due to arrive "tomorrow" three times. Why so much repetition? The writer was aware of the possibility that some readers would interpret the statistics to mean, perhaps, that 750,000 DPs were arriving, or that 205,000 European Jews

17 See, for example, editors' responses to a United Press Associations survey, *Editor & Publisher*, January 31, 1953, p. 11.

were admitted every year under the existing law, and so forth.

"Economizing" the receiver's attention: Compliance with most of the rules of writing—as Herbert Spencer [18] so clearly pointed out as long ago as 1865—insures that the reader's or listener's attention is "economized." These rules require that ideas be presented so they "may be apprehended with the least possible mental effort:"

A reader or listener has at each moment but a limited amount of mental power available. To recognize and interpret the symbols presented to him, requires part of this power; to arrange and combine the images suggested requires a further part; and only that part which remains can be used for realizing the thought conveyed. Hence the more time and attention it takes to receive and understand each sentence, the less time and attention can be given to the contained idea; and the less vividly will that idea be conceived . . . .

Carrying out the metaphor that language is the vehicle of thought, there seems reason to think that in all cases the friction and inertia of the vehicle deduct from its efficiency; and that in composition, the chief, if not the sole thing to be done, is, to reduce this friction and inertia to the smallest possible amount.

In some cases, redundancy has the effect of economizing the reader's time and effort in the sense that Spencer refers to. How this is done is explained in a later section.

Understanding radio and print: There is some reason to believe that a radio newscast is somewhat more difficult to understand than the same matter in print. The data derived from an experiment by Chall and Dial,[19] who used reading ability formulas on a group of college freshman subjects, seem to indicate that, beginning with fairly difficult material (ninth grade and above), the listening difficulty is probably a grade or two above the reading difficulty. For example, a

[18] "The Philosophy of Style" in *Essays: Moral, Political and Aesthetic* (New York, 1865), pp. 11-12.

[19] J. S. Chall and H. E. Dial, "Listener Understanding and Interest in Newscasts," *Educational Research Bulletin*, 27:141-153, 168 (Sept., 1948).

story rated approximately eleventh-to-twelfth-grade reading level probably rises to a level of thirteenth and fourteenth grade when heard. Flesch [20], quoting other studies, says: "If material is put on the air rather than on the printed page, easy matter becomes easier but difficult matter more difficult. Radio will therefore magnify differentials in difficulty detected by the writer's formula.[21]

Chall and Dial,[22] in 1948, found that state news on the WOSU radio wire was more difficult than national and foreign news, and that national news was more difficult than foreign news. Probably the main reason for these differences in news of different geographical origins is that the readability formulas they used included number of personal references as one of the measures. State news, because it relates primarily to governmental activities, probably contains fewer personal references than national or foreign news. The same fact would probably explain the difference between national and foreign news, because foreign news on the radio is of such dramatic character.

Summary: This chapter has described those factors in mediated communication that restrict the encoder and decoder of a news communication and, hence, reduce communication efficiency. Those factors reside in the medium and in the decoder, and can be compensated for only by the high efficiency of the encoder.

The key terms in this chapter are *channel noise, semantic noise, regression, context,* and *redundancy.* The student should be sure that he comprehends them, for he will meet them again in later chapters.

[20] Rudolf Flesch, *Marks of Readable Style: A Study in Adult Education,* p. 43. Contribution to Education No. 897 (New York, Teachers College, Columbia University, 1943).
[21] For an explanation of the Flesch formula, see pp. 94-98.
[22] *Op. cit.*

Chapter II

THE AUDIENCE FOR NEWS

THE FACSIMILE of a newspaper front page found on the next page shows the percentage of adult male readers and the percentage of adult female readers of the individual items. These percentage scores do not mean that the readers have read an item clear through—although they may have; the scores mean that the readers have read the headline and a significant part of the item. (The symbol "M" refers to men and the symbol "W" refers to women.)

The scores do not tell us a great deal about the nature of reading behavior. They do tell us, however, a few things— especially the differences between men's reading and women's reading. The news story under the banner headline, for example, is about the action of a United States Senate committee, which passed a resolution to require the consent of Congress before our troops could be sent to Europe. It is the highest read story by men—68 per cent. Although *some* item on the front page was read by 98 per cent of the men, about one-third of the men (32 per cent) did *not* read this item that the editor thought was the most important one. The same item was read by only 38 per cent of the women. An examination of the other scores will show that the items most interesting to women were about people—the accidental death of a United States senator and an airplane accident. The women were much more interested in the death of an obscure senator than in the action of a committee of the United States

Ene... Hordes Flee ...ed Smash

The Bakersfield Californian

Vol. 64   7 CENTS PER COPY   FOUR SECTIONS   BAKERSFIELD, CALIFORNIA, THURSDAY, MARCH 8, 1951   48 PAGES   7 CENTS PER COPY   ★ ★ ★   No. 188

SOLONS APPROVE TROOP CHECK

Prosecution Asked in RFC Inquiry

Dunham Tells of Approach as "Fall Guy"

WASHINGTON — (AP) — Senator investigating the RFC Director Walter L. Dunham...

Earlier, they had held a short closed door cross-examination of RFC Director Walter L. Dunham and had quoted him as saying a fellow board member urged him to resign and "become the fall guy" in the subcommittee's investigation.

Fulbright and Dunham caused Director C. Edward Rowe as the man who made the proposal.

Documents Filed

Another subcommittee member, Senator Capehart (R-Ind.), said Dunham used the words "become the fall guy" in describing the incident.

Continued on Page 2

Witness Balks at Red Hunt

WASHINGTON — (AP) — ...

Atomic Spy Plot Unfolded

D.C., in June 1944. This in halt, was five years after he had been recruited into the Communist party by a member of the defendants. — Martin Sobell.

The third defendant is Rosenberg's wife, Ethel. All are accused of gathering atomic secrets for Russia in wartime.

Foe Loses 11,600 Men in 24 Hours

Eighth Army Drives Ahead Up to 2½ Miles on Wide Front

TOKYO — (AP) — The 8th ... up to ... mile front ... Red ... from ... hours of ...

 ...

signs of a general withdrawal taking place along the defenses of five Chinese armies and three North Korean corps—perhaps 200,000 men.

The U.S., Canadian, Australian, Greek and South Korean troops killed and wounded 11,600 Reds in ground action since yesterday—new record for the Korean war. At least 250 prisoners were taken.

The air forces accounted for ad—

Continued on Page 2

Senator Dies of Injuries After Crash

 ... Senator ... Kentucky died ... suffered ... collided with a ...

Admiral M. D. Willcutts, commanding officer of the hospital, said Chapman suffered ... lung and other internal injuries.

Veteran of House

Although Chapman was serving his first term as a senator, he had been a member of the House for 22 years before he moved up to the Senate in 1948. He defended former Republican Senator John Sherman Cooper, who is now a state department consultant.

In the House he was considered to be an expert on tobacco and farming. He carried the farm subsidy.

Continued on Page 2

Six Aboard Crashed Plane Saved From Sea

ROME, Italy — (AP) — Seven of the persons aboard the plane which disappeared on a flight from Trieste to Rome...

The Privateer crashed in the shortly after the pilot radioed Rome's Ciampino airport at 1 p.m. (6 a.m. E.S.T.) yesterday that he was having engine trouble.

The plane, en route to Rome from Udine, Italy, apparently overshot the Italian capital, officials here said.

Girl, 12, Burned in Cooking Meal

SAN DIEGO — (AP) — ...

condition in a hospital.

Plane Falls; 9 Crewmen Bail Out

WOODLAND — (AP) — Seven of the ...

The airmen were accounted for others were ...

number was ... firefighter flew to Sacramento in a ...

Three were the March and May positions, meaning certain able in those months.

Prices showed gains of as much as 200 points or $10 a bale. A cotton contract of 100 bales bought just before the market closed January 26 on the price freeze order, would have brought a gross profit today of $1000 on three free months. Other positions showed gains between $7 and $10 a bale. The $10 rise is the limit of fluctuation permitted by the exchange.

COTTON PRICES UP $10 BALE TO HIT CEILING

NEW YORK — (AP) — ...

Writer of Hit Plays Is Dead

Forty-five minutes later the main part of the wreckage was blazing furiously.

The plane dug a huge crater where it landed. Deputies estimated it buried itself 12 feet in the ground. They said the crater was about 60 feet by 20 feet in area.

Richard Walton Tully, the beloved playwright, who wrote "The Bird of Paradise." They were divorced in 1914.

Phone Men Return Pending New Talks

SAN FRANCISCO — (AP) — ...today morning. A union spokesman said the men were tried by the technician...

Offer Own Resolution

Bradley Eyes Rocking Chair

NEW YORK — (AP) — ...

14-10 Vote Favors Voice for Congress

Major Contribution by Europe Also Asked by Committees

WASHINGTON — (AP) — ... control. ... Johnston ... requiring ... house approval of the North ...

The Senate foreign relations and armed services committees approved a proposal by Senator Lodge (R-Mass.) to put the Senate on record as saying European nations must make the "major contribution" to ground forces under the command of General Dwight D. Eisenhower.

This reversed a 13-12 tie vote by which a similar proposal by Lodge was defeated yesterday.

Chairman Connally (D-Texas) and nine other Democrats were outvoted in the two moves by a coalition reported to have been made up of all of the Republicans members of the joint group plus three Democrats.

Democrats Named

Although Connally refused to make public the roll call, the three Democrats were reported to have been Senators George (D-Ga.), Byrd (D-Va.) and Stennis (D-Miss.).

Eleven Republicans were registered, but Senator Vandenberg (R-Mich.), ill and absent, was not recorded.

The proposals were within line a resolution which Connally and Senator Russell (D-Ga.) have sponsored to put the Senate on record as favoring the administration plan to send troops to join Eisenhower's western European army.

The committees, which held lengthy hearings on the issue, approved the plan in principle yesterday.

Offer Own Resolution

Connally said members of the coalition served notice that while they will support the Connally-Russell resolution, they want it supplemented by an identical resolution which would require action by both houses and have the form of law.

The administration has announced plans to send four more divisions, bringing to six the total number of U.S. units available there for the North Atlantic defense command of General Dwight D. Eisenhower.

Yesterday's 12 to 11 vote came on a motion to proceed with the

Continued on Page 2

Senate. Men read more of the news stories about government and business than did women, but they also were interested in stories about people.

By averaging the scores, we note that the men read 43 per cent of the items and women read 35 per cent. Thus, the "average man" did *not* read half of the items and the "average woman" did *not* read two-thirds of them. In the discussion which follows, we shall pay some attention to the kinds of news that people do not read—as well as to the kinds they do read.

This chapter, however, is not so much about the kinds of news that people read and do not read as it is about why people read and listen to news. Nor is it a definitive explanation of news reading behavior. In the first place, we still have a great deal to learn about reading behavior. In the second place, the only reason for such a chapter in a book of this kind is to tell the student something about the people to whom the news writer addresses his news communication. The statements that follow, therefore, are provisional explanations.

Why do people read and listen to news? [1] A few people read news for a prestige reason: the news supplies an agenda for conversation, and the reader likes to appear well-informed when he talks to others in his business and social circles. Probably all people read news to conduct a surveillance of their environment so as to adjust their behavior and thought to situations they feel the need to control—to control either by their own acts or by the acts of a group they belong to. Probably all people read news as a social activity: they become acquainted in the news with persons and personages mentioned there and they sometimes experience vicariously the actions of these news subjects. People also read so as to relive their own experiences, as, for example, when they read

[1] In this and the following sections of this chapter, "reading" means generically "reading *and* listening"; this is to avoid repeating a long phrase.

on Sunday morning about the football game they saw on Saturday afternoon.

News reading gives pleasure: The gratification that people get from reading news is what psychologists call *reduction of tension*. The newspaper reader, responding to the headline cue, anticipates novelty and this mental state arouses tension. Reading reduces the tension and this reduction of tension is pleasurable, rewarding. The reward may be what Schramm [2] has called "immediate." The following oversimplified explanation of this process is adequate for our present purpose. The reader sees, for example, a news story about an auto accident. He reads it to find out if it relates to somebody he knows. By reading it, he is rewarded immediately, whether he recognizes a name or not. Of course, he may also feel pain if the person he knows has been injured or killed, but he was rewarded originally because refraining from reading would not have reduced the tension: the reader experiences a reduction of tension even though tension was also aroused by the bad news.

The reader, however, may also read for an *instrumental* reason; that is, to solve a problem of some kind. Two examples will suffice. In the first instance, the reader may see a news story about the enactment of a new law which requires auto owners involved in an accident to post bond unless they carry liability insurance. Reading the dull provisions of the new law is anything but a pleasure, but the reader reduces his anxiety by learning what he must do to comply with the law. In the second instance, the reader during a war reads about the military situation to learn how close his side is to victory or defeat and to peace. The reader, in other words, feels the need to read so that he can do something about or think something about the specific situation—so that he can readjust his

[2] Wilbur Schramm, "The Nature of News," *Journalism Quarterly*, Vol. 26 (1949), pp. 259-269. The student should read all of this important explanation of news reading behavior.

plans to achieve his goals or readjust his thoughts to the change in his environment.

Which news is selected? The individual reader chooses to read those items that relate to his personal needs and to his experience. Many persons will probably read, for example, a news story that tells them what to do when they get a cold. Some readers will probably also read an item such as this one: "Excessive cigarette smoking is the cause of most lung cancer, in the opinion of a famous chest surgeon. . . ."

The reader is not attracted to those items that he cannot relate to his experience. Each reader has a unique experience-world that he has acquired through face-to-face contacts with others and through reading. Some readers, as is well known, have a very limited experience-world, and that fact causes them to read less than persons with a larger experience-world.

In every item that a particular reader is attracted to read there is some degree of ego involvement. This may be considerable, for example, to a young man who reads that the selective service quotas for his state have been increased or decreased. The ego involvement is less for the reader who reads about a house burning down which is owned by a person he knows. And so on down the scale.

Although the usual reader does not know a great many other persons, he *identifies* with certain persons in the news or *associates himself* with them in some way. An example: readership studies of two daily newspapers in different communities were conducted on the same day. Both newspapers carried the same dispatch about a national coal strike. In one of the newspapers the headline was: "Miners Agree to Wage Offer"; in the other newspaper the headline was: "John L. Lewis Says He'll Settle." Twice as many readers read the second story. (Both were on the front page with equal display.)

Whether or not the reader identifies with the subject of the news story depends upon the reader. Take the following story as one example: "Four-year-old Donald Compton died today after dropping a milk bottle in his mother's kitchen and fall-ing on the broken glass." Many parents and grandparents of children of about that age read it, imagining this accident happening to their children or grandchildren. Another ex-ample: teen-age readers seem to be attracted to news stories about youths of their own age much more than to stories about adults.

In another way, the reader identifies when he reads stories about cute children and animals and about the discomfiture of adults when the consequences are harmless. His point of view is that of a superior person observing the eccentric be-havior of the object which he compares with his own behavior. The observer's feeling of superiority to the subject of the story is at the basis of all humor.[3]

Another way in which the reader's ego is involved in cer-tain news stories is his association with *reference groups*.[4] Any group to which a person relates his attitudes is called a reference group. He may formally belong to a particular group (member) or he may relate himself to a group as a "reference point for making evaluations of himself and oth-ers." This conception may be expanded to mean *our com-munity, our nation, our region, our allies,* and so forth. It is a *we* aspect of ego involvement. A reader, for example, may perceive in a certain news story a threat to *our* national se-curity, *our* labor union's solidarity, *our* team's win record, or *our* community's welfare.

The interaction of *we* and *they* groups gives rise to prob-lems of conflict and co-operation. But the complexity of these interactions is not understood by some readers and they do not, therefore, perceive a subject-matter in a specific news story that would cause their ego to be involved. We usually say that such readers are not well-informed. Hence, to them

[3] See Sigmund Freud, "Wit and Its Relation to the Unconscious," in A. A. Brill, ed., *The Basic Writings of Sigmund Freud* (New York, 1938).

[4] See H. H. Hyman, "The Psychology of Status," *Archives of Psychology*, No. 269 (1942).

"news is what a chap who doesn't care much about anything wants to read," as a character in Evelyn Waugh's novel *Scoop* [5] so aptly put it. The chaps who don't care much about anything read sports and crime news and the dramatic aspects of political and economic news because that is all they adequately understand.

Some readers perceive more in a specific item than do others; in fact, sometimes more than do editors. What they perceive or do not perceive is related to the magnitude of their experience-world. The following news story is an example: "TOKYO—The edge of a typhoon hit Japan today and left at least 65 persons dead." Only a few readers, as would be expected by an editor, would relate this happening to their own experience or needs. One reader, however, projected her own ego into the item: her soldier son was stationed in Japan, and the item, therefore, was of more interest to her than were many local news items. Another reader, a telephone lineman, was interested in reading more details in the news story to learn what was the typhoon's effect on the communication facilities.

When we say that proximity [6] is a standard for estimating reader interest in a particular news item we really mean *psychological*, not geographical, proximity. The two dimensions are practically the same as to many news stories because most of the people one knows live in our community and most of the reference groups one associates himself with are local ones. The resident of Seattle who used to live in Cedar Rapids, however, is probably always interested in reading about a happening in Cedar Rapids.

The subject-matter of a news item does not necessarily have the same meaning for every reader because of (*a*) the varying life histories of individuals (i.e., their experiences), and (*b*) their varying personality structures. We have already illustrated the first of these factors. As to the second, some

5 P. 69.
6 See F. L. Mott, *The News in America* (Cambridge, Mass., 1952), p. 27.

people wish to control their environment more than do others. This is illustrated by varying reader reactions to the following news story:

> Michael Holden, the TV comedian and his wife, Nita, are "having a wonderful time" during their stay at the local hospital.
> That's what Nita said today in explaining that neither of them is sick—just having a checkup.
> "We've got two pretty corner rooms," Nita said. "Michael has a pretty nurse, and they're feeding us well."

Many readers perceived this item as something interesting about the private life of a well-known person who was regarded as a delightful "friend" of the members of his large TV audience. But some readers, whose experience told them of the overcrowded situation in the hospital and the difficulty that local taxpayers were having in getting in at all perceived the item as presenting a problem. Reading of the item stimulated a "what's-going-on-here?" reaction and the thought of doing something about the situation. The latter type of reader was well informed in that he was aware of the crowded condition of the hospital. Many news stories evoke in readers —especially readers with a certain personality structure—the thought of controlling the situation they are reading about. Some such persons are of the "reformer" type.

What is news? There is no adequate definition of news and we shan't attempt one. News, of course, is what the editor decides to print or the radio news director to broadcast. As good a definition as any, perhaps, is this one: News is the report of an event that the reader can and will understand. (This is as broad as the jurists' definition of law, viz., those rules of conduct that the courts enforce.) There is some evidence to suggest that this definition of news could be revised to read as follows: News is the report of an event that the reader *can* understand. The evidence mentioned [7] indicates that *interest in a radio news item correlates so highly with the listener's ability to understand it* that "can and will understand" means the same thing as "can understand."

News, naturally, is "the new"—something novel. But it must also be "the old" or the reader does not relate himself to the subject-matter. Some news items that get printed are more old than new: the routine accident story, for example, is what we could call a "constant." But in most news stories the reader perceives something novel because he assumes the usual. It is the idiosyncratic aspect of an event—the unexpected role of the news object, whether a train, a person, a business, or an institution, that makes it a good news story. The worthy item then is not just about an auto accident but about a very bad one with an unusual cause or effect; one that involves people we have heard of; and to some readers one that is a social problem (i.e., what can be done to stop all of these terrible accidents?).

Even when only a fragment of the reader's ego is involved (that is, when he is not emotionally concerned), a news story may be read for the instrumental purpose of solving a puzzle. An example is the story on page 20 about the child dropping a milk bottle and killing himself by falling on the broken glass. Many readers without children or grandchildren wanted to read the details to find out how such an unusual fatality could have happened.

Some events are of the kind that permit of little identification by the reader and that have little instrumental value for him. An earthquake in Java, for example, does not permit of much identification and is a situation about which the reader cannot do anything by way of controlling it. Possibly some skillful writer—if it were worth-while—could treat that event in such a way as to permit of more identification; that, however, is an aspect of news to be discussed in a later section.

[7] Chall and Dial, *op. cit.*

Anxiety as a factor in news reading: It is generally assumed that intellectually sophisticated persons read news for an instrumental reason more often than do unsophisticated persons. While this is doubtless true, it is also possible that people with a low anxiety load read more of those items that permit of only slight identification than do people with a high anxiety load. There is also some evidence that, since a person of high anxiety tends to be self-centered, he identifies often with the subjects of news stories. He probably also rejects certain news stories with anxiety stimuli. We are not sure about all of this, for psychologists are not even sure what anxiety is. Yet there turn up very frequently in reader interest studies persons who reject stories about a war "because it is so terrible." The meaning of this for the newspaper and radio editor is, perhaps, that the news content should be better balanced between news that presents a threat and news that is optimistic.

Episodic news: Some events are completed actions in the historical sense; as, for example, the report of the result of a presidential election or of a baseball game. But most of the events reported daily are only *episodes in the course of a larger event;* as, for example, the action of a United States Senate committee (like the banner headline story in the facsimile of a front page opposite page 16). A great proportion of public affairs news is about *the steps being taken*—or speculation about the steps that may be taken—in connection with a major piece of legislation in Congress or the city council or a démarche in a foreign chancellery or the United Nations General Assembly or Security Council.

This episodic news is understood by well-informed readers and is ignored by uninformed readers to whom it has little meaning. The reader who does not know the difference in function and authority between the United Nations General Assembly and the Security Council or who does not understand what is meant when he reads that a proposed city ordinance "passed second reading" in the city council cannot be expected to read such items with much understanding.

A certain amount of news that is printed in the newspaper is mere chronicle of those events that are the easiest to report. Newspapers and news agencies station reporters at strategic places where certain kinds of events happen or are recorded, such as police stations, courts, state capitols, and the federal capitol. Some of this available news does not relate to the personal experience or personal needs of many readers. Perhaps newspapers should invent some new techniques of reporting so that other kinds of news gets reported oftener. There is considerable truth in the statement of a former editor of *Time* news magazine that "journalism is a crude experiment in communicating facts (not truth) which is in its very early stages; that some day far in the future, if any of its flimsy records should survive, present-day journalism will be regarded in the same way we now regard the earliest wall-scratchings of the prehistoric cavemen." [8]

The treatment makes it news: Whether or not a certain set of facts is news depends sometimes upon the way the facts are treated by the writer. A leaf falling from a tree would not be news if that event were treated in the conventional way by the ordinary writer, but it might be news if the writer were John Keats or another poet who had the literary ability to relate the facts to a reader's personal experience or needs. "News is," as one discerning newspaper man expressed it, "anything *selected for treatment by a newspaper* that is so *treated that* it interests a number of persons." [9]

Whenever the news can be told by connecting it with a specific individual it will have meaning for the reader because the reader can identify with the individual. Few readers, for example, were attracted to read a statistical summary of United States casualties in the Korean war, whereas a great

[8] T. S. Matthews, quoted in *Editor & Publisher*, April 11, 1953, p. 70.
[9] Gerald W. Johnson, *What Is News?*, p. 48.

many readers were interested in a news story about the death of one Marine by an accidental shot while he was writing a letter to his teen-age bride. That kind of treatment can sometimes be used to give more meaning to stories about strikes, new laws, taxes, science and invention, and health and medicine. The news writer sometimes can relate the story by even addressing the reader directly. An example of that technique are the following two versions of an Associated Press lead (the original filed at 6:12 P.M. and the rewrite of that lead filed at 8:50 P.M.):

> CHICAGO—The strain of deciding whether their baby should be left to live several more years or undergo an operation which could kill or cure her, brought a mother and father into court today.

> CHICAGO—If she were your little girl would you have her undergo an operation at once, believing there was only a tiny chance she would pull through? Or would you leave her as she is—probably to die before she is five?
> The tragic question today. . . .

Summary: News is read and listened to mainly because people conduct a surveillance of their environment so as to adjust their behavior and thought to the changes they perceive in the environment. News reading and listening is pleasurable because the headline stimulates tension and the reading reduces that tension. The receiver of the news gets an immediate reward by identifying with a subject in the news either directly or as a member of a reference group. He is also rewarded when he reads for an instrumental reason, viz., to solve a problem.

The reader tends to select news that relates to his personal needs and experiences.

Sometimes the news writer can treat a set of facts in such a way that he enlists more reader interest in the news story, and the reader achieves a better understanding of the event.

Chapter III ··

GETTING AND PROCESSING NEWS

THE EDITORIAL department of a newspaper is so organized that it can get or receive a great amount of news each day,[1] select and process it, and deliver it to the reader within a very few hours. The radio station also receives a considerable amount of news and puts some of it on the air immediately after receiving it.

The following explanation of how a newspaper staff is organized to handle the daily news is not typical of any specific newspaper, especially of the small daily newspaper. But it suffices for the purpose of this chapter—which is to supply the student with that minimum of information he needs to understand some of the conditions that will limit his writing of news. On the small daily, a reporter at some time may find himself performing the functions of copy reader and makeup man as well as of reporter. Wire copy, too, is now delivered to many small dailies on tape directly to teletypesetters so that the copy reader uses the teleprinter copy only to monitor the operation of the typesetters.

Local news reporting: The newspaper has a staff of reporters to get local news, regional correspondents to get regional news, and a staff of copy readers and rewrite men to process this and other news supplied by the news agencies from all parts of the world. The reporters are stationed at certain strategic places where news happens or is recorded, such as the

[1] For the usual metropolitan newspaper this is 200,000 to 300,000 words.

police stations (where reporters also cover by telephone hospitals and fire stations), court rooms, and the city, county, and federal buildings. Other reporters have "beats" (or "runs") that relate to certain types of activity, such as business, labor, shipping, social welfare, and education. General assignment reporters also go to places where unexpected or scheduled news happens, such as conventions and meetings, and to any other local places at which anything happens that is worthy of reporting. Some of the news they get is telephoned to rewrite men and some is written by the reporters after they have returned to the newsroom.

The news executive who supervises the staff of reporters is the *city editor*. The executive who selects the wire news and supervises its processing by copy readers is the *telegraph editor*. Over both of these executives is usually a *news editor* who is also sometimes the *makeup editor*. (These titles do not correspond to these duties on all daily newspapers.) The executive who supervises all of the news procedures is the *managing editor*.

The "newshole": The number of pages in each day's issue of the newspaper depends upon the amount of advertising scheduled for that issue. The publishing executives adopt a general policy which fixes the percentage of advertising and editorial matter but which also provides for a minimum "newshole"—say, 110 columns. A dummy that shows for each page where scheduled advertising will run is supplied by the advertising department to the editorial department on the day preceding publication. The newshole—exclusive of sports, women's news, comics, and features—is divided between local and regional [2] news, on the one hand, and wire news, on the other hand. The newspaper has a rule that applies in general to the apportionment of space for each of these kinds of

---

[2] An edition that circulates outside of the city of publication often carries a good deal of regional news which is replaced by local news in the later editions that are delivered within the city.

news, but on certain days alters the rule so as to emphasize particular news stories without regard to their geographical origin. This decision is made in a brief conference of the news executives; in some situations there is a certain amount of competition between the executives for more space for local or wire news.

Although the conference mentioned above is held very early on the day of publication (for an afternoon newspaper), the news executives know pretty well what news will be available. In the first place, the wire news agencies, at the beginning of a news cycle, send a "budget" that lists about ten news stories that are regarded as "top" news. The city editor, likewise, has a fairly good estimate of the local news that will develop. He keeps a "future book" that reminds him ahead of time about matters that should be reported on certain days, and some of the beat reporters also keep a kind of future book for their particular beat. Some events, too—such as trials —continue over a period, and their coverage is planned for. Of course, during any day, unexpected news happens, thus causing the news executives to alter their plans to some extent. Such plans call for the omission of some planned news stories and for the trimming of others.

Copy readers process all of the news stories that are selected to run, trimming some stories to meet space requirements, checking some of the facts, improving diction and sentence structure, editing to conform to the newspaper's style as regards capitalization, abbreviation, punctuation, etc., writing captions for pictures, and finally writing the headlines. During all of this time, the amount of copy is being controlled by keeping a count of the accumulated number of column inches of type. (When the news stories are set in 8-point type, for example, one column-inch of type corresponds to about four lines of teletype or typewriter copy.)

We shall now take a look at a specific wire news story as it comes to the telegraph desk so the student will know about another situation that causes the conventional news story to take the form that differentiates it from the usual literary composition.

The form of a wire news story: Much wire copy is received on a teletype printer in "takes"; that is, parts of certain stories are received at different times instead of the whole story. The reason for this is that the news agency must "move" as many different important stories as possible within a very brief time so that the various newspapers on the circuit can include the latest news in each of their editions. If this were not done, certain editions would go to press with more details of some stories but entirely without certain other stories. An example of this process follows:

```
AR1
     SEATTLE, FEB. 7.--(UP)--FATE OF THE MISSING
SEINER VARSITY, WHICH RADIOED IT WAS AGROUND AND
SINKING OFF TATOOSH ISLAND IN THE STRAITS OF
JUAN DE FUCA, REMAINED A MYSTERY TONIGHT AS THE
SECOND DAY OF WIDESPREAD SEARCH FAILED TO
DISCLOSE ITS LOCATION.
     COAST GUARD HEADQUARTERS HERE WERE UNABLE
TO CONFIRM A REPORT THE CREW OF "10 OR 11" HAD
ABANDONED THE VESSEL.
     A U.S. PATROL SHIP, TWO COAST GUARD CUTTERS,
AN AIRPLANE AND 13 SURF BOATS FROM COAST GUARD
STATIONS ALONG THE OREGON AND WASHINGTON COAST-
LINES RESUMED THEIR SEARCH.  THEY REPORTED NO
TRACE OF THE VARSITY, ANY LIFEBOAT, SURVIVORS
OR WRECKAGE.
     SEARCH WAS HAMPERED BY RAIN, SNOW AND A
46-MILE WIND.  CAPT. HUBERT URSICH OF THE 61-TON
SEINER, WHICH LEFT SAN FRANCISCO LAST WEEK,
RADIOED YESTERDAY THE VESSEL WAS SINKING OFF
THE ROCKS IN THE VICINITY OF TATOOSH ISLAND.
     A RECOMMISSIONED U.S. NAVY MINELAYER, THE
BREESE, ENGAGED IN PATROL, ENTERED THE SEARCH
WITH THE COAST GUARD CUTTERS ONONDAGA OF
ASTORIA, ORE., AND THE REDWING OF PORT ANGELES,
WASH.
     THE VARSITY WAS BUILT TWO YEARS AGO IN
```

TACOMA, WASH., AT A COST OF $40,000. SHE WAS
OWNED BY JOE CLOUD AND MIKE KATICH OF GIG
HARBOR, WASH., AND HAD BEEN FISHING IN
CALIFORNIA WATERS SINCE SEPTEMBER FOR SARDINES.
    CLOUD WAS ONE OF THOSE ABOARD THE SHIP.
KATICH WAS AT HOME WHERE, HE SAID, HE PICKED
UP THE REPORT OF THE VESSEL'S ABANDONMENT ON
HIS SHORTWAVE RADIO. THE MESSAGE, HE SAID,
REPORTED THE CREW MEMBERS HAD "GOT OFF IN A
SKIFF."
    RELATIVES OF THE CREWMEN, HEARING OF
KATICH'S REPORT, ANNOUNCED THEY WERE ORGANIZING
A LAND SEARCH FOR THE SEAMEN IN HOPE THEY HAD
MADE THEIR ESCAPE FROM THE SINKING SHIP.
                                        GJ438PM

At the top of the story is the symbol *AR1*. This means
book 1 [3] of the report of the United Press *AR* wire (from
Seattle). At the bottom of the story, the symbol *GJ438PM*
gives the initials of the tape puncher and the time he signed
off sending the news story.

AR5
    BULLETIN
        1ST LEAD
    SEATTLE, FEB. 7.--(UP)--COAST GUARD
AUTHORITIES ADMITTED TONIGHT THERE WAS LITTLE
HOPE FOR NINE CREW MEMBERS OF THE MISSING
SEINER VARSITY, WHICH RADIOED IT WAS AGROUND
AND SINKING OFF TATOOSH ISLAND IN THE STRAITS
OF JUAN DE FUCA.
                        (MORE)
                                        GJ529PM

Although the book above does not indicate it, this story
has been given a label by the news agency; that is, it has been
"slugged" as "Varsity." Since book 1 was sent at 4:38 P.M.

---

[3] These separate messages are called books because the Morse telegraph
editors, before the teleprinter, typed each message on a "book" which consisted of several sheets of paper with alternate sheets of carbon paper. They
are also sometimes called takes, which is the name of the pieces of a news story
that the copy cutter in the composing room gives to the individual linotype
operators; this procedure expedites composition of a news story because more
than one operator is setting the story at the same time.

three other books had been received, but these related to some other subject-matter. Book 5, it will be noticed, was sent at 5:29 P.M. It is headed "Bulletin" and also "1st lead." "Bulletin" means the news is of first importance as compared with some other news stories in the report. This paragraph supersedes the first paragraph of the story as sent earlier. If the newspaper has an edition coming up immediately, the news editor will substitute the new lead.

```
BULLETIN
        2ND LEAD
        SEATTLE, FEB. 7--(UP)--A NAVAL RADIO
DISPATCH FROM VANCOUVER ISLAND TONIGHT SAID
THREE CREW MEMBERS OF THE AMERICAN SEINER
VARSITY HAD REACHED THE ISLAND IN SAFETY,
PRESUMABLY AFTER THEIR BOAT SANK OFF THE ROCKS
OF TATOOSH ISLAND AT THE ENTRANCE TO THE STRAIT
OF JUAN DE FUCA.
                        (MORE)
                        WD544PM
```

The 2nd lead was received 15 minutes later and superseded the 1st lead. Note the line "(more)" at the bottom of the book. This means that additional details will follow in a succeeding book.

```
BULLETIN
        ADD 2ND LEAD VARSITY, SEATTLE X X X FUCA
        THE RADIOED MESSAGE FROM PACHENA POINT,
NORTHWEST OF VICTORIA, B.C., SAID:
"THREE MEN FROM VARSITY REPORTED FOUND FOUR
MILES EAST OF HERE.  PLEASE ADVISE MRS. ULRISCH
4106 NORTH 30TH TACOMA UBERT (CORRECT) ULRISCH
IS OKAY AND HAS WITH HIM HUBERT ANCISCH
(CORRECT) AND ANTONE MAZER.  REST OF CREW NOT
LOCATED."
                        (MORE)
                        WD545PM
```

This copy, received one minute later, is an "add" to the 2nd lead. Note, after "Add 2nd lead Varsity," the words "Seattle X X X Fuca." Seattle refers to the point of origin of the story and Fuca is the last word in the preceding book; the latter symbol indicates to the telegraph editor that the "add 2nd lead" is to be a paragraph coming just below the paragraph ending with the last word of the preceding paragraph.

(In this chapter, we do not mean by *lead* the same thing we mean in Chapter VI. In that chapter *lead* means the *beginning* of the news story. In this chapter it refers either to the *whole news story* or *the top part of a news story* when the news agency rewrites all or a part of the news story either to accord with new developments or to supply a different story for the succeeding news cycle; hence *day lead* and *night lead* as well as *2nd lead* and *3rd lead*.)

```
ADD 2ND LEAD MISSING VESSEL SEATTLE XXX LOCATED.
    THE MESSAGE WAS BELIEVED TO REFER TO THOSE
IDENTIFIED EARLIER AS CAPT. HUBERT URSICH,
TACOMA; ANTONE NARVER, GIG HARBOR; AND ANTONE
ANCICH, TACOMA.  COAST GUARD HEADQUARTERS
RECEIVED THE MESSAGE FROM THE KLIPSAN BEACH,
B.C., NAVAL RADIO OPERATOR.  NO OTHER DETAILS
WERE IMMEDIATELY AVAILABLE.
    EARLIER HOPE HAD BEEN GIVEN UP FOR MEMBERS
OF THE SEINER'S CREW AFTER SEARCHING PARTIES
REPORTED FAILURE FOR THE SECOND SUCCESSIVE DAY.
    A NEUTRALITY PATROL SHIP, TWO COAST GUARD
CUTTERS, AN AIRPLANE AND 13 SURF BOATS
PATROLLED THE COAST.
    OTHER OCCUPANTS OF THE BOAT WERE JOSEPH
CLOUD, CO-OWNER; VINCENT KARNELICH, GIG HARBOR;
PETE PULJAN, ABERDEEN; NED MALICH, HOQUIAM;
CHRIS CHRISTENSEN, POULSBO; AND STEVE LEMCKE,
TACOMA.
    (PICK UP 4TH PGH EARLIER; SEARCH WAS ETC)
                                        GJ6PM
```

Note at the bottom of this book the line in parenthesis "(pick up 4th pgh earlier; search was etc)." The meaning of this line is that (*a*) all of the matter in the first three paragraphs of book 1 has been superseded by the matter sent later, and (*b*) the matter in book 1 beginning with the fourth paragraph ("search was, etc.") will remain in the news story.

At the time this last book was received (6 P.M.), if the copy had been printed in an early edition, the editor would now cross out on a proof sheet the superseded matter and would substitute the new matter so that the story in the next edition would present at the top of the story the latest developments and still retain (i.e., "pick up") the latter paragraphs of the original story. (The slug has been changed from "Varsity" to "Missing Vessel"—possibly because the latter is more descriptive.)

```
INSERT 2ND LEAD MISSING VESSEL SEATTLE AFTER 4TH
PGH XXX AVAILABLE
        IT WAS BELIEVED THE VARSITY MIGHT HAVE
BEEN WRECKED OFF VANCOUVER ISLAND RATHER THAN
TATOOSH ISLAND, INASMUCH AS THE RESCUED MEN
WOULD HAVE HAD TO SWIM MORE THAN 10 MILES FROM
TATOOSH TO PACHENA POINT.
        THE THREE MEN WALKED UP THE ISLAND'S WEST
COAST TRAIL WHERE THEY MET PATROLS WHO HAD
ACCESS TO TELEPHONES.   THE SEAMEN SAID THE
SEINER WAS WRECKED AND LOST.   TWO COAST GUARD
CUTTERS SEARCHING FOR THE VESSEL WERE IMMEDI-
ATELY DISPATCHED TO VANCOUVER ISLAND.
        (PICK UP 2ND LEAD AT 5TH PGH: EARLIER
HOPE ETC)
                                        GJ748PM
```

This book is an "insert" for the 2nd lead. Note that the insert is to be between the fourth and fifth paragraphs of the 2nd lead. This matter was sent as an insert instead of as an add because the matter relates to what is in the 2nd lead, not to the later matter in the original story.

```
INSERT 2ND LEAD MISSING VESSEL AFTER 6TH PGH
XXX ISLAND.
        ADVICES FROM PACHENA POINT, HOWEVER,
WARNED THERE WAS VIRTUALLY NO CHANCE FOR THE
CUTTERS TO LAND IN THAT VICINITY.   MEDICAL AID
AND FOOD WERE BEING RUSHED TO THE SURVIVORS
FROM NEARBY KLIPSAN BEACH.
        (END INSERT PICK UP AS BEFORE)
                                        GJ751PM
```

This fast breaking news story now has a second insert. Note how the news agency writer used "however" as a transitional device.

3RD LEAD

SEATTLE, FEB. 7.--(UP)--THREE SEAMEN OF THE WRECKED AMERICAN SEINER VARSITY REACHED VANCOUVER ISLAND IN SAFETY TONIGHT WITH INDICATIONS THE OTHER SIX CREW MEMBERS OF THE 61-TON CRAFT PERISHED.

A NAVAL RADIO DISPATCH FROM PACHENA POINT, NORTHWEST OF VICTORIA, B.C., IDENTIFIED THE RESCUED MEN AS:

CAPT. HUBERT URSICH OF TACOMA, WASH., ANTONE NARVER OF GIG HARBOR, WASH., AND ANTONE ANCICH OF TACOMA.

THERE WAS NO WORD OF THE OTHER CREWMEN, LISTED AS JOSEPH CLOUD, TACOMA, A CO-OWNER; VINCENT KARNELICH, GIG HARBOR; PETE PULJAN, ABERDEEN, WASH.; NED MALICH, HOQUIAM, WASH.; CHRIS CHRISTENSEN, POULSBO, WASH.; AND STEVE LEMCKE, TACOMA.

THE VARSITY RADIOED EARLY YESTERDAY IT WAS AGROUND OFF TATOOSH ISLAND IN THE STRAITS OF JUAN DE FUCA AND SINKING RAPIDLY. IT WAS BELIEVED, HOWEVER, THE SEINER MIGHT HAVE BEEN WRECKED OFF VANCOUVER ISLAND INASMUCH AS THE RESCUED MEN WOULD HAVE TO SWIM 10 MILES FROM TATOOSH TO PACHENA POINT.

TWO COAST GUARD CUTTERS PATROLLING THE STRAITS IN SEARCH OF THE VESSEL WERE DISPATCHED TO VANCOUVER ISLAND BUT IT WAS LEARNED THERE WAS VIRTUALLY NO CHANCE TO LAND AT PACHENA POINT. MEDICAL AID AND FOOD WERE RUSHED TO THE SURVIVORS FROM NEARBY KLIPSAN BEACH.

THE SEINER LEFT SAN FRANCISCO LAST WEEK AFTER FISHING IN CALIFORNIA WATERS SINCE SEPTEMBER FOR SARDINES. CLOUD AND MIKE KATICH OF GIG HARBOR OWNED THE VESSEL, BUILT TWO YEARS AGO IN TACOMA AT A COST OF $40,000.

DURING THE DAY A RECOMMISSIONED U.S. NAVY MINELAYER NOW ON PATROL JOINED THE COAST GUARD CUTTERS AND AN AIRPLANE IN SEARCH FOR THE MISSING BOAT.

(INCLUDES ALL EARLIER) GJ818PM

Some time before the 8:18 P.M. signoff, the Seattle United Press editors had completed their coverage of this news to the point at which they thought it desirable to write a new story that contained the latest facts and that was a smoother and a summarized version of the event. Hence, the 3rd lead. This story, in some newspapers, would replace the earlier one. The earlier editions, however, would only have presented the "running" story.

At 9:42 came this "correction":

```
EDITORS:
    IN 3RD LEAD MISSING SEINER, SEATTLE, PLS
READ IN 1ST PGH X X X THE OTHER F O U R CREW
MEMBERS ETC., AND IN LIST OF MISSING MEN PLS
ELIMINATE NAMES OF NED MALICH, HOQUIAM,WASH.,
AND CHRIS CHRISTENSEN, POULSBO, WASH.
                    UPA SEATTLE FEB 7
                                    GJ942PM
```

At this point the San Francisco bureau (SX call letters) broke in on the wire with a query. The immediate reply was given by Seattle with notice also that an add to the 3rd lead was coming up. Here are the query and the reply:

```
SX
95
  AR
    WERE THOSE TWO MEN NOT ABOARD, OR WERE THEY
FOUND?
            SX FEB 7
                    RM955PM

SX
    NOT ABOARD      ADD UPCMG SOON
                            GJ958PM
```

(The "95" in the first message above means it is fairly urgent.)

```
ADD 3RD LEAD SEINER SEATTLE X X X BOAT.
    THE SURVIVORS SAID THEY AND THE FOUR MISSING
MEN PUT OUT IN A SKIFF AFTER THE VARSITY RAN
```

OFF ITS COURSE IN A HEAVY FOG AND STRUCK A REEF
SIX MILES SOUTH OF PACHENA POINT.
 THEY ABANDONED THE SHIP AS IT BEGAN TO
SETTLE. THE SKIFF WAS SWAMPED BY HEAVY WAVES
BUT THE THREE MEN FOUGHT THEIR WAY TO THE BEACH
UNDER A CLIFF, REMAINING THERE UNTIL LATE TODAY.
THEY DID NOT KNOW WHAT BECAME OF THE OTHERS.
 CAPT. URSICH SAID NEITHER NED MALICH OF
HOQUIAM, WASH., NOR CHRIS CHRISTENSEN, OF
POULSBO, WASH., ACCOMPANIED THE SHIP ON ITS
RETURN FROM SAN FRANCISCO. BOTH HAD BEEN LISTED
AS ORIGINALLY MEMBERS OF THE CREW.

GJ1008PM

The full meaning for the news writer of the foregoing illustration of the handling of wire copy will become apparent
in the next chapter which relates to the structure of the conventional news story. We could also present an illustration
of a somewhat similar handling of certain local news stories,
but it is not necessary. Local stories about fires, major accidents, and certain crimes are handled in somewhat the same
way. As the story develops, the rewrite man writes adds, inserts, and new leads (and sometimes corrections) so as to keep
the readers of each edition up to date on the happening. He
must compromise, therefore, with his desire to present a
smoothly-flowing and logically-organized story such as the
weekly news magazine can present.

The radio station: The news organization of a radio station is much simpler than that of the newspaper, and the
processing of its news is a simpler operation. Only a small
amount of news is broadcast—20 to 30 items in each 15-min-
ute show. The writers have enough time between newscasts
to prepare each program even when one considers the requirement for keeping a story up to date. Much of the wire
news is received on a radio wire after being specially prepared
for broadcasting instead of printing; this wire delivers "pack-
aged" 5-minute and 15-minute programs as well as individual
news stories. Some stations emphasize and some neglect local

news coverage. Except for those stations that are affiliated with a newspaper, the local station provides its own local coverage; some stations make extensive use of tape- and wire-recorders for such purposes as eye-witness interviews and live reports of city council meetings. The recorded matter is usually edited to conform to the format of the particular newscaster's show.

In Chapter V, we examine the structure of the conventional news story. That structure, as will be explained, is influenced by some of the factors mentioned in this chapter.

Chapter IV

CHARACTERISTICS OF NEWS STYLE

STUDENTS OF communication frequently classify a communication by the purpose of the communicator: the communication is directive, affective, or informative. A directive communication is intended to influence human behavior; it is a command or an appeal such as is contained in editorials and advertisements. An affective communication is intended to arouse a feeling tone: to affect the receiver pleasantly or unpleasantly. An informative communication is intended to apprise the receiver of something that the communicator thinks the receiver will want to know; it is, in short, a report.[1]

A news story almost never is directive; usually it is informative, although parts of it may be affective. Some news stories —those that describe rather than recount an event—are mostly affective. Except for Chapters IX-XI, we are concerned in this text almost exclusively with the informative type of news story. The conventional news story is, in a broad sense, a narrative, but for the purpose of our discussion, we distinguish the news story that is mere *chronicle* (i.e., a simple report of an event) from the news story in which the incidents are consciously arranged to produce a literary effect; the latter type we refer to as *narrative*. In addition, we shall refer to

[1] Not all students of communication distinguish these three types. One of them, for example, defines communication as "a process whereby one or more individuals transmit words or ideas to modify the behavior of other individuals." Some semanticists hold that all communication is directive: that it is not possible to form a sentence that does not express a command.

certain types of news stories as *descriptive, explanatory,* and *interpretive.* A news story, of course, often contains elements of several of these types.

The discussion which follows refers to the conventional news story, which is chiefly chronicle.

The conventional chronicle type of news story has two characteristics that differentiate it from the usual prose found in magazines and books. These are (1) its objectivity and (2) its structure. In this chapter we shall discuss the objectivity and in the next chapter the structure of the news story.

Point of view of the writer: The perspective of the writer of chronicle is that of a detached observer. His purpose is simply to report, for example, what happened at the meeting of the city council and how the automobile accident happened and its consequences for the persons involved. A trend has started in American journalism for the writer of news to evaluate events at the same time that he writes about them. The argument for this departure from traditional objectivity is that the writer can make the news more meaningful to the reader or listener by reporting it in a specific frame of reference. This, of course, is true, for the method supplies the reader or listener with more context. The argument against such a practice, however, is that the well-informed reader or listener, who already has an adequate context is inhibited from receiving the news in his own frame of reference.[2] *Time* news magazine, some people say, "insults my intelligence."

Objectivity: attribution: A characteristic of the conventional news story is the attribution of statements of fact and evaluation to a specific news source—such as an official, a pub-

---

[2] Some semanticists assert that it is not possible to make a *neutral* statement —because the meaning of a statement is in terms of its context. "The Governor finished his breakfast at 10 o'clock" is not necessarily a neutral statement, they hold, because its meaning depends upon what kind of man the Governor is (the context). We do not need to analyze that argument in a textbook of this limited scope.

lic speaker, or an eye-witness.[3] This practice is a recognition of a well-known principle of perception: "As soon as we experience any facts they will be perceived as organized into some sort of meaningful whole." [4] This means that the human mind does not suspend an evaluation until it has acquired all of the facts, but structures the facts, as the psychologists say, into some pattern of meaning immediately. The structuring is in terms of the context: a statement means one thing in context *A* and something different in context *B*. This characteristic of the cognitive process was demonstrated in the following experiment in which the context was the author of a statement.

A statement which was actually made in 1944 by the then president of the Chamber of Commerce of the United States, Eric A. Johnston, was submitted to a group of subjects. In one part of the experiment, some of the subjects were told that the statement was made by Mr. Johnston and some were told it was made by Harry Bridges, radical labor leader. The statement was as follows:

Only the wilfully blind can fail to see that the old style capitalism of a primitive freebooting period is gone forever. The capitalism of complete laissez-faire, which thrived on low wages and maximum profits for minimum turnover, which rejected collective bargaining and fought against justified public regulation of the competitive process, is a thing of the past.

None of the second group of 33 subjects questioned the authorship of Mr. Bridges, but 7 of 35 of the first group ques-

[3] The author, in a study of an election campaign in twelve newspapers in 1950, found that only 14 per cent of all statements in the news stories were not attributed to some source. Nearly all of these were *neutral* in direction, as for example, "Mr. Nixon will speak at Oakland Wednesday night." One-fourth of the nonattributed statements about each of the candidates were *favorable* and about 6 per cent were *unfavorable.*—See *Editor & Publisher,* Jan. 27, 1951, p. 12, and C. R. Bush, "The Analysis of Political News," *Journalism Quarterly,* 28:250-52 (1951).

[4] D. Krech and R. S. Crutchfield, *Theory and Problems of Social Psychology* (New York, 1948), p. 86.

tioned the authorship of Mr. Johnston; that is, they could not believe that such a statement could be made by the president of the Chamber of Commerce of the United States. Those subjects who were told that the statement had been made by Mr. Johnston and who accepted that authorship interpreted it to mean that the business leader was advocating an "enlightened" form of capitalism which would be in the best interests of business. Those who were told that Mr. Bridges had made the statement interpreted it to mean that labor had won out over capitalism and intended resolutely to defend its gains from attack. What some of the readers of this statement did was to *alter the content of the communication* to fit their own context.[5]

So inattentive are some readers and listeners that the news agencies require their writers, in some instances when an accusation is made, to precede the accusation with the name of the accuser.[6] Thus: "Congressman Henry Thomas told a Republican rally last night that his opponent, Ferris Cotten, left Louisiana to escape disbarment for misuse of a client's money." The disapproved version would be: "Ferris Cotten, Democratic candidate for Congress, left Louisiana to escape disbarment for misuse of a client's money, his Republican opponent, Congressman Henry Thomas, charged last night at a Republican rally." It is thought that the rule mentioned above is more likely to cause the reader or listener to refer the accusation to the context of the accuser instead of merely to the context of the newspaper or of its writer.

It is a general practice, also, of newspapers and news agencies, when publishing an accusation, to obtain a state-

---

[5] This experiment is reported in S. E. Asch, *Social Psychology* (New York, 1952), pp. 420-426.

[6] The *A. P. Reference Book* says: "Don't be afraid to begin a story by naming the source. It is awkward sometimes, but also it sometimes is the best and most direct way to put the story in proper perspective and balance when the source must be established clearly in the reader's mind if he is properly to understand the story."—p. 36.

ment from the person accused and to publish both statements in the same news story; when the person accused is not available or declines to make a statement, that fact is also published simultaneously. Some newspapers began in 1953, when a fear of Communism was prevalent, to go even further in protecting the reputations of accused persons: they inserted in parentheses after an accusation that was known to be false a statement about the falsity or the evidence of the falsity.

In the propaganda battles waged by various interests, organizations with virtuous sounding names are formed (usually by "public relations counsel") to issue publicity.[7] Since some of the publicity is newsworthy it gets published. A few newspapers, which are aware of the purpose and sponsorship of a particular organization, take the trouble to qualify the attribution with a parenthetical statement as to who the sponsors of the organization are.

Some newspapers, also, are careful in distinguishing organizations with similar names: there is a considerable difference in philosophy, for example, between the Federal Council of Churches of Christ in America and the American Council of Christian Churches.

The following leads to news stories indicate two different ways of handling an attribution. It would appear that the second version has the effect of reinforcing the reliability of the prediction. Or has it?

> LONDON—Kenneth de Courcy, editor of the "Intelligence Digest," said today he had received information that another atomic explosion will occur in Russia at midnight Saturday, Jan. 7 (7 P.M. EST).

> LONDON—You can look for a second Russian atomic explosion Saturday, Jan. 7 at 7 P.M. (EST), according to the man who predicted last year that Russia would attempt an atomic explosion in 1949.

[7] For example, see Drew Pearson in the *San Francisco Chronicle*, April 16, 1953.

The practice of using impersonal attribution, such as "police say" and "according to a Foreign Office spokesman," is declining. Newspapers and news agencies are insisting more than before on specific attribution. They are also banning *useless* attributions: as long as the writer makes it clear to the reader and listener that he is objectively describing an event, he need not include in his news story an overabundance of attributions. In the usual crime story, for example, he can make it apparent to the reader or listener that all or almost all of his information was obtained from policemen, and thereafter omit attribution. He is thus able to write more easily and more clearly.

Use of evaluating expressions: The writer of a news story tries to avoid using adjectives—at least certain kinds of adjectives. He generally uses adjectives that merely *particularize,* but seldom adjectives that *evaluate.* For example: "The *seventy-eight-year-old* leader ... died at 5:45 P.M. with his head cradled in the lap of his *sixteen-year-old* granddaughter, Mani." The italicized expressions help the reader to form a clear image of the personalities mentioned in the news story; they are particularizing adjectival phrases. If the writer, however, had said "*pretty* sixteen-year-old granddaughter," the evaluating adjective would be considered as editorializing.

This is not to say, however, that the writer never uses evaluating adjectives. Sometimes evaluation is a necessary part of the description of an event—unless the editor of the newspaper is satisfied with deadpan reporting. For example, the writer may say: "The mayor was angry." (More effective, however, would be to suggest anger by reporting objectively a sign of anger, such as "The mayor flushed" or "The mayor pounded the table.")

In some instances, an evaluating statement is what makes an event news. When the writer says, for example, "For the third time this year, a C. X. & Y passenger train was wrecked ...," he is including a fact that, as a newspaperman, he can scarcely omit. But when he does say it, he is also saying, "There must be something wrong with the way the company is operating; maybe the employees are disgruntled, and so forth." Of course, he could report news according to the rule that the reader or listener should always supply his own context. But he realizes that most readers—because of the conditions under which news is read or listened to and because of the receiver's poor memory—will not have such a context, and he supplies it. We return to a discussion of this question in Chapter X.

Typographic style: In this chapter we have meant by *style* the manner of choosing and arranging words so as to produce in the reader an intended meaning. In newspaper making there is another kind of style—*typographic style*. It is a sort of printer's style. Every newspaper has its own typographic style; that is, it has specific rules about capitalization, abbreviation, punctuation, the use of numerals, compound words, and preferred spelling. Nearly every newspaper has a style guide or style book. The reason for it is *to achieve a consistency* in these matters: it doesn't look well in a newspaper to capitalize *street* in one place and not capitalize it in another place, to spell it out in one sentence and to abbreviate it in another, to write *60* in one sentence and *sixty* in another.

There is no *right* style: style is a matter of preference. Newspapers vary as to the rules they adopt. Some adopt, as to capitalization, an *up* style in which the generic words are capitalized (Third Street) and some adopt a *down* style in which the generic words are in lower case (Third street). Nevertheless, it is important for the student to adhere to the style that his instructor adopts: when he begins work on a newspaper he should have acquired the habit of complying with a newspaper's style rules, whatever they happen to be. The style guide in the appendix may be used when the instructor does not supply a different one. One that the student will use professionally, if he happens to work for a news agency or for the newspaper that receives wire copy on tele-typesetter tape, is the *Associated Press Style Book (1953)*.

Summary: When one begins to learn to write informative news he should adopt the point of view of the disinterested observer and reporter.

There are certain circumstances that allow for affective elements in informative news stories, and there are a few types of news stories in which the point of view of the writer is wholly affective. We discuss both of these situations in following chapters. At this point in his laboratory work and his outside-class assignments, however, the student should not try to do affective writing.

Chapter V

STRUCTURE OF THE NEWS STORY

THE FUNCTION of the conventional news story is to tell what happened. In reporting the usual accident, for example, the writer does not begin with "Joseph Hemming and his wife, Marie, left their home this morning at 9 o'clock." He reports, first, the *completed* action, viz., "Mrs. Marie Hemming was killed and her husband, Joseph, was injured today, and so forth." In the rest of the news story the writer relates certain details in connection with the accident. Usually he assembles these facts *in a descending order* of their relative importance or interest value.

News about routine fatal accidents is published because the victims may be known by a certain number of readers and because the readers relate the accident to the safety of themselves or of others. The conventional news story tells who were the victims, where the accident happened, and what caused it. Only when some unusual factor—as when Mr. and Mrs. Hemming were on their way to the funeral of their daughter who had been killed in an automobile accident just two days before—does it occur to the writer to assemble the facts in a climactic order. In such an instance, he may decide to recite the events *in the order in which they happened* and in a way in which an omnipresent observer might have seen them; that is, "Joseph Hemming and his wife, Marie, left their home at 9 o'clock this morning for the Todd-Williams

Funeral Parlor in Oakdale. . . ." The news magazine *Time* reports such fatal accidents in climactic order. But that is because *Time* reports only those accidents to ordinary people that are bizarre.

The inverted pyramid structure: Most news stories are mere chronicle. The structure of such news stories is like that of an *inverted pyramid* and they often have two parts. The first part (called the *lead* or the *intro*) is the gist of the report and is usually separable from the *body* of the story, which is an elaboration of the first part. This is illustrated by Fig. 3.

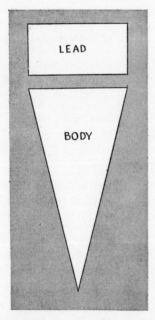

Fig. 3. Structure of the chronicle type news story with a summary lead.

The lead need not be separable from the body in all chronicle-type news stories, however: parts of the lead can be distributed to the first three or four paragraphs. Examples will be presented in Chapter VI.

The following United Press story is typical in its organization:

Gandhi Killed
By Hindu Fanatic

The gist

NEW DELHI, Jan. 30—Mohandas K. Gandhi was assassinated today by a Hindu extremist whose act plunged India into sorrow and fear.

Effect

Rioting broke out immediately in Bombay.

Death scene

The seventy-year-old leader whose people had christened him the Great Soul of India died at 5:45 P.M. (7:15 A.M. EST) with his head cradled in the lap of his sixteen-year-old granddaughter, Mani.

Just half an hour before, a Hindu fanatic, Ram Naturam, had pumped three bullets from a revolver into Gandhi's frail body, emaciated by years of fasting and asceticism.

Gandhi was shot in the luxurious gardens of Birla House in the presence of one thousand of his followers, whom he was leading to the little summer pagoda where it was his habit to make his evening devotions.

The main incident

Dressed as always in his homespun, sacklike dhoti, and leaning heavily on a staff of stout wood, Gandhi was only a few feet from the pagoda when the shots were fired.

Gandhi crumpled instantly, putting his hand to his forehead in the Hindu gesture of forgiveness to his assassin. Three bullets penetrated his body at close range, one in the upper right thigh, one in the abdomen, and one in the chest.

He spoke no word before he died. A moment before he was shot he said—some witnesses believed he was speaking to the assassin—"You are late."

The assassin had been standing beside the garden path, his hands folded, palms together, before him in the Hindu gesture of greeting. But between his palms he had concealed a small-caliber revolver. After pumping three bullets into Gandhi at a range of a few feet, he fired a fourth shot in an attempt at suicide, but the bullet merely creased his scalp.

The shots sounded like a string of firecrackers, and it was a moment before Gandhi's devotees realized what had happened.

Arrest of assassin

Then they turned on the assassin savagely and would have torn him to bits had not police guards intervened with rifles and drawn bayonets. The assassin was hustled to safekeeping.

Gandhi quickly was borne back to Birla House and placed on a couch with his head in his granddaughter's lap. Within a few moments she spoke to the stricken throng, among them Pandit Jawaharlal Nehru, Premier of India: "*Bapu* [father] is finished."

Shift of scene

Then Mani rose and sat cross-legged beside the body of the man whose life was forfeit for the cause of peace and humanity. She began to chant the two-thousand-year-old verses of the Bhagavad-Gita, the Hindu scripture.

Over all India the word spread like wildfire. Minutes after the flash was received in Bombay rioting broke out, with Hindu extremists attacking Moslems. A panic-stricken Moslem woman echoed the thoughts of thousands with a cry: "God help us all!"

Development of the riot angle

In Delhi itself, in the quick gathering gloom of the night, the news set the people on the march.

They walked slowly down the avenues and out of the squalid bazaars, converging on Birla House. There by the thousands they stood weeping silently or moaning and wailing. Some sought to scale the

People on the march

high walls and catch one last glimpse of the Mahatma. Strong troop contingents strove to keep order.

Tonight in response to the insistent demand of the people, his body was shown to them.

Exhibition of the body

The balcony window of the house opened and the body was borne outside. The people gasped and surged forward as it was placed in a chair, facing them. A brilliant spotlight blazed on the wrinkled, brown face. The eyes were closed, the face peaceful in repose. A white sheet covered the bloodstained loincloth. . . .

In this skilfully organized news story, the first thing the writer tells is what happened—a well-known political figure was assassinated. The writer also hastens to tell who the assassin was: he realized that many sophisticated readers and listeners would be wondering whether or not the assassin was a Moslem. The writer also hastens to report the main effect of the event—sorrow and fear, and a secondary effect—the rioting. He manages to communicate all of these facts and impressions in twenty-two words. (Only one of the words, it will be noted, is adjectival—the attributive noun *Hindu*.)

A news story about this kind of event tries to fulfill the need of the reader for a picture of the scene or scenes. The present writer discharges this function of the reporter by presenting first the death scene and then the assassination scene. The reader will note how the writer achieves the *transition* of these scenes by the phrase at the beginning of the fourth paragraph, "Just half an hour before. . . ." The writer then shifts the scene from the garden back to the house in which Gandhi died.

Next, he devotes three paragraphs to developing the riot angle, *achieving the transition* by beginning the paragraph with a phrase, "Over all India. . . ." Finally, he returns the reader's attention to the streets of New Delhi to present a picture of the crowds around Birla House and their behavior. This *transition* is achieved by the phrase, "In Delhi itself. . . ."

This, of course, is not a typical news story because it is more important than most news stories and contains more description. Yet it is a conventional news story in its structure. That is to say, it tells first what happened and then presents blocks of subject-matter which are not assembled in any logical or chronological sequence. One reason for this is that it is often necessary in daily journalism to relate the facts in a descending order of their importance. It is less important to the reader, for example, to know about the behavior of the crowds around Birla House than to know about the rioting throughout India; the latter fact, therefore, is related earlier than the former. And it is of more interest to the reader to know exactly how Gandhi was assassinated than to read the second part of the death scene. The facts have been assembled so that the least important can be cut off from the bottom by an editor if necessary.

Nearly all news stories that break for late editions of newspapers are organized in this way. Although the reader is sometimes confused by such a structure, the conditions of newspaper making described in Chapter III frequently require it.

It will be noted that in the Gandhi death story—the limiting conditions being considered—it was better to subordinate chronological order to an order of importance and interest. In some cases, the writer should pay little attention to chronological order. In the report of a trial, for example, the order in which witnesses testify is seldom important. Such phrases as "The next witness was John Smith" or "The last witness said thus-and-so" or "At this point the defense concluded its case" add nothing to the reader's understanding of the event and are almost always superfluous. In some instances, however, the use of such phrases achieves a necessary transition.

What is more important in some types of stories with

inverted pyramid organization is for the writer to *increase the probability of the reader's understanding of each successive paragraph.* Thus, the writer must make sure that a recital of certain facts necessary to the understanding of other facts is presented in the appropriate order. This is especially important in most accident stories.

The same requirement applies to the inclusion of names. While the writer need not present at the beginning all of the dramatis personae, he should mention the principals first and bring in the names of less important persons later. The writer can also confuse the reader when he uses too often an appositional term to identify certain names. Some readers, for example, forget as the story proceeds whether Smith is the plaintiff or the defendant; it is better, therefore, to use the parties' names instead of referring to them always as the plaintiff and the defendant.

The radio news writer has less of a problem with names than does the writer for the newspaper. Since the newcast is only a summary that is never longer than twelve and one-half minutes (about 1800-1900 words, the equivalent of less than two newspaper columns), it contains fewer details, especially fewer names.

The medley type of story: One type of news story must nearly always be organized like beads on a string—that is, the blocks of subject-matter are little related to each other or to any specific theme. The story is a medley of miscellaneous items. The usual report of a meeting of a public body—such as the city council—is an example. In assembling the facts, the writer leads off with one salient piece of business (for example, passage of an ordinance to permit dancing in places where liquor is sold) and follows that with such unrelated actions as the appointment of a new recreation director, the enactment of an ordinance to prohibit peddling, and the adoption of a new pension plan for city employees.

A somewhat similar type of news story is one that "rounds

up" two or more events of the same kind. Examples are burglaries and auto accidents that are reported in the same news cycle. Some stories of this kind are very confusing to the reader when the writer (*a*) mentions all of them in the lead, and (*b*) relates the details of each of them separately. When the facts are poorly organized by the writer the reader confuses the persons in one event with those in another event. When, in reporting auto accidents, the writer includes the dead and injured in *both* accidents in a single list and then proceeds to relate the details of each of the accidents, the reader has to reread the news story at least once to find out which persons were killed or injured in one accident and which in another. The best rule: *write a separate story for each event* unless the events are commonplace.

Climactic organization: An increasing number of stories in newspapers are now reporting events *in the order in which they occurred.* Instead of just telling what happened, the writer tries to reconstruct the happening with the view to sharpening the images which he wants the reader to perceive. The following news story is from the *San Francisco Chronicle* (with the names changed):

Police Stop Holdup On Third Try

Police Officers Richard Lollar and Denny Austin spotted a stolen car at a gas station last night. They recognized it as one taken earlier in Modesto by a trio who had held up a Chowchilla tavern.

When the officers approached the car, their guns and car were taken and they were dispatched on foot into the fog by the fugitive trio, who then held up the service station.

Next Policeman Ernest Liddle and Virgil White arrived. They also were re-

lieved of their arms. But they were held
captive as the holdup proceeded.

Officers Lollar and Austin meanwhile
trudged to a downtown intersection and
flagged down Police Chief Walter Feller.

The holdup was still in progress when
Chief Feller arrived. He held on to his
pistol and a free-for-all followed.

Richard Burns, 27, an ex-convict, was
wounded by his own gun. Finally he was
arrested along with his companions,
Richard Robinson, 20, and Bert Bollweg,
19, both AWOL sailors from Alameda
Air Station.

It will be noted that, although the story contains eight
names, they are presented to the reader in a sequence that
does not confuse him as to their respective actions: each
person is mentioned in the order of his appearance on the
scene. The names of the arrested men are mentioned last,
whereas the conventionally organized news story would have
begun with a statement of their arrest.

A story with that type of organization does not confuse the
reader about names, but automatically sets the reader straight
as to the time of each separate action.

Some kinds of subject-matter lend themselves to climactic
organization and some do not. When the story involves *suspense,* climactic organization is natural, as when a person
intending suicide from a high building delays his plunge. The
following news story is an example of subject-matter that can
be organized climactically:

William Cullen, 3, recovered from
diphtheria in time to sit at the Christmas
dinner table yesterday with his brother
and sister.

He snatched a nut from his mother's
hand and tried to swallow it. The nut
lodged in his throat. Hurriedly, his father
picked up the choking boy and carried
him to an automobile.

> But on the way to the family physician's office, a few blocks away from the Cullen home, the gasoline gave out.
>
> Frantically Mr. Cullen pushed the car to the crest of a hill and rolled down to the doctor's office, but the slight delay proved tragic. The boy was dead.

Most news stories, *unless they are fairly short,* must take the inverted pyramid form because (*a*) the reader wants to find out quickly what happened, and (*b*) because of the limited conditions of newspaper making that were described in Chapters I and III; that is, the necessity for transmitting news by wire and telephone in "books" and "takes" and the makeup problem of having to fit some stories into an available block of space on the page.

When the subject-matter of a news story is not of considerable interest to the reader the writer who organizes it climactically risks losing his reader before the end. The usual reader of the daily newspaper does not have the same mental set as does the reader of the weekly news-magazine who devotes an evening or a part of a week-end to that type of reading. The writer of a climactically-organized news story, therefore, should be fairly certain before beginning it that the subject-matter and his treatment of it will arouse interest: suspended interest is also sustained interest.

The paragraph: In books and magazines, the paragraph indicates to the reader a progression. A new paragraph signals the reader that one of the writer's thoughts has been developed and the writer is now ready to present a new thought. One requirement is that the paragraph have unity; that is, relate to one topic or to one aspect of a topic. A second requirement is that the paragraph contain a topic sentence; that is, a sentence that states in a general way the subject of the paragraph and summarizes it. The topic sentence is usually—but not necessarily—the first sentence. Such a paragraph is from 50 to 300 words in length.

The newspaper paragraph cannot meet these requirements, although the news writer tries to achieve some degree of unity. The newspaper paragraph is a division of a news story that is indicated by a one-em indentation at its beginning.[1] It is not so much a unit of thought as it is a unit of type. It averages 20 to 25 words—about one inch of type. It has only one or two sentences. The narrow column width and the small size of the type require a frequent indentation to avoid presenting the reader with a mass of type that has a gray and uninviting appearance. The indentations break up the type mass and stimulate the reader to continue through the news story. The frequent indentations also facilitate rapid reading and take into account the conditions under which newspaper reading is done.[2]

In the newspaper, a *block of paragraphs* is somewhat the equivalent of the literary paragraph. Insertions of new material and deletions must frequently be made and new leads be written to keep a developing news story up to date. This can be done with a minimum of alteration of the story (which already may be in type) when the writer does not have to meet the requirements of the literary paragraph.

Transition: The lack of adequate transition in news stories is a weakness that derives from the writer having to compromise with the several types of channel noise mentioned in a preceding section and in preceding chapters. Because the news writer is so much aware of this necessity for compromise he has the tendency not to value highly enough the advantages of transition.

As a substitute for transition, a kind of paragraph emphasis is striven for by the news writer. To persuade the reader to continue reading the story (and also to assist his understanding), the writer tries to begin each paragraph with significant

---

[1] Newspaper paragraphs in standard-size newspapers vary in width from 11½ to 12 ems. Twelve ems equal two inches.

[2] See p. 9 for a discussion of these conditions.

or key words. This is on the principle that, since the first line of a paragraph contains only about five words, advantage should be taken of this opportunity for emphasis. This first line is sometimes referred to as the show window of the paragraph. Actually this objective cannot always be realized, but the effort results in most sentences having emphatic beginnings (for example, few sentences begin with "there are" or with weak participial modifiers).

Transition is a sign of continuity: it indicates a progression. It urges the reader to continue. Most transitions refer back to the preceding sentence or (newspaper) paragraph so that the reader's mind is carried forward without much effort by this connection. But if one is to write a news story to accommodate insertions and deletions, he is inhibited from using many connectives. If he did so, he would risk disturbing the organization of the news story—so that the preceding or following matter would be inconsistent with the standing matter.

This book argues that news writers have compromised too much with the conventionalities. The news writer nearly always knows at the time he is writing whether or not the story is likely to stand up as written; in most instances it will. If the news writer would make more use of transitional devices, he would eliminate much of the semantic noise that interferes with efficient communication and would, therefore, enlist a larger audience for his story.

Most transitional devices are some kind of *restatement* of the preceding matter. The reader, having perceived a specific pattern, expects it to be preserved in the next sentence or paragraph. A 1-2-3 listing is one example of such a device. The following excerpt from a news story about testimony before a United States Senate committee is an example:

> ...Here are some of the things the committee was told:
> 1—Sen. Wilson: "If the Russian program continues as predicted, within three years most of the Soviet air force will be..."

2—Undersecretary Martin: "We have got to do all we can..."
3—Secretary Thomas: "We have an object lesson which should teach,..."

The story below illustrates several types of transitional devices, which are italicized. One repeats a name. Another uses a pronoun instead of repeating a name. Another refers back in time. Two repeat a word or expression.

Three Areas Study Flood Control Actions

Three Peninsula communities launched studies of their storm-created flood control problems last week.

The most concrete action was taken by the Redwood City council at a Monday night meeting. Paul Adamson, a local engineer, was authorized to begin a $10,-000 to $15,000 preliminary study of an overall community project to control street and house floods.

Major problems assigned *Adamson* were what to do about trash-clogged catch basins and drainage in areas in which building has outstripped drainage and sewerage system capacity.

At a San Mateo city council meeting the *same night,* County Manager Robert Stallings proposed state legislation to permit a county-wide drainage district.

Such a *district,* Stallings said, would supplement a proposal made in both the San Mateo meeting and a council meeting at Burlingame—that these two cities join with Hillsborough and Belmont in a four-city flood control district.

He emphasized the importance of coordination of any such *four-city* project with the efforts of unincorporated areas of the county.

The connective and the adverb—unless they are too conspicuous—are excellent devices for supplying transition. *And,* *but,* and *or* could be used more often by the news writer to begin a sentence. So could such adverbs as *next, later,* and *meanwhile.* The radio writer makes considerable use of adverbs that express time and of expressions that change the scene or the subject-matter. Some of these are: *While the storm was raging in Texas, on the other side of the Pacific, down in Georgia, on the labor front, more recently,* and *the year before.* The writer for the newspaper, although not under the same necessity as is the radio writer, should use more such devices—provided he does not use them in a way that is monotonous.[3]

Transition is achieved naturally when the details of the event are narrated in the order in which they happened; the *momentum* of the story provides an intrinsic continuity that carries the reader along. The following news story from the *San Francisco Chronicle* illustrates how transition is achieved both by the repetition of words and by the momentum given to the narrative by the writer:

Youth Sucked Into Barley Vat, Dies

A whirlpool of sodden barley, draining swiftly from a huge hopper in a malt plant, sucked Martin Drake, 18, to his death yesterday.

Drake died alone, with no one to notice his flailing arms as he groped in vain to save himself from suffocation.

The young State University student was working during his summer vacation at the Pacific Hop and Malt Co., 524 Lucas Street.

With only two weeks experience on the

[3] For an excellent use of transitional devices, see the news story about Gandhi's assassination on pp. 50-52.

job, according to Plant Superintendent J. J. Kearney, Drake was assigned to a task in the *tank room* normally done by two men.

The *tank room* is located high up under the roof of the three-story plant. Yesterday, however, the work force was short-handed and Drake climbed down alone from a catwalk overlooking the *vat*.

It was filled with 14 tons of wet barley. The towering *vat,* funnel-shaped at the bottom, was to be drained of the barley by a hopper at the lower end.

Drake's job was to stand on the slithering top surface of the barley pile and scrape the smooth sides of the vat as the level of the grain diminished.

His instructions, Kearney said, were to stay close to the sides of the round tank, avoiding the center where the downward suction of the draining barley was strongest.

In a room below the hopper, Foreman Frank Cusick opened the tank valve and stood by to watch the barley flow into a conveyor and on to the fermentation tanks where the grain is transformed into malt.

Suddenly the rush of barley stopped, and only a few wet grains came through the hopper. Cusick sent another worker to see what was clogging the foot-wide valve.

The big tank was still nearly full, but Drake was missing and the surface of the barley bore not even a trace of the young employee.

Quickly Cusick reached up through the bottom of the hopper, groping through the wet mass of grain. He felt something hard, pulled, and his hand came out clutching one of Drake's heavy rubber-soled boots.

A Fire Department rescue squad, three engine companies and an ambulance speeded to the plant. While the rescue squad cut through the bottom of the tank with acetylene torches, other firemen ran hoses up the steel catwalks and played water on the grain to keep it from catching fire.

It took more than an hour before the tons of barley were drained out and Drake's body was found. He was standing upright, with his feet jammed in the hopper valve. It was another hour before his body could be extracted....

Ending the news story: Since the facts of very few events can appropriately be organized in a climactic order, very few news stories can have an ending that summarizes the facts or that carries a punch. News stories would be more interesting if it were always possible to have an ending that was separable from the body of the facts. The writer, therefore, should keep looking for opportunities to supply an ending. The following news story by Gordon Brown, of the Associated Press, has an appropriate ending although the story is not organized climactically. The story was written at the time of a disastrous flood at Kansas City and in its environs.

WASHINGTON—Army engineers have poured cold water—in reasonable quantities—on a suggestion they might turn the Missouri River around and run it in another direction.

The idea was advanced yesterday at a Senate Appropriations subcommittee hearing on funds for various flood control projects. Senator Thye (R-Minn.) started the discussion with Brig. Gen. C. H. Chorpening, deputy chief of Army engineers.

"I notice on the map," Thye said, "that the Missouri flows south about to Kansas City and then almost turns a right angle (to the east). Would it be possible, General, perhaps to change the river and divert it south or southwest where its waters might be more in demand?"

"Well," said Chorpening, "there's almost no limit to what engineers could do —if they had the money. What you suggest probably could be done but I wouldn't estimate the cost."

"Then it's not feasible?" Thye asked.

The general shook his head and said, "It's not feasible."

He added that cities along the Missouri probably wouldn't like it if someone took their river away....

Senator Ellender (D-La.) suggested it might be possible to divert headwaters of the Missouri southward by tunneling under the Great Divide.

That's where the matter ended. The Missouri apparently is going to stay right where it is—just as soon at it gets back in its bank, that is.

Summary: The conventional chronicle type of news story usually has the inverted pyramid structure, with the lead nearly always separable from the body. The necessity for this kind of organization derives from (a) the need of the reader to find out quickly what happened and (b) the limiting conditions of newspaper making that were described in Chapters I and III. In such news stories transition helps the reader to understand and enlists his interest in reading further into the story.

Some events permit of a climactic organization of the news story; a story organized in that way is more clearly understood by the reader.

THE LEAD

THE NEWS WRITER may begin a story in several ways. The skilled craftsman nearly always knows which is the best way. The kind of beginning the skilled writer uses is pretty much inherent in the subject-matter.

We cannot adequately define the "lead" or "intro" since it now has various forms. Some years ago the lead was thought of as being the first paragraph (or sometimes the first two paragraphs) and it was thought essential that the lead should answer most of these six questions: "What? Who? When? Where? Why? and How?"

Many leads are now written in that form for these reasons: (1) the reader's desire to know quickly what happened; (2) the urgency connected with the publishing of fresh news in each edition; and (3) the necessity for making it possible to edit a news story by cutting some of it from the bottom. The conventional lead, therefore, was constructed so as to fulfill two purposes: (1) to give the gist of the news, and (2) to interest the reader.

The conventional form of the lead, however, did not always fulfill the second of these purposes. In recent years editors of newspapers and news agencies have been influenced by radio news writing. They have also become more conscious of the desirability of efficiency in communication. Hence, they emphasize more than formerly the second purpose of the lead, viz., to interest the reader.

We can still consider the lead as the first *part* of the news story, but we no longer think of it as being completely separable from the body of the story. Answers to some of the six questions are now often placed somewhere in the body of the story so as to make the lead more effective as a way of getting the reader into the story.

In the discussion that follows, the emphasis is on keeping the *first sentence* in the lead short. It doesn't matter very much how many sentences there are in the lead or whether or not all of the six questions are answered in the first sentence (that is, whether the lead is a complete summary of the event).

The gist of the event: When the news story reports a *completed action*, the lead is the gist of that action. For example, when the Norfolk *Virginian-Pilot*, on December 18, 1903, reported the successful airplane flight of the Wright brothers at Kittyhawk, North Carolina, the lead was:

> The problem of aerial navigation without the use of a balloon has been solved at last.

When Charles A. Lindbergh completed the first airplane flight across the Atlantic ocean on May 21, 1927, the lead in the *New York Times* was:

> PARIS—Lindbergh did it.

The usual lead, in other words, reports what happened and tells it in pithy language. Every day we read in our daily newspapers leads like these:

(1)

> A water driller struck oil yesterday near La Honda.

(2)

> Moving an automobile sideways into a tight parking space has long been the

dream of new drivers and the subject of
cartoons about helpless women drivers.

Now it can be done.

(3)

A pill to protect children against polio
is on its way, it appears from results announced by Dr. Herald R. Cox, of Lederle
Laboratories.

(4)

By court decree, a union had the right
today to picket a juke box.

(5)

BUENOS AIRES—Argentina's atomic
energy project has exploded with the force
of a bursting soap bubble.

The lead and the headline usually tell the same facts. In
many instances, the main fact is not as salient as in the leads
just quoted: the writer sometimes must decide which of two
or more facts he will emphasize by putting one of them in the
lead sentence or as they say within the craft, which "angle"
should be "featured." Two large bomber planes collided—a
very unusual happening; only four of the twenty-two men in
the planes were saved—a major tragedy. Which fact should be
emphasized? The Associated Press decided to write the first
paragraph this way:

> STOCKTON, CALIF. (AP)—Two air
> force B-29 Superforts collided 26,000 feet
> above Stockton at midnight Wednesday.
> One fell in flames. The tail of the other
> fell off and it crashed.

And the second paragraph was written this way:

> Four of the 22 men aboard the planes
> were saved. Seven were found dead in the
> wreckage. Eleven were missing.

The following news story could have been written in two ways. Which is the better way?

> An unemployed bartender admitted to police last night that he had stabbed his wife to death.
>
> The police said that Ralph Hodges, 54, admitted he killed his wife, Miriam, 51, in the kitchen of their apartment at 2182 Bell Court, because "she gave me a bad time about being out of work. . . ."

> The first thing Ralph Hodges did after he stabbed his wife to death was to make sure his pet cocker spaniel would have a nice home during his anticipated absence, police said yesterday.
>
> They said Hodges, 54, unemployed bartender, admitted he killed his wife, Miriam, 51, in the kitchen of their apartment at 2182 Bell Court Monday night because "she gave me a bad time about being out of work."
>
> . . . Hodges put down his hunting knife, the murder weapon, on the kitchen drainboard, and took his dog, Amber, to the apartment of his landlady, Mrs. Bertha Harrison, 32.
>
> He asked Mrs. Harrison to take care of the dog—and to call police.

The following news story also could have been written in two ways. Which is preferred, and why?

> The lifeless body of Murray Roberts, an airline technician, was found by police last night on Nursery Road with nine pistol wounds in his face and head. His wife has been missing for three days, neighbors said.
>
> On his forehead were imprints of a kiss, and a thin trail of lipstick was smudged across the bridge of his nose.
>
> Roberts was formerly a staff sergeant

with a battalion in Germany, where he
met his wife.

The ragged, threadbare romance of an
American staff sergeant and the buxom
Bavarian fraulein he married in Germany
five years ago came completely unravelled
yesterday—in murder. . . .

The suspense lead: A lead that relates a completed action
can sometimes, however, spoil an interesting story. Most
"shorts"—i.e., anecdotal news stories—depend for their effect
on suspense. Consider, for example, the difference in these
two lead sentences:

A blonde bathing suit model walked
into the district attorney's office today and
shoved a sackful of fine jewelry and a blue
mink coat across a desk. . . .

A young apprentice printer was booked
on a burglary charge today because his
girl friend became suspicious of his gifts
of expensive gems and a blue mink
coat. . . .

And these two:

Mrs. Ruth Bogen, 26, was reading the
morning mail. One letter from the Veteran's Administration read: "We have
learned with regret of the death of your
husband." She was asked to fill out a form
to collect the $10,000 life insurance.
Mrs. Bogen, the wife of Harold Bogen,
a World War II veteran, looked surprised
and then smiled across the breakfast table
at her three children . . . and her husband.

Mrs. Ruth Bogen read the letter from
the Veteran's Administration, and then
glanced at her husband drinking his
breakfast coffee. . . .

The image of the event: To understand the report of some events the reader or listener has to visualize the happening. The image he perceives is in terms of his own experience-world. Unless he is assisted adequately by the news writer, his image may be blurred. The writer has the obligation to the reader and listener to omit no part of the communication that is necessary to the latters' perception. When the happening relates to such a commonplace as an automobile accident, the writer's task is fairly easy, but often the writer is narrating a happening more remote from the receiver's experience-world. It is especially important for the writer when he is writing the lead to keep in mind that he is presenting an image.

The following leads are good examples of presenting the image of the event:

(1)

Trying to pass another car while going 90 miles an hour brought death to two youths last night on Highway 99 when their automobile struck an overpass.

(2)

FAYETTEVILLE, N. C.—*The sky was filled with silk today* as 1,500 paratroops jumped from 70 C-82 flying boxcars over the North Carolina hills.

It was the largest such demonstration in the nation's peacetime history.

(3)

WASHINGTON—Feb. 6 (UP)—A Polish mystery witness, *wearing a pillow case over his head,* said today he watched from a treetop while Russian soldiers slaughtered 200 Polish officers and dumped their bodies into a mass grave.

When his testimony was complete, Capitol police ... kept spectators back until he was escorted from the room.

(4)

The middle-age couple known here as Mr. and Mrs. Howard Newman sat in their night robes at dawn today and nodded—yes, they were the man and his secretary who disappeared from Toledo 22 years ago....

Both had long since been declared legally dead....

(5)

For an hour and a half yesterday, while the predawn darkness gave way to daylight, a jealous husband sat astraddle another man who was already bleeding from one stab wound, holding a knife at his throat.

Three policemen and the man's wife stood there in the little living room, arguing with the jealous husband.

"Don't kill him," the policemen argued. "He's not worth it."

"He doesn't deserve to live," the husband would tell them.

Eventually, the husband's uncle, a married man himself, persuaded him to give up his weapon and submit to arrest....

There are two ways the lead to the following news story could be written. The writer of the second version is more skilfull in presenting the image because he causes the receiver to identify with the object (i.e., the man inside the ball).

Dr. Otis Barton, forty-eight-year-old undersea explorer, went farther under the ocean today than man had ever gone before when he dived 4500 feet into the dark Pacific in a five-foot round steel ball.

A man in a steel ball saw weird and wondrous marine life 4500 feet down in the Pacific Ocean today, the deepest descent in history.

The writer sometimes has a problem of figure-and-ground. He must so write as to cause the figure he wants the reader to perceive to stand out from the background. In some types of news stories, the figure is the reader himself. One of the following leads does this; the other does not.

> Volunteer airmen are subjecting themselves to "mock airplane crashes" on rocket-propelled sleds in Air Force experiments designed to save lives in accidents, it was announced here today.

> Airplane passengers of the future may ride backward for protection against crash injuries. . . .

The Science Service writer who composed the following lead was trying to communicate to the reader in terms of the reader's personal needs, instead of describing objectively a scientist's research results:

> In case of an A-bomb blast, it may be safer to stay out in the open and cover your head with some cushioning material than to try to hug a wall.
> Dr. Benedict Cassen, of the University of California at Los Angeles' Atomic Energy Project, makes this recommendation. His research has shown that. . . .

The writer, in some situations, is able to include certain details in the lead that help the reader to imagine the happening. Lee Pitt, of the *Houston Press,* did this by putting the principal character in the news story at the place at which the event happened just before it happened and by describing the principal's state of mind. He might have written a lead like this: "A 27-year-old woman was kidnaped by four youths from the steps of a church early this morning and raped in Milby Park." Instead he wrote this lead:

> A 27-year-old girl, her black-and-gold prayer book in her hand, stopped for an

instant on the steps of Immaculate Conception Church.

It was 5:50 A.M.

She was there especially early for Lenten Mass this morning, for her mother was sick and she wanted to attend Mass, get home quickly, cook breakfast and go to her job at an insurance company.

Suddenly two young men came from behind her, pinned her elbows. A car pulled up. The girl was thrust violently into the car, screaming for help that didn't come.

Thus began what Homicide Lt. Frank Murray calls "one of the most vicious crimes ever committed in Houston."

The lead orients the reader: As several of the foregoing leads have indicated, one purpose of the lead is to *get the newspaper reader into* the story. Some of those leads got the reader into the story by assisting his ability to perceive: they provided a clearer image or they caused the reader to identify. Another way to get the reader into the story, when the subject-matter is appropriate, is to achieve a *rapport* with the reader through informality. This does not mean writing down to the reader; it merely means that the writer tells the reader a story as if he were conversing with him in the reader's living room. When relating a story in conversation one does not begin by using formal language such as is found in some leads, but says, "A taxidriver was killed uptown a while ago," or "Did you hear that So-and-so (a famous film actor) got swindled at a clip joint last night?" The radio news writer has to begin in something of that fashion—what Dr. Rudolf Flesch has called a throat-clearing—*because the radio has no headlines* to synopsize the story. The newspaper should do more of it anyway so as to communicate more efficiently. The following news story, for example, is a "translation" of formal "press release English." The writer tries to talk to the reader in terms of the reader's personal need.

> INDIANAPOLIS, Jan. 2 (AP)—Are you shivering in this cold weather? Well, go gnaw a hunk of cabbage.
>
> It all simmers down to a matter of Vitamin C, says the state board of health.
>
> "Cabbage," says Miss Leila Ogle, nutritionist for the board, "is one of. . . ."

The newspaper lead should also, in some instances, orient the reader so that he will not be misled by the facts in the lead —even when they are explained later in the story. That will prevent the reader from jumping to an immediate conclusion. The following Associated Press "one-two" lead is an excellent example of a writer anticipating that some of his readers would not finish reading the news story:

> The Federal Rent Control Act was held unconstitutional today by a federal district judge. But that doesn't mean controls are off now.

Here is another example of how the writer anticipated confusion in the decoding of a communication:

> AMES, IOWA (AP)—A rule of the college at Iowa State College requires that administrative officials retire on the July 1 after they reach 65 years of age. Dr. Charles E. Friley has bowed to the rule and quit office as president of Iowa State College.
>
> The rule doesn't apply to teachers. Dr. Friley will, accordingly, join Iowa State's faculty as a teacher and researcher.

Why did the writer first state the retirement rule before he announced the president's retirement? Because he anticipated that many inattentive readers and listeners would assume that the president was severing his connection completely with the college, whereas he was to remain for a term as a teacher.

The writer sometimes does not take enough pains to write a lead that will orient the reader as to background. The first of the two leads below puzzled readers; the second version oriented readers adequately.

> The fingerprints of young Tommy O'Neill "do not compare" with those taken from the playthings of Ronnie Thompson, who was kidnapped from his home here five years ago, Chief of Police M. G. Kirkpatrick said tonight.

> Fingerprint tests tonight dashed the hopes of Mr. and Mrs. Arthur Thompson that a Michigan orphan might be their son who was kidnapped five years ago . . .

Length of the lead: The traditional rule for writing the "summary" lead required that it contain all of the "5 *W*'s" (*who, what, when, where, why,* and sometimes *how*). That usually meant a lead of one sentence or sometimes of two sentences in the same paragraph. Such lead paragraphs consisted of 50 to 75 words. Here is an extreme example of the summary lead:

What	Registering "an acute sense of disgust" with the practices of the National Labor Relations Board as revealed in the current Congressional investigations, Judge
Who	Thomas D. Thatcher, former solicitor general of the United States, told the
Where, When	State Bar Association yesterday that most of the evils of administrative agencies performing judicial or quasi-judicial func-
What	tions, Federal and State, have resulted from violation of "the most fundamental principle of common justice, that a man cannot be a judge in his own case."

The length of the average lead *sentence* of the Associated Press *AAA* wire report is now about 23 words (including "shorts") because many of the leads are not in summary form.

The summary type of lead has three advantages. One of these is that such a lead goes far to insure the objectivity of the reporter-writer; working within such restrictions, it is difficult (although not at all impossible) for him to color the facts with connotative words and certain twists of emphasis. A second advantage (especially for a news agency and a newspaper with several editions) is that it is the quickest form in which to present the main facts of a news story. A third advantage is that the editor can quickly delete all of the story except the lead and the reader will know the gist of the event. The disadvantage of the summary type of lead is that *it is seldom an efficient wedge into the reader's mind.* It contains more facts, ideas, or names than the usual reader can comprehend without regression.

The best practice, in most situations, is to distribute some of the *W*'s to second and third (and even fourth) paragraphs. The following is an example:

Who *When*	*Glenn McMains,* a husky, self-confessed holdup man, *yesterday* told his version of the robbery-slaying of bookie Martin Breslauer.
What	McMains, 33, is the top prosecution witness in the *murder trial of Roy (Fat) Teller, 27, and John (Midge) Ruano, 34.* Teller and Ruano are accused of killing Breslauer last September 29 in Daly City.
Where	Yesterday was the second day of the trial, which is being held before a jury of eight women and four men in the *court of Superior Judge Murray Draper.*

Names can cram the lead: The following is an example of a lead that forces the normal reader to regress:

Dan Lombardi, South San Francisco police officer, testified in superior court today that *Cecil Barbi,* plaintiff in an assault and battery suit against *Julio Bigazzi,* bartender, was drunk and disorderly at the time of the alleged assault.

Lombardi's charges came under the direct examination of *Frank Fehi,* attorney for the defendant. Lombardi asserted that Barbi was. . . .

When several persons are to be mentioned in a news story, the minor ones can be omitted from the lead, or a phrase can be substituted, such as "Five men were convicted. . . ." Often, too, some of the persons can be identified in the lead but with mention of their name deferred until later in the story. Thus, the foregoing lead could be improved somewhat, as follows:

> A South San Francisco police officer testified in superior court yesterday that Cecil Barbi, who is suing Julio Bigazzi, a bartender, for assault and battery, was drunk and disorderly at the time of the alleged assault.
> The officer, Dan Lombardi, was examined by Frank Fehi, attorney for the defendant.

It will be noticed that many of the leads quoted in this chapter do not contain the name of the person or persons in the news. The reason is, of course, that the lead sentence, being shorter, is a better wedge into the reader's mind. When a widely-known person is the subject of news his name should always be in the lead sentence. In most of the news stories quoted here, however, the name is not as important as the happening.

The use of nameless leads, however, does have one disadvantage: the newspaper may be full of such stories and the reader may feel a monotony in reading that "a taxi driver" did this and "an Eastside business man" did that and "an unemployed plumber" did thus-and-so.

Facts can cram the lead: The following is an example of a lead that forces the reader to regress—or even to cease reading before he has reached the end of the sentence:

> Paper that will not burn, a thin coated fabric that is difficult to tear, layers of impregnated paper that are not marred by boiling water, glass fibers used to increase the beauty of a plastic rather than add to its strength are the interesting

> items included in the latest "Things of
> Science" unit just issued here.

When two or more facts are of equal importance and it is not
desirable to "play" one more than the others, they all can
sometimes be included in the lead by the device of enumeration, as illustrated in the following lead:

> The President said today the refusal of
> State Department officials to disclose (1)
> their policy directives on the controversial
> book issue and (2) the names of books
> removed from overseas libraries was not
> in line with his views.

When this is done, however, it sometimes causes the subject
to be widely separated from the predicate as, for example,
in the foregoing lead.

When the facts are *modifiers* of substantive facts, some of
the modifiers can be distributed to later paragraphs. They do
not all have to be included in the lead.

The transferring of certain modifiers from the first sentence,
however, can have the effect of prescinding an essential part
of the context—and thus preventing the reader or listener
from perceiving the whole meaning of the event. In certain
news stories, some of the substantive words in the lead derive
their full meaning from their directly connected modifiers.
The following Associated Press dispatch is an example of an
instance in which the modifiers should *not* be transferred so
as to shorten the lead sentences. (The essential modifiers are
italicized.)

> JACARTA, JAVA—The 77,000,000
> people of Indonesia snapped their colo-
> nial bond with Holland today and took
> their place as a new nation in *Communist-
> threatened Southeast Asia.*
> *Throughout the chain of islands stretch-
> ing nearly 3000 miles between the Pacific
> and Indian Oceans,* Indonesians tonight

> *peacefully* celebrated their first hours of
> freedom *after 347 years of Dutch rule.*

Scarcely one of the italicized facts was known to the usual American reader or listener. Few of the receivers had a correct conception of the size of the new nation, either as to population or geographic extent. Few of them realized its location—its nearness to Communist China and to Communist-invaded Indo-China. Many did not know the islands had been Dutch colonies. And, except for the modifier, *peacefully*, many readers, at the beginning of the story, would have perceived an image of violent revolution. The modifying facts, of course, could have been prescinded from the lead and recited later in the story, but the total impression of the communication would have been weakened.

In the following instance the modifier is a part of the gist of the story. If the modifier had been omitted from the lead, the story would have been routine and of less interest to the readers; it would not have presented the readers with a mystery.

> A *financially well-off* couple was arrested
> in a raid early today and the husband
> admitted selling his wife's favors to other
> men.

It is better to write a long lead sentence than to write one that omits some essential qualification or one that overgeneralizes as to the gist of the happening.

The grammar of the lead sentence: An analysis of the numerous lead sentences quoted in this chapter up to this point shows that only three varied from the normal sentence order. In one of these the sentence was interrogatory; in another the sentence began with an adverbial phrase; in the third the sentence began with a participial phrase (which was quoted only as a "horrible example"). The normal sentence order (omitting modifiers) is: first, the subject, next the finite verb, next the indirect object (when there is one) and, finally, the direct object of the verb. Thus: "John gave Mary plums." This is a *fixed* order; it is fixed by the habits and logic of language which English-speaking people have developed through the years. We cannot say, for example, "John gave plums Mary" and expect it to be understood easily.

Any deviation from the normal sentence order can be justified only for purposes of emphasis, and in most of those situations the element that is permuted is a modifier of one of the basic sentence components, not one of the basic components. Thus, it was to achieve emphasis that the lead quoted on page 67 read: "By court decree, a union had the right today to picket a juke box."

Deviation from normal sentence order very often creates semantic noise, which is sometimes a greater evil than lack of adequate emphasis. The following lead, which begins with a participial phrase, is an example of inefficient communication:

> Climaxing an intensive drive staged during the past two years by the State Federation of Women's Clubs, groundbreaking exercises were held yesterday for the new hostess house at Yountville, and all is in readiness for the immediate start of the new $60,000 building.

Beginning a lead sentence with a participial phrase is sometimes justified when the *time* or *place* element needs to be emphasized. A sound rule, however, is to stick to normal sentence order except when the emphasis seems to be very necessary. An example of the emphasis on time (and circumstance):

> After living fourteen days on a rubber raft, Taylor Spence was rescued today from the Pacific Ocean.

The reader of this book may have noticed that in nearly every lead quoted the time element was buried in the most unemphatic part of the sentence.

Here is an example of the emphasis on place:

> Beside the grave of his wife, who died only two days ago, ex-Governor Burton Wallis was interred in Glenview cemetery today.

Quotation leads: If there is a rule of writing which has universal application by editors, it is: "Never—almost never —use a quotation in a lead sentence." A quotation, if it is of normal length, does not get the reader into the story. The inverted commas are a sign to the reader that somebody is talking, and what the reader wants to read about is action. In a speech report, the best practice is to convert the lead quotation into indirect discourse (see Chapter XI). In any type of news story, a quotation lead is justified only when it is brief, is a part of the gist of the happening, or contributes to the imagery the writer is striving for. Here are three examples of quotation leads which appear to be justified:

(1)

> "I went swimming, Daddy."
> Those were the first weak words of 3-year-old Glenn Machos when he was revived Tuesday from a "swim" in a rain-filled pipe-line excavation hole which almost cost him his life.

(2)

> "He was ugly looking and he made me that way," explained a young lady who yesterday beat her sleeping father to death with a hammer.

(3)

> "I'll show you suckers where I'm going," Bernard Martin shouted, and then plunged ten floors to his death yesterday from a window at City Hospital.

The tone of the lead: When the writer intends to adopt the point of view of a narrator of a human interest story or other type of affective writing he establishes a tone at the beginning that is a signal to the reader or listener that his intent is affective. Some stories of that type will be discussed in Chapter XI. As one example of a situation in which the writer tells the reader immediately that he is not writing with a straight face is this lead from a news story that was presented in full on pages 63-64.

> WASHINGTON—Army engineers have poured cold water—in reasonable quantities—on a suggestion they might turn the Missouri River around and run it in another direction.

Once in a while a news writer violates the reader's sense of the fitness of things by adopting a frivolous tone for a story that is essentially serious, such as one involving death. The thoughtful writer just doesn't write in the same key about a tragedy and about flying saucers.

Here is the lead of a front page story (with a 3-column picture of an automobile and a locomotive) in which a woman driver of an auto struck by a locomotive at the street crossing was unhurt, although she remained in the auto while the locomotive carried the car for nearly a block. If she had been killed or badly injured, this lead, by Ed Cony of the Portland *Oregonian,* would have been inappropriate:

> You know how it is when you're late for work. Everything that happens seems cunningly contrived to delay you.
>
> That was the situation as Martha Jensen drove down S.E. Hawthorne Boulevard Saturday night bound for the west side and work at the China Clipper restaurant. Sure enough, there was a southbound train just coming into the intersection at Hawthorne and S.E. First Avenue....

The second-day lead: For a story that has broken for an afternoon newspaper, the morning newspaper tries to develop a new angle in its lead (and vice versa for the other news cycle). In that situation, the second-day lead should include, if possible, the essentials that were in the first lead.

First day:
A committee of citizens announced *today* it is circulating a petition for the disincorporation of Los Altos.

Second day:
State law may delay the Los Altos disincorporation movement that was launched *yesterday.*

Dr. Morris Winslow, chairman of the Committee for Incorporation, said the courts had held that a petition for disincorporation could not be filed until two years had elapsed.

In trying to fulfill two purposes, however, the writer of the second-day lead risks overloading it with facts. The following example turned up in the Associated Press readability survey in 1948:

CHAMPAIGN, ILL.—The Supreme Court's ruling that voluntary religious instruction in Champaign public schools is unconstitutional is viewed by opposing parties as "a severe blow" to religion and having "safeguarded our school system from sectarian domination."

Dr. Flesch, the AP consultant, rewrote the lead as follows:

CHAMPAIGN, ILL.—The attorney who lost in the Supreme Court's ruling that voluntary religious instruction in Champaign public schools is unconstitutional *today* called the high court's decision a severe blow to religion.

(Then go on with the other side's view.)

In rewriting for a second-day lead, as these examples show, two lead sentences are nearly always necessary if the writer is to fulfill both purposes of the lead. To avoid writing two sentences, the writer of the second-day lead sometimes resorts to hyphenate expressions, as for example: "Rebel-seized ships of the Peruvian navy entered Callao harbor today flying white flags of surrender. . . ." Such expressions are sometimes meaningful in print but seldom are meaningful when spoken on the radio.

Here is an example of a rewrite when there is no new development; the writer simply features a fact that was not featured in the preceding news cyle.

First day:

A young woman bank teller pretended a faint just before noon *today,* foiling an attempted holdup at the First National Bank.

The holdup man walked out of the bank before an alarm could be sounded and escaped in a new gray Studebaker car.

He did not get a cent.

The teller, Mrs. Joan Osborn, 22, said a young man in his early twenties walked up to her window and handed her a note and a $1 bill. . . .

"When the other man came to the window and threw down a note and a $1 bill I knew what it was," Mrs. Osborn said.

Second day:

A pretended faint frightened away a holdup man and made a $1 profit for the First National Bank shortly before noon *yesterday.*

Sometimes the writer, striving for a second-day lead that sounds fresh, produces something that is ridiculous, as in this one: "Siwash College *today* held a 21 to 7 football victory over State U. as the result of a game *last night.*"

Empty and irrelevant leads: Sometimes when the writer has difficulty in deciding which fact to feature in the lead he writes an empty lead; this happens most often in the report of a speech that itself is rather empty. The following is an example:

> Mayor Miller Ingram addressed the
> League of Women Voters yesterday.

Sometimes, when the writer is trying for some effect he isn't sure about, he features an irrelevant fact. The following lead, for example, is about a trial being held in a Montana barroom:

> A cigarette-eating deer today peered
> through a saloon to watch this gold-mining
> camp's first trial in 40 years.

Summary: Depending upon the subject-matter of the news story, the lead should (1) tell the reader the gist of the event; (2) present the image of the event; or (3) orient the reader as to what is to follow. Except in certain circumstances, the lead should get the reader into the news story. This means that, in general, the lead sentence should not be long: it will then cram the lead with facts or names. Some leads are better if they contain two short sentences instead of one long one. (The headline writer gives the gist of the story in ten or fewer words.) The lead sentence should be in the normal sentence order except when a different order will emphasize an element such as time or place. The subject-matter of some news stories permits of a suspense lead in which the writer relates the details of the event in the order in which they happened.

Chapter VII ··

SENTENCES

WE ASSUME THAT the student, having taken the usual English composition course, does not need in this chapter a treatment of the elementary facts about the sentence. The discussion here is confined to those points that need some elaboration in relation to efficient communication.

These are the main faults in making sentences that cause inefficient communication: (1) changing the expected pattern; (2) improper sentence emphasis; and (3) unnecessary interruptions within the sentence.

Changing the pattern: A major fault in sentence construction for communication is the instance in which the writer— unaware of what he is doing to the mind of the reader or listener—fails to continue the pattern the receiver expects. By what he has first written or spoken he has presented a certain frame of reference, but he then shifts away from it. He has prepared the reader to anticipate a certain structure or a certain meaning, but he presents a different one. In brief, he hasn't said what he intended to say. This mistake puzzles the reader and causes him to regress. There are two kinds of such mistakes: (1) the dangling modifier, and (2) the lack of parallel construction.

The dangling modifier: The writer sometimes states or implies a subject and then changes it in the sentence. The change is the result of his not placing a modifier adjacent to the subject he had in mind. For example:

Bad: The robbers shot the cashier and, having robbed the vault, their fast automobile speeded away.

Right: The robbers shot the cashier. Then they robbed the vault and speeded away in a fast automobile.

Bad: In reaching for the rope, her neck got caught in the loop suspending her three feet above the garage floor.

Right: When she reached for the rope her neck got caught in the loop, suspending her three feet above the garage floor.

Bad: Dickey the pitcher fell behind the count immediately. After striking out Garbowski and Vico, Jimmy Rivera hit a scorching grounder past second base.

Right: After Dickey had struck out Garbowski and Vico, he immediately got behind the count on Jimmy Rivera. Jimmy hit a scorching grounder past second base.

Parallel construction: Because there are so many ways to say something in English, the writer sometimes says it two ways in the same sentence. This confuses the reader who expects that the second element will have the same form as the first. For a like meaning there must be a like construction. In some "bad" instances, the first sentence element is a substantive and the succeeding one is a gerund; in other instances, the first element is an infinitive ("to swim") and the second is a gerund ("hunting"). An example:

Bad: The accused men denied the *theft* and *dumping* the woman in a ditch.

Right: The accused men denied stealing the jewels and dumping the woman in a ditch.

Writers have more trouble with two relative clauses that are not parallel in construction than with infinitives and gerunds. An example:

Bad: He said he had met many people in Denmark whom he had seen before but did not know their names.

Right: He said he had met many people in Denmark whom he had seen before but whose names he did not know.

A requirement somewhat similar to parallel construction is that sentence elements of like *importance* be joined as equals. The rule can be stated negatively as follows: do not subordinate an important idea to one of less importance. An example of joining unequal ideas:

Bad: Councilman Mitchell pointed out that the city is growing rapidly and that an improved system for distribution of electricity is needed.

Better: Councilman Mitchell pointed out that *since* the city is growing rapidly an improved system for distribution of electricity is needed.

Sentence emphasis: The excerpt just quoted is an aspect not only of the requirement for parallel construction but also of the requirement for sentence emphasis. For example, the improved version presented above could be further improved by changing the passive voice to active voice in the last clause:

Councilman Mitchell pointed out that, since the city is growing rapidly, it needs an improved distribution of electricity.

The most emphatic part of a short or a fairly short sentence is the beginning; the reason for this is that the first word or group of words is the first perceived. The most emphatic part of a long sentence is the end; the reason for this is that the ultimate meaning of the sentence is suspended and, hence, the greater is the impression on the receiver's mind when he perceives that the writer has reached his goal. In the fairly short sentence, the end, as well as the beginning, is an emphatic part although not as emphatic as is the beginning. Since informative writing does not employ long sentences as much as does affective writing, the main problem of sentence emphasis in the newspaper relates to the beginning.

The newspaper sentence, as mentioned earlier,[1] *should not usually have a weak beginning,* such as the following sentences:

[1] Pp. 59.

Bad: There are many tenants who expect to oppose the ending of rent controls.

Better: Many tenants are expected to oppose the ending of rent controls.

Bad: It was decided to instruct the assessor not to devalue the land in the light industrial district.

Better: The council directed the assessor not to devalue the land in the light industrial district.

It will be noted that some sentences in this book have a weak beginning, such as this one. That practice is appropriate in a textbook because the author is addressing sophisticated readers and, hence, does not wish to appear patronizing by addressing them directly ("you will note that"). Newspaper writing, however, is more direct because sentence emphasis is more necessary for communicating to all kinds of readers who read under less than ideal conditions.

The time element in the newspaper lead sentence should be buried in the most unemphatic part of the sentence except when there is a good reason for emphasizing time.[2] Thus, the usual lead should read: "A water driller struck oil *yesterday* near La Honda."

Another aspect of emphasis is *voice*. Whether the writer uses the active or the passive voice depends upon whether he wishes to emphasize the actor or the thing done (that is, the goal of the action). In the following example there is no good reason for emphasizing the object of the verb:

Passive voice: The telephone pole was crashed into by the speeding car.

Active voice: The speeding car crashed into the telephone pole.

In one situation, however, the writer should disregard the need for emphasis and use the passive voice just to avoid the monotonous repetition of the subject in a series of sentences. An example is the report of a city council meeting by a writer

[2] See p. 80 for examples of emphasizing the time element in the lead sentence.

who has repeatedly written, "The city council directed the city attorney. . . ." and "The city council appropriated $7,500 for . . . ." To avoid this repetition of the subject the writer begins the next sentence, "An ordinance to require . . . was passed by a 12 to 3 vote."

The passive voice is also appropriate in those instances when it assists transition and when it preserves the unity of a section of the discourse. (The next sentence is an example of both instances.)

Emphasis can also be achieved by the repetition of a word within the sentence when the repeated word is followed by a modifier of the former word. This is an example: "Still there were rumors—rumors that connected her with the strange death of Nancy Hulton." That is more effective than "Still there were rumors. These connected her with the death of Nancy Hulton."

Since newspapers seldom use italics or bold face for emphasizing a word or a phrase, the writer has to rely for emphasis on skillful repetition and skillful sentence construction. In radio writing, however, the writer sometimes underlines or capitalizes certain words or phrases so the announcer will stress them. It is a good practice for the newspaper writer to read aloud what he has written so as to improve his sentence emphasis.

Interruptions within the sentence: The news writer increases the probability that readers will understand him when he uses normal sentence order, that is, (1) subject, (2) finite verb, (3) indirect object, and (4) direct object.[3] When he varies it—as he sometimes must for emphasis and for transition—he risks creating semantic noise. And even when he uses normal sentence order he may decrease the efficiency of his communication by careless arrangement of the modifiers of the basic sentence elements. Some modifiers are interruptions of the thought because they intervene between the subject

[3] See p. 79-80.

and the verb; in one sense they are digressive. Modifiers may be so placed as to create ambiguity and, hence, confusion.

One example of the mishandling of modifiers relates to the *identification* of the persons in the news. In the following sentence, the subject of the sentence has two modifiers: "MILAN, Italy—Mrs. Carla Toscanini, wife of conductor Arturo Toscanini, ill with a heart condition . . ." Who is ill? Mr. or Mrs.? Usually, a good remedy for this fault is to divide a sentence that has several modifiers into two sentences.

Wide separation of the subject and the verb does not usually cause ambiguity, but it retards the speed of reading and causes regression. One example, which is not extreme, will suffice:

Bad: The electrical manufacturing firm says persons suspected of party leanings who refuse to sign affidavits that they have never supported the Communists will be fired.

Better: The electrical manufacturing firm says it will fire persons suspected of party leanings who refuse to sign affidavits that they have never supported the Communists.

Rhythm of sentences: It is only when a news story contains descriptive elements that sentence rhythm becomes very important either for the newspaper writer or the radio writer.[4] But since unrhythmic sentences detract from clarity, the writer has another reason for sometimes reading his copy aloud. One example of rhythmic sentences will suffice at this point; the excerpt is from a report of a prizefight by W. W. (Red) Smith of the New York *Herald Tribune:*

> . . . Now Wolcott was in full flight, and
> the crowd was booing him. He ducked
> and danced and ran. He was caught and
> hit; he clinched and held; he ran again.

The writer of news that is to be broadcast should read his copy so as to improve those sentences that are sing-song, are

[4] For a discussion of descriptive news writing, see Chapter IX.

too alliterative, or that contain too many sibilants (as "He said certain subjects cannot be discussed!").

Tense: The beginning news writer sometimes is careless in his use of tenses. He sometimes uses, in certain situations, the past instead of the past-perfect tense and the past instead of the present tense.

The past tense should refer to an action that was *completed* in the past, as in "We won the game." The past-perfect tense should refer to an action that happened in the past *before some other action that happened in the past,* as in "Senator Magruder died today. He *had been* ill several months." In many situations, strict adherence to the use of the past-perfect (instead of the past) tense is not required: the writer may choose the past tense *unless it will result in ambiguity.* Thus, "The driver *surrendered* before the highway patrolman learned of the accident," violates the strict rule but is not ambiguous.

The news writer often could use the present tense more than he does. For example, he could change the italicized verbs in the excerpts below from past to present tense:

> A preliminary budget of record proportions for the next fiscal year was submitted to the board of supervisors by the county auditor yesterday.
> The budget *totaled* [totals] $54,771,640, an increase of $2,883,650 over the current budget. That budget *called for* [calls for] an increase of 27 cents in the property tax rate. . . .

Unlike the radio news writer, the newspaper news writer in some situations has the problem of making the story stand up for several hours although contingencies may change the facts he has just written. For example: he writes a story at 5 o'clock in the afternoon for a morning newspaper that will not be available to the reader until the next morning. He must write the story so it will stand up when it is read. Hence

he writes: "Workers *were* on strike today." Should the strike
be settled at a late hour, the story still would be correct since
the context implies that a settlement is possible at any time.
The radio news writer, however, publishes his news immediately. Hence, he may use the present tense: "Workers *are*
on strike today."

The news writer, of course, uses the present tense in statements that are permanently or historically true; as for example: "His new play *describes* life in a small Kansas town."

Punctuation: No good purpose will be served by reviewing
in this book the rules about punctuation that the student presumably learned in his English composition course. Compliance with some of the rules varies with writers anyway. One
basic rule will be stated: *Use a punctuation mark whenever
it will make the expression less ambiguous;* and use the punctuation mark that will assist the reader's understanding and
accelerate his reading speed. Sir Ernest Gowers [5] illustrates
this point when he discusses whether to use a comma after
the next to last item in a series. He advises this punctuation
in the following sentence: "The company included the Bishops of Winchester, Salisbury, Bristol, and Bath and Wells."
Since the writer intends to mention only four bishops, the
last comma conveys that intended meaning. Without that
comma, as Sir Ernest shows, the sentence could be construed
in two other ways.

Sentence length: For communicating understandably, the
writer should not use complex sentences; that means they
should not, *on the average,* be long. Very often the writer
can divide one sentence into two. But he does not need to
make all of his sentences short; that practice produces a stac-
cato style. The writer, unconsciously, may write sentences of
about uniform length; if he does so, he should deliberately
strive for some variety of length so as to avoid a monotony
of rhythm. The average sentence length of the Associated

[5] *Op. cit.,* p. 32.

Press *A* wire report is 19 words, but many local stories and some important Associated Press stories have a higher average. (The average sentence length of the matter in various types of magazines is shown in Table 1.) Fig. 4 shows the range and average length of sentences in a fairly typical chronicle type of news story.

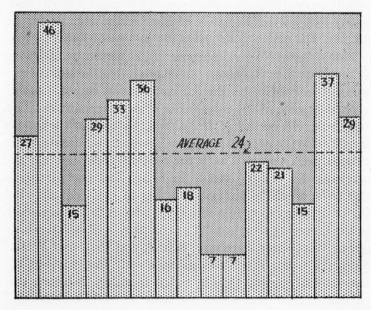

Fig. 4. The length of sentences in a fairly typical news story in the *Wall Street Journal*.

The Flesch readability formula: Dr. Rudolf Flesch, in 1943, developed a formula to measure readability,[6] and in 1948 revised it into twin formulas.[7]

We are discussing here the revised formulas. The first one measures "reading ease." It uses two elements: (1) average

[6] *Marks of Readable Style: A Study in Adult Education*, Contribution to Education No. 897 (New York, Teachers College, Columbia University).

[7] "A New Readability Yardstick," *Journ. of Applied Psychology*, Vol. 32 (1948), pp. 221-233. By permission of the author and publisher; copyright 1948 by The American Psychological Association, Inc.

TABLE 1: Pattern of Reading Ease Scores

Reading Ease Scores	Description of Style	Typical Magazine	Syllables per 100 Words	Average Sentence Length in Words
0 to 30	Very difficult	Scientific	192 or more	29 or more
30 to 50	Difficult	Academic	167	25
50 to 60	Fairly difficult	Quality	155	21
60 to 70	Standard	Digests	147	17
70 to 80	Fairly easy	Slick-fiction	139	14
80 to 90	Easy	Pulp-fiction	131	11
90 to 100	Very easy	Comics	123 or less	8 or less

TABLE 2: Pattern of Human Interest Scores

Human Interest Score	Description of Style	Typical Magazine	Percentage of Personal Words	Percentage of Personal Sentences
0 to 10	Dull	Scientific	2 or less	0
10 to 20	Mildly interesting	Trade	4	5
20 to 40	Interesting	Digests	7	15
40 to 60	Highly interesting	New Yorker	11	32
60 to 100	Dramatic	Fiction	17 or more	58 or more

sentence length in words; and (2) average word length in syllables. The second formula measures "human interest." It also uses two elements: (1) average percentage of "personal words" (i.e., all nouns with natural gender, all pronouns except neuter pronouns, and the words *people* when used with the plural verbs and *folks*); and (2) average percentage of "personal sentences" (i.e., "spoken sentences, marked by quotation marks or otherwise; questions, commands, requests, and other sentences directly addressed to the reader; exclamations; and grammatically incomplete sentences whose meaning has to be inferred from the context").

The importance of human interest in news communication has been discussed in Chapter II. One value of the Flesch human interest formula is that it relates to *comprehension;* that is, it measures (perhaps partially but yet directly) the extent to which "human interest in a given text will make the reader understand it better." [8] A major value, however, is that the human interest in a written discourse motivates the reader to read it.

Both formulas yield a score of from 100 to 0. Table 1 shows

[8] For an explanation of why this is so, see Flesch, *ibid.,* p. 226.

the range for the reading ease scores and Table 2 for the human interest scores. The numerical scores, it will be noticed, correspond to the average scores of the matter in various types of magazines and to verbal descriptions of style, such as "easy," "fairly easy," and "very difficult," for reading ease; and "dull," "interesting," and "dramatic," for human interest. A reading ease score of 100 corresponds to "reading matter that is understandable for persons who have completed fourth grade and are, in the language of the U. S. Census, 'functionally literate' "; a score of 90 to 100 is designated as "very easy." The lowest score—from 30 to 0—corresponds to the description, "very difficult."

The reading ease formula is more important to the news writer than is the human interest formula because the writer only infrequently controls the subject-matter he writes about. Since the elements in the reading ease formula are average sentence length in words and average word length in syllables, the formula is a useful tool to use now and then as a check on one's writing. It is not a recipe for writing, but a way to tell whether or not one has been writing in a way that decreases the efficiency of his communication. The reader of this book will be more able to appreciate the value of this tool after he has read the next chapter.

How to apply the formula: Dr. Flesch, in the article referred to in footnote 7, explains how to apply the formula:

Step 1. Unless you want to test a whole piece of writing, take samples. Take enough samples to make a fair test (say, three to five of an article and 25 to 30 of a book). Don't try to pick "good" or "typical" samples. Go by a strictly numerical scheme. For instance, take every third paragraph or every other page. Each sample should start at the beginning of a paragraph.

Step 2. Count the words in your piece of writing or, if you are using samples, take each sample and count each word in it up to 100. Count contractions and hyphenated words as one word. Count as words numbers or letters separated by space.

Step 3. Count the syllables in your 100-word samples or, if you are testing a whole piece of writing, compute the number of syllables per 100 words. If in doubt about syllabication rules, use any good dictionary. Count the number of syllables in symbols and figures according to the way they are normally read aloud, e.g., two for $ ("dollars") and four for 1918 ("nineteen-eighteen"). If a passage contains several or lengthy figures, your estimate will be more accurate if you don't include these figures in your syllable count. In a 100-word sample, be sure to add instead a corresponding number of words in your syllable count. To save time, count all syllables except the first in all words of more than one syllable and add the total to the number of words tested. It is also helpful to "read silently aloud" while counting.

Step 4. Figure the average sentence length in words for your piece of writing or, if you are using samples, for all your samples combined. In a 100-word sample, find the sentence that ends nearest to the 100-word mark—that might be at the 94th word or the 109th word. Count the sentences up to that point and divide the number of words in those sentences by the number of sentences. In counting sentences, follow the units of thought rather than the punctuation: usually sentences are marked off by periods; but sometimes they are marked off by colons or semicolons—like these. But don't break up sentences that are joined by conjunctions like *and* or *but.*

Step 5. Figure the number of "personal words" per 100 words in your piece of writing or, if you are using samples, in all your samples combined. "Personal words" are: (*a*) All first-, second-, and third-person pronouns except the neuter pronouns *it, its, itself,* and *they, them, their, theirs, themselves* if referring to things rather than people. (*b*) All words that have masculine or feminine natural gender, e.g. *Jones, Mary, father, sister, iceman, actress.* Do not count common-gender words like *teacher, doctor, employee, assistant, spouse.* Count singular and plural forms. (*c*) The group words *people* (with the plural verb) and *folks.*

Step 6. Figure the number of "personal sentences" per 100 sentences in your piece of writing or, if you use samples, in all your samples combined. "Personal sentences" are: (*a*) Spoken sentences, marked by quotation marks or otherwise, often including so-called speech tags like "he said (e.g. "I doubt it."—We told him: "You can take it or leave it."—"That's all very well," he replied, showing clearly that he didn't believe a word of what we said). (*b*) Questions, commands, requests, and other sentences directly addressed to the reader. (c) Exclamations. (d) Grammatically incomplete sentences whose full meaning has to be inferred from the context (e.g. Doesn't know a word of English.—Handsome, though.—Well, he wasn't.—The minute you walked out). If a sentence fits two or more of these definitions, count it only once. Divide the number of these "personal sentences" by the total number of sentences you found in Step 4.

Step. 7. Find your "reading ease" score by inserting the number of syllables per 100 words (word length, *wl*) and the average sentence length (*sl*) in the following formula:

R.E. ("reading ease") $= 206.835 - .846\ wl - 1.015\ sl.$

The "reading ease" score will put your piece of writing on a scale between 0 (practically unreadable) and 100 (easy for any literate person).

Step 8. Find your "human interest" score by inserting the percentage of "personal words" (*pw*) and the percentage of "personal sentences" (*ps*) in the following formula:

H.I. ("human interest") $= 3.635\ pw + .314\ ps.$

The "human interest" score will put your piece of writing on a scale between 0 (no human interest) and 100 (full of human interest).

In applying the formulas, remember that Formula *A* measures *length* (the longer the words and sentences, the harder to read) and Formula *B* measures *percentages* (the more personal words and sentences, the more human interest).

Our discussion of the Flesch formula is resumed in the next chapter. The student will profit from reading some or all of these books by Dr. Flesch: *The Art of Plain Talk* (1946); *The Art of Readable Writing* (1949); *The Way to Write* (with A. H. Lass, 1949); *How to Test Readability* (1951); *The Art of Clear Thinking* (1951); and *How to Make Sense* (1954).

Chapter VIII ∙∙∙∙∙∙∙∙∙∙∙∙∙∙∙∙∙∙∙∙∙∙∙∙∙∙∙∙∙∙∙∙∙∙∙∙

WORDS

THE USUAL news writer has a large stock of words and phrases. If he does not consider which of them to select in terms of the receiver's capacity to comprehend them, he will narrow his potential audience. He can perform like the virtuose pianist—either for himself and a few colleagues in his studio or for the popular audience in the concert hall.

Words in context: Some words evoke a specific meaning *only in context.* Suppose a reader sees this elliptical sentence:

He . . . rifle. . . .

The word *rifle,* with no other context except *he* and the two sets of leaders, either evokes no specific meaning at all or is ambiguous. The word can evoke several meanings, depending upon its verbal context; as for example:

He shot the *rifle* and ran.
He found that the *rifle* in the gun barrel was different from the groove on the bullet.
He allowed the burglars to *rifle* the premises.

A good many words evoke a specific meaning only when considered in their context: think, for example, of the various meanings of such simple words as *run, fly, strike,* and *pool.*

The dictionary is not an authority: All that the usual dictionary does is to record usage. A dictionary is made in this way. The editors assign a large number of part-time collaborators to keep a record of certain assigned words as they read. When a collaborator encounters one of these words he excerpts the passage in which he found it, copying it on a card. After the collaborator has done an exhaustive job of collecting quotations, he delivers his cards to the editors. The editors formulate definitions of these words in terms of the various contexts in which the words had been actually used by the various writers. The unabridged dictionary publishes the definitions and the illustrative quotations. The editors have devised a dictionary in about the same way that all of us have made our own mental dictionary as we have grown up: we have attached a specific meaning to a word as we have heard it or read it in a specific context. For example, we first learn that a "rifle" is "something we shoot"; later, through conversation or reading, we learn that "rifle" has other meanings. The definition of a word in the dictionary, therefore, is not what the editors think the word means: it is what the word meant to the writer who used it. Thus, a dictionary is descriptive rather than prescriptive or proscriptive.

When the usual reader or listener to news meets a word he does not recognize he almost never looks up its definition in the dictionary. He either skips the passage without gaining much understanding of its meaning or he acquires a meaning from the context.

The most common words: There are some words that almost all adults in the United States recognize. E. L. Thorndike and Irving Lorge have made studies to find out which are the most common. Their method was to count the frequency of usage of all words in a large number of books and magazines—a task that required the reading and counting of several million words. An analysis of their findings shows that the most common 1000 words make up 80 per cent of all words they found in print. The next 9000 most common words made up an additional 18 per cent. That is to say, the most common 10,000 words make up 98 per cent of all of the words in print.[1]

[1] See S. S. Smith, *The Command of Words* (New York, 1949), p. 266.

The reader's range of vocabulary, however, should not be equated with his ability to discriminate. This distinction has been illustrated by Professor Allison Davis in a criticism of one of the standard intelligence tests. Scoring of the following test question, for example, *apparently* indicates that children of the upper socio-economic classes are more intelligent than those of the lower socio-economic classes by a ratio of 81 to 52: "A symphony is to a composer as a book is to an. . . ." (the correct answer, of course, is "author"). When this type of question is changed to "A baker goes with bread as a carpenter goes with . . ." (a house), the scores of the two groups are equal. Vocabulary, then, is related to environment; that is, to social context. When we say a word is "familiar" we mean that it probably is recognized by most persons because it has appeared in print or in speech very often in a context that is universal.

Prefer a concrete to an abstract word: Let's look at this sentence:

The cessation of home construction, which operated throughout the war period, developed an accretion of demand.

Several words in this sentence are abstract words. Look, first, at the phrase *home construction*. It is an *abbreviated* way of presenting an image of many homes being built—Joe Jones' home in Pittsburgh, Mrs. William Tyler's home in Nebraska, the Metropolitan Life Insurance Company's apartment houses on Long Island, and thousands of other homes being built. It is equivalent to the mathematical expression "$home_1 + home_2 + home_3 + \ldots home_n$." The phrase *home construction* is an abstract one because it presents a concept that describes no single concrete instance but includes all things of the same kind. It is a *general* term that includes all of the particulars. Look at the words *cessation, accretion,* and *demand,* which also are abstract words. Other abstract expressions we often see in print are *cost, business, consumption,*

system, work, the press, farm assets, and *criminal element.*
None of them refers to a unique object or state or situation.

Hayakawa,[2] after Korzybski, has illustrated the process of
abstracting by a "ladder of abstraction" with which he shows
the different *levels* of abstraction. An abbreviated list of these
levels is as follows: (1) The word *Bessie* for cow $_1$ as distinguished from cow $_2$, cow $_3$, and so forth; (2) the word *cow;*
(3) the word *livestock,* which classifies *Bessie* with those other
animals whose characteristics she shares; (4) the term *farm
assets* which classifies *Bessie* with other items whose characteristics she shares; (5) the term *assets;* and (6) the term
wealth—an extremely high level of abstraction.

If we did not use *some* abstract words in writing and speaking, we could not communicate without an intolerable redundancy. But we do not always have to use them; often we
can use concrete words. When we do use abstract words—
especially a succession of them in the same sentence—we re-
tard the decoding procedure. When a reader or listener meets
an abstract word he has to translate it into something concrete: *he has to choose from his stock of images one that fits
his experience.* For example, when he reads or hears "Business is profiteering," he has to sort out in his mind as a particular for "business" retail stores, wholesale firms, or large
industrial corporations.

This necessity for the receiver to select a particular sometimes turns up in opinion polling. For instance, the question,
"Do you think business men are making higher or lower
profits than before the war?" The administrator of the poll
thought the question referred to the profits of corporations.
But, unfortunately, he had structured the context for many
respondents by asking a previous question: "About how
much has the cost of living increased during the past twelve
months?" Many respondents, therefore, thought the term

[2] S. I. Hayakawa, *Language in Thought and Action* (New York, 1949),
p. 169.

business men referred to retailers, and they interpreted the second question to mean, "Are retailers charging me too much for the goods I buy?" These responses invalidated the findings of the poll.

Communication—especially mediated communication—is more efficient when the writer, in advance of writing a sentence, takes the pains to translate his own thoughts into a more concrete language instead of requiring the receiver to do so. For example, he could translate the sentence on page 101 to read:

Because so few homes were built during the war the demand accumulated.

In this recast sentence we have not succeeded in replacing all of the abstract words, but we have got rid of all of the "tion" words.

The reader of this book might like to try to translate the following news story which contains many abstract words.

> An intensification of the drive against tax-evading racketeers was promised yesterday by the Secretary of the Treasury as part of the reorganization of the Bureau of Internal Revenue.
>
> Speaking at ceremonies in which the newly-appointed officials of the bureau took their oaths of office, he said:
>
> "In recent years the criminal element has attempted tax evasion with greater persistence than ever before. It is our determination that this persistence will be met with even greater enforcement diligence."

Or this paragraph from a news story:

> Neither police nor District Attorney Sparks were present for the recantation and exculpation, although they were ostentatiously invited by the Public Defender's office.

Concreteness contributes so much toward making a piece of writing readable (i.e., "easy to read because [it is] interesting or pleasing") that Dr. Rudolf Flesch published in 1954 an experimental formula to measure that quality in writing which he calls "realism, specificity, concreteness." The formula ranks a piece of writing according to this quality (the r score) by counting "all references to one or more specific human beings and their attributes and possessions, plus all references to named or numbered things, location on a map, dates in the calendar, times on the clock, and colors on the spectrum." By this formula, writing that relates to abstractions (e.g., most academic and professional writing) rates very low and much fiction and drama rates very high. For a complete explanation of this formula and also Dr. Flesch's e score, which measures the quality of "communicative energy" in a piece of writing, the reader is referred to his book, *How to Make Sense*.[3]

Prefer a "familiar" word: How can the writer know which words are and which are not familiar to most of the members of his large audience? He could refer, of course, to the Thorndike-Lorge word list which will tell him which words readers of print have been exposed to most often. *But the writer, in practice, cannot work from a word list.* Nor is the number of syllables in the word a certain clue to familiarity. For example, the following two-syllable words—and a good many others—are outside of the 20,000 most common words; that is, they are words that the reader of print has had only slight opportunity to meet.

defer	evict	inept
delete	evince	rebut
demise	fatal	recede
demote	fracas	recoil
dour	furor	rile
dowdy	grisly	roil

[3] Rudolf Flesch, *How to Make Sense* (New York, Harper & Brothers, 1954). Copyright 1953 by Rudolf Flesch.

Some four- and five-syllable words, on the other hand, are included within the 5000 and 10,000 most common words; for example:

Within 5,000	*Within 10,000*
administration	approbation
anniversary	conspicuous
authority	controversy
development	determination
establishment	fundamental
examination	negotiation
extraordinary	preliminary
institution	responsibility
recommendation	simultaneous

Some polysyllabic words are just about as "familiar" as their one-syllable synonyms. (The numerals after each of the following words indicate in which of the *thousands* of commonest words it was found by the Thorndike and Lorge counts.)

fundamental (7)	basic (11)
sufficient (3)	enough (1)
endeavor (4)	try (1), attempt (2)
assist (2)	help (1)
construct (3)	build (1)
confer (4)	meet (1)
acquire (3)	get (1)
encounter (3)	meet (1)

The writer can surmise correctly that nearly all words with a special meaning—regardless of their length—are unfamiliar to those persons in his audience who are not in certain professions, who are not associated with government, and who live in a certain section of the country. A few of these are *escrow, unilateral, collateral, cloture, devaluation, therapy,* and *bituminous.* The news writer should either not use them at all or, if he does, he should explain them.

Context is a clue to meaning: Some words, not instantly recognized by a reader, can yet be understood by him *pro-*

vided the writer has built in the appropriate context. The reader may not be able to define the unfamiliar word, yet its meaning is clear enough for him to understand the relevant part of the news story. Context can be extended in several ways:

1. By a definition that is a *restatement* of the expression in familiar terms:

(1)

Judge Keegan said he would admit the *holographic* will to probate even though the subscribing witnesses could not be located.

The judge explained that when the will is *holographic* it is not necessary for a subscribing witness to testify that the testator's signature is genuine. The whole document is in his handwriting, he said.

(2)

The government today won its first Chinese *derivative citizenship* case.

Federal Judge Martin E. Colebaugh handed down an opinion denying two Chinese a declaration of American citizenship because they failed to prove they are children of an American father.

2. By a definition that builds in *a contrast* to the expression:

The Senator was astonished.

"How can you say," he demanded of the treasurer, "that your investment committee was *bullish* when they sold so many stocks on a falling market?"

3. By building in *an example* of the expression:

... The Boston publisher asked the court for an *injunction* to force the Hale-Persons Publishing Co. to withdraw its own book from the market and to destroy all copies and plates.

When the writer is able to build in defining context he does not need to worry too much that the word is unfamiliar or long. One unfortunate effect of the Flesch formula has been to cause some writers to shun certain words whose meaning can be made plain. The word *injunction*, used in the last example, is an instance: some news writers have been writing all around the word, calling it a "court action" and "an action to halt thus and so." Injunction is not an abstract word and it is included in the Thorndike-Lorge 8000 most common words; it is, however, a three-syllable word and a technical word, but, like another technical word, *mortgage*, it is understood by most people when it appears in its usual context.

Wilson L. Taylor [4] has demonstrated that the ability of readers to supply a word that has been prescinded from a passage is a measure of the readability of that passage. The procedure calls for the deleting of every *n*th word in a passage and for the supplying by readers of the missing words. Scores made by groups of readers correlate highly with the standard comprehension tests, and seem to predict readability as accurately as do the readability formulas. *Thus, it is a test of how closely the reader's way of decoding a message corresponds to the way that the writer encoded it.* Since the clues to meaning reside in the context of the passage, it appears to be a demonstration of some of the points mentioned in this book.

The writer who tries to convey the meaning of a hard word by building in context should not, however, construct a sentence or sequence of sentences that forces the reader to puzzle very long over the meaning of the word. When he does that he retards the decoding process and is creating semantic noise. He should either use a short or familiar synonym or explain the meaning of the word.

Technical terms: A technical term is devised by a specialist

---

[4] " 'Cloze Procedure': A New Tool for Measuring Readability," *Journalism Quarterly*, Vol. 30 (1953), pp. 415-433.

or scientist to stand for a concept or a process when ordinary language does not suffice. Since it has no referent outside the technical frame of reference, it can seldom be defined for the lay reader by context. In such instances, the news writer should not use the term unless he has the space to define it parenthetically. For example, in most news stories about a "suit in equity," it is not necessary to use the term at all. The term would need to be used and defined, however, in an important legal action in which one of the main questions for determination by the judge was whether the action was a "suit in equity" or an "action at law." In that situation the writer would need to define the term by some parenthetical device. The same rule applies to the use of medical terms when the patient is a person of considerable importance or notoriety and the public is eager to know more exactly what is the ailment.

Some terms—and, therefore, some events—are not adequately understood by most readers unless the writer supplies a brief parenthetic definition or illustration. These terms about labor, for example, need explanation: *secondary boycott, closed shop,* and *featherbedding.* Certain medical terms can be defined in a parenthesis that will add to the reader's understanding even though the definition is not complete. One example: "coronary occlusion (a blocking off of blood to the heart)."

The following words are examples of terms frequently used in government that are unfamiliar. The news writer should consider whether to use them or to define them—either by built-in context, by a defining synonym, or by parenthesis:

attest	insolvent
autonomy	moratorium
bilateral	plenary
constitutionality	rejoinder
disburse	retroactive
espionage	revocable
felonious	tripartite

Synonyms: Words that have the same or almost the same essential meaning are called synonyms. The writer sometimes selects a synonym to avoid repeating the same word. In another situation he selects a synonym deliberately to express precisely what he means.

Some words and expressions are interchangeable in their meaning—or at least they are when used within a certain context. Examples are *sea* and *ocean, doctor* and *physician,* and *hear* and *listen to.*

The "right" word is right when it has the same meaning for both the communicator and the reader or listener. This means that the writer may use any synonym which the receiver of the communication understands. But his choice of expressions should conform to prevailing usage. For example, *provisional* and *tentative* both refer to something that is not final but the former refers to adoption temporarily and the latter to adoption on an experimental basis. ("The society adopted a *provisional* constitution" and "The thirty-day parking ordinance is only a *tentative* approach to the problem.") Until these words come to have identical meanings through use—as is possible—the writer should not adopt them interchangeably.

The precise word should be chosen to express certain comparisons; for example, *annoyance, irritation, anger,* and *exasperation* express varying degrees of frustration. The word *old* is used in an indiscriminate way by some news writers: how old is an "old" person?

The appropriate synonym should apply in situations in which dignity or formality is to be considered. A single example should suffice. A class of students at Stanford University were asked to supply the missing word in the following lead: "MANILA—Ramon Magsaysay last night resigned his _____ as National Defense Secretary in a rift with President Elpidio Quirino...." All of the students inserted in the blank either *post* or *position,* either of which was appropriate;

the news agency writer, however, had used the word *job*. A more frequent fault is that of using a word that is more formal than the situation calls for, such as *emolument* for *pay*.

Value connotations: By his choice of synonyms which have a certain connotation the writer exhibits either his own attitude or his low or high evaluation of somebody or something ("editorializing"). Some examples are: *scheme* instead of *plan, alien* instead of *foreign,* and *capitalist* instead of *business man.* A *scheme,* for instance, is a plan whose author is crafty, self-seeking, or visionary.

Euphemisms: With respect to certain delicate matters, the writer sometimes chooses a euphemistic synonym; that is, one that is milder and less offensive than the situation calls for. Examples are: *tumor* instead of *cancer,* and *unclad* for *nude.*[5] Newspapers are not as euphemistic or as prudish now as they were a generation ago (e.g., *social disease* for *syphilis* and *statutory offense* for *rape*), but editors of newspapers realize that their large audience includes individuals with varying tastes and mores, and they try to respect them. Radio stations and radio networks are even more sensitive to the taste of certain sections of their audience because the radio is often heard by the whole family at the same time.

Levels of abstraction: In some contexts, a general word may be used as a synonym for a particular word when both words are used. An example:

> ...He denied that *Detective Wilson* had a right to search the suspect's home. *"Police,"* he explained, "must have a search warrant, which can issue only on probable cause."

[5] The story is told of a London "class" newspaper, which is very sensitive about the established religion in England, that when the subeditor put the innocuous headline "Clerical Question Raised" on a news story about a bishop being accused of the theft of church funds, his superior editor changed the headline to read, "Prebendiary Act of 1787."

See A. M. Barnes and P. I. Lyness, "How the Wire Services Reported the Rutledge Murder Trial," *Journalism Quarterly,* Vol. 28 (1951), pp. 161-178.

These expressions, it will be noted, are on different levels of abstraction, as are *cow* and *beast,* and *horse* and *animal.*[6]

Colloquialisms: The writer should not be afraid to use new words which he has heard often in conversation—provided the word expresses the concept well. English has retained its vigor because it has adopted many of the expressions of the street. These expressions often stimulate imageries that are more penetrating than those of the conventional expression. Why this is so was explained by a scholarly newspaper man:[7]

The closer to daily life and speech is the writer's pen or the click of the typewriter keys, the more active, the more efficient, the more effective is the utterance of the writer and the life of the people. So long as accepted and acceptable writing accepts and shares the daily changes of the vocabulary of the market place, so long as both live and move and have their being in the sun of passion, action, and achievement, the more lasting, pungent, and penetrating is the literature of the period. . . .

Confucius and the earlier classics wrote in the tongue they used daily. This became the tongue of letters. The language of the mass has changed to a local patois, unintelligible from province to province. While the words have changed, the characters that represent them are unchanged. Letters and official life keep the tongue of the past, unintelligible to the many. This thin film stretches over the great empire, the only means of communication. Below are the vast millions with no common medium. . . .

If Samuel Johnson had had his way we should have become like the "Doktoren" of the German leader writers, men who write in a literary tongue. . . .

One, Benjamin Franklin, saved us. He and Johnson lived parallel lives. Johnson was born three years later and he died six years earlier than Franklin. Both wrote early and they wrote to the last. Each turned to the periodical. They knew men, letters, and affairs. On opposing sides, they fought the issues and the battle of our Revolution. Johnson died just as Franklin signed the treaty of peace and independence. In the lists of public opinion, the style

---

[6] See the discussion of Korzybski's "ladder of abstraction" on p. 102.

[7] Talcott Williams, *The Newspaperman* (New York, 1922), pp. 94-110. By permission of the publishers, Charles Scribner's Sons.

of Franklin was pitted against the style of Johnson. He was the inventor of newspaper English, direct, immediate, knowing humor as well as argument, using the speech of the people. The literary world in England and here accepted the style of Johnson; the world of men and events the style of Franklin.

The world is unconsciously ruled by it today. We all walk in Franklin's path for ill or well. Samuel Johnson is a back number. . . .

The temptation was to make the prose of the eighteenth century a standard. Instead, the current of the talk of the many and the diction of the writer merged. The new words and phrases, the changes in the details of speech, slang, and the imagery of our American speech, all these, through the newspapers, found their way into print and acceptance in the American newspaper.

Some colloquial words are abbreviations of longer words used frequently in speech. Some of these truncated words that are acceptable are *movie, gas,* and *auto.*

Cant, jargon, and slang: Writers define these terms in various ways, but in this text the definitions below apply. Both cant and jargon are expressions which have been taken by the writer or speaker from some sphere of life, occupation, or profession, such as sports, the stage, aeronautics, and the criminal underworld. *Flop* and *spotlight,* for example, are derived from the theatrical world; the latter is more acceptable than the former. *Holdup* and *racket* come from the criminal underworld and are acceptable words. To *get the project off the ground* is more expressive, in some contexts, than is either *establish* or *install.*

Jargon, in this text, is further distinguished from cant in that jargon is a special vocabulary which is not as reputable as cant and not as well understood. Jargon is not only a special vocabulary but one that usually clusters abstract words and uses weak verbs such as are found in press releases by officials in government bureaus. An example: "The cessation of home construction, which operated throughout the war period, developed an accretion of demand." The best way to avoid jargon is to use concrete words and finite verbs (i.e., not infinitives and participles).

Very few slang expressions ever achieve acceptance. Slang derives from the desire of some persons (e.g., youths in their group life and sports writers) to say an old thing in a novel way; the expressions enjoy a temporary vogue within a limited circle because of the urge of some to comply with the prevailing fashion. Since the new expressions are seldom as effective as the old they usually pass out of existence. The news writer should not generally use them because (a) too few members of his audience understand them, and (b) they are inefficient ways of expressing a thought.

Repetition: The repetition of a fact or a thought, as was stated before, increases the probability of the communication being understood—especially by a listener since he cannot regress as does a reader. It is not the repetition of words so much as it is the repetition of facts and ideas that assists the reader or listener. Yet a key word repeated is often more emphatic than a pronoun. For example:

> Although there is considerable news about Russia in American newspapers, little of [it] *this news* is actually reported from behind the Iron Curtain.

Radio news writers generally repeat a name or a title when it is important *instead of using a pronoun,* as in the following example; newspapers could afford to adopt this practice more than they have so far.

> Mayor James Martin announced today he would veto the ordinance to regulate taxicab rates.
> [He] *The mayor* said he was opposed to the monopoly possibilities which the ordinance contained.

As Fowler [8] has said, "A dozen sentences are spoilt by ill-advised avoidance of repetition for every one that is spoilt by ill-advised repetition." And again Fowler: [9] "The fatal influence . . . is the advice given to young writers never to use the same word twice in a sentence—or within 20 lines or other limit." Fowler warns against what he calls "elegant variation," that is, using a synonym *just to avoid repeating the word itself:* for example, "The total number of farming properties is 250,000. Of these only 800 *have* more than 600 acres; 1600 *possess* between 300 and 600 acres, while 116,000 *own* less than eight acres apiece." A news story about a strike that needlessly refers to it as a *work stoppage* and a *walkout* would be a better communication if it used *strike* more often. A feature news story about state legislators serving their first term referred to them as *newcomers, first termers, freshmen, frosh, fledglings, yearlings,* and *embryo statesmen.*

Verbosity: The most disreputable type of repetition is what is variously called verbosity, wordiness, and tautology. It consists of saying something over again—usually in other words and in the adjacent context—without increasing the emphasis. It is pointless and needless repetition, for example, to say "an empty barrel with nothing in it." In other instances it is just loose writing. A few examples:

(1)

Existing city ordinances *now* call for lots of only 6,000 square feet.

(2)

The city council voted last night to authorize payment to Mrs. Virginia Mason.

[8] H. W. Fowler, *A Dictionary of Modern English Usage* (London, 1950), p. 495.
[9] *Ibid.,* p. 131.

(3)

Attorney Henry Tuckman, representing
the Marshall family, spoke to the city
council and said that he did not believe
such action would be necessary.

Wordiness is sometimes the result of using superfluous adverbs and adjectives to achieve emphasis. Some examples of
this overlapping of symbols are: *forward progression, con-
sensus of opinion, almost imminent, violent tornado, present
incumbent, in a more superior way, too ultraconservative,
over-saturated, bolt of lightning, advance preparation,* and
completely exaggerated. The word *definitely* is often superfluous and is used unnecessarily to mean *very,* as in *definitely
harmful.* So, too, with *serious* as in *serious danger* and *currently* as in "they are currently undergoing a setback." Such
words, as Gowers [10] has said, "hang on so loosely you may
blow 'em off." The word *very* is not only overlapping, as in
very excellent, but is generally so superfluous that most editors bar its use almost entirely.[11]

Formal words: How often does the newswriter think first
of the simple word and then translate it to a formal word before he writes it? When he does that he often compels the
reader to translate the formal expression back into the simple word which first came into the news writer's mind. News
writers, it is true, have generally abandoned these more formal expressions: *inaugurate* for *begin, transpire* for *occur*
and *happen, conflagration* for *fire,* and *obsequies* for the
funeral rites of the ordinary deceased person. But they still
sometimes use *expedite* for *hasten, sustain* for *suffer,* and
numerous other words that create semantic noise for some
readers.

[10] Sir Ernest Gowers, *Plain Words* (London, 1948), p. 35.
[11] The late William Allen White had a device for keeping *very* out of his
Emporia Gazette. The newspaper's style guide directed the writer to use *damn*
instead of *very* (because the copy desk would then delete *damn*).

Prefer the short word: The short word is less likely to be abstract and more likely to be familiar. In a series, it prevents regressive eye movements. When a short word has the same essential meaning as the long word it should be preferred. The following brief list is illustrative:

Instead of:	*Use:*
presently	now
apprehend	capture, arrest
resuscitate	revive
approximately	about
effervescent	bubbling
repercussion	effect, echo
incapacitated from	unable to

It is less important to use a short and familiar word in the body of the news story than in the lead. When the lead has supplied adequate context the longer word in the body will be more easily understood and the unfamiliar word will be explained.[12] An example:

> LONDON—Government financial officials today denied a plan is being considered to *cheapen* Britain's money.
>
> Many business men also agreed that *devaluation* of the pound is unlikely as long as British exports continue at the current level.

The Flesch formula appraised: As was explained in Chapter VII, the factors in the Flesch formula for computing reading ease are average sentence length in words and average word length in syllables. We are concerned in this chapter only with the number of syllables in words. The formula, it is true, does not directly measure abstract words, unfamiliar

---

[12] Something like the opposite practice is necessary when the initials of an organization are used instead of the full name. There are a few exceptions, such as AFL, CIO and UN, but as to names of most organizations it is better to write the full name in the lead and the initials in the body of the story. When the organization is not widely known, initials should not be used at all.

words, or formal words—the kind of words we have advised
the reader not to use when he has a choice. A formula which
did directly measure such words would be of little help to
the writer because, in practice, the writer cannot work from
a list of words. The formula, to a considerable degree, however, does measure such words indirectly because abstract
words, unfamiliar words, and formal words tend to be longer
than concrete words, familiar words, and simple words.[13]

The writer should not comply with the formula in a slav-
ish way. Many a hard word can be understood by the reader
provided the writer skillfully builds into his sentence a defining context.[14]

The formula is not meant to be a guide for writing. As
one editor has said, "It is a tool, not a command." Its main
value is that it provides a definite measure that the writer,
from time to time, can use as a check. Editors have always
directed writers to use average short sentences and short
words but the writers, after an initial conscious effort to comply, have drifted back to the easier method of long sentences
and long words. Now, with this formula, editors have a way
of keeping the writers in line.

We repeat that the formula measures only an *average*. It
does not require every sentence and every word to be short.
It does require that there not be a succession of long sentences and long words.

Verbs: Compliance by the writer with these three rules
will help the reader and listener to decode the writer's symbols:

1. Substitute, when possible, action verbs for those that
express only a state. Instead of writing "All of the charges
represented recommendations of the Planning Commission,"
substitute "All of the charges *had been recommended* by the

13 For a more scientific explanation of why this is so, see Rudolf Flesch,
"A New Readability Yardstick," *Journal of Applied Psychology,* Vol. 32 (1948),
p. 226.
14 See pp. 105-107.

Planning Commission." Instead of writing "Search planes *are out* for the missing plane," substitute "Search planes *are looking* for the missing plane."

2. Instead of a verb and an adverb, use a verb that *implies* an adverb—except when such a verb is long and unfamiliar. Thus, instead of "The spectators *ran rapidly away* from the plane," write "The spectators *scurried* out of the plane's path." The verb *scurried,* it will be noticed, has a built-in modifier, viz., *rapid.* A very large number of verbs that express motion have built-in modifiers that imply direction, speed, and method. A few examples:

to move forward	advance
to move backward	retreat
to move sideways	sidle
to move upward	ascend, rise
to move downward	descend, fall
to move upward at a high rate of speed ..	zoom, rocket
to move stealthily	slink, sneak, creep

The reader of this book is certainly familiar with a great many similar verbs that describe motion and speech, such as *surge, approach, trudge, stagger, lurch, amble, glide, wobble; murmur, babble, gasp, prattle, chatter,* and *wail.* He should remember to use them.

3. Instead of a long and unfamiliar verb, substitute a *simple verb plus a simple adverb.* This is the opposite of the last-mentioned rule except for the attached proviso. It means that instead of writing *append* and *supplement* you write *add to,* instead of writing *circumvent* you write *go around,* and instead of writing *disintegrate* you write *break up.* Dr. Rudolf Flesch [15] has devised a list of 50 verbs and 20 adverbs that may be combined into pairs to express about a thousand abstract ideas. Many of these ideas are verbal nouns, such as *breakthrough, checkoff, sitdown,* and *takeoff,* as well as verbs.

One of the most frequently used words in a news story is

[15] *The Art of Readable Writing* (New York, 1949), p. 134.

said. A study of names in the news showed that the leading role of persons in the news is that of being quoted in a speech, a report, or a statement; from one-fifth to one-fourth of all persons mentioned in the newspapers were quoted.[16] Because the news writer must so often use *said* he uses some of its synonyms interchangeably although they are stronger verbs than *said.* Some of these are *declare, assert,* and *state.* Some editors, however, do not permit the use of some of these synonyms to mean mere utterance as does *said.* When a quoted statement is addressed to an audience (at a convention, on a jury, on the city council, and so forth) the writer may also use *told. Claim,* used sometimes as a synonym for *assert,* is regarded as inappropriate by many editors except when it refers to a right, title, or possession of the speaker.

Numerous other verbs that denote utterance are used in certain contexts. Some of these are *recited, recounted, related, averred, alleged, protested, argued, explained, added,* and *pointed out.* They should be chosen by the writer to fit the appropriate context; *pointed out,* for example, suggests that the news writer agrees with the speaker (editorializing).

Speakers are sometimes quoted as saying they *felt* that thus-and-so was true; a more correct word for this indirect quotation is *believed.*

Revealed is sometimes used in connection with something that has never been hidden; usually the appropriate word is just *said.*

Clichés: The editor of *A Dictionary of Clichés* [17] has defined cliché as follows: "an outworn commonplace; a phrase or short sentence that has become so hackneyed that careful speakers and scrupulous writers shrink from it because they feel that its use is an insult to the intelligence of their audience or public." When first used the expression was very

[16] C. R. Bush and R. K. Bullock, "Names in the News: A Study of Two Dailies, *Journalism Quarterly,* Vol. 29 (1952), pp. 148-157.

[17] Eric Partridge, *A Dictionary of Clichés,* 4th ed. (London, 1950), p. 4.

effective, but it has lost its literary value—at least for sophisticated persons—through persistent use.

News writers today seldom use such hackneyed idiomatic clichés as *heart and soul* or such figurative clichés as *sea of faces,* but they sometimes use hackneyed idiomatic phrases derived from the journalism of another day. Some of these are:

launch an investigation	collided in midair
fusillade of shots	innocent bystander
took the witness stand	play host to
rushed to a hospital	unshakable alibi
appear on the scene	wave of optimism
explore every avenue	up in arms
shattering effect	heavily armed policeman
sickening thud	grim faced policeman
took to his heels	gained access through
traffic was at a virtual standstill	vanish into thin air
sustained an injury	made his appearance
long-felt want	cloak of secrecy *
the stage was set	meteoric rise †

* A mixed metaphor: "The cloak of secrecy was clamped down Thursday when the plane left Tokyo."
† Does a meteor rise?

Sports writers use more clichés than the city desk permits. A few of them are *spine-tingling finish, coveted trophy, pile-driving right, won by an eyelash, stout-hearted defense, circuit clout,* and *four-ply clout.*

News writers should have more freedom to use clichés than writers who address only a sophisticated audience. A cliché that is not too outworn is a more effective symbol of communication for many readers and listeners in the newspaper and radio audience than are more carefully chosen words. The cliché often stimulates an imagery that an alternative expression does not. The list of clichés presented above could have been extended, but would then have prohibited some expressions that would increase the decoding efficiency of a good many readers.

A cliché, however, is certainly out of place when the writer uses it in a news story of a high literary order about a subject of dignity or tragedy, as for example, in some of the stories quoted in Chapter IX.

Prepositions: Some news writers fall into the habit of using idiomatic prepositional phrases instead of just prepositions. Examples of such circumlocutory phrases are *in relation to, in the case of,* and *with the result that.* Instead of writing "The fares will vary in relation to the distance traveled," the writer can better say, "The fares will vary *with* the distance traveled." Instead of *in relation to,* the prepositions *with, for,* and *towards* make the sentence easier to understand. The prepositions *in* and *by* are generally better in news stories than *in the case of;* and *so that* is better than *with the result that.* Usually a simple preposition is better than *in connection with, in respect of, due to the fact that, with reference to,* and *for the reason that.*

Some writers have difficulty in deciding which is the proper preposition to use in certain idiomatic phrases, such as *compared to* and *compared with.* The unabridged dictionaries indicate the proper usage. There is also available the *Standard Handbook of Prepositions, Conjunctions, Relative Pronouns, and Adverbs* by the Funk & Wagnalls editorial staff.[18]

A doubtful rule that a sentence should never end with a preposition bothers some writers. A better rule is for the writer to let his ear be his guide.

Adjectives: Although objectivity is the main characteristic of journalistic style, some chronicle type news stories have elements that are affective: adjectives are used not for the purpose of stimulating a feeling tone in the reader but to present a clear image of the event. The following lead is an example:

> The *slashing* blades of a *giant* cement mixer *ripped* Harley Ashburn to death today after he had gone inside it to make repairs.

18 New York, 1953.

While the italicized words are not essential for an understanding of the event, they do increase the vividness of the happening. Some editors would prefer to use a more matter-of-fact version of this event because they feel that a good many readers would not want to experience such horror vicariously.

Summary: Because of the average reader's limited vocabulary, the news writer should, generally, use concrete instead of abstract words, familiar instead of unfamiliar words, and short instead of long words. Sometimes, however, he can use an unfamiliar word by carefully building in context.

A readability formula is meant to be a check on the writer, not a guide on how to write.

The writer should repeat a word for emphasis when it will help the reader understand rather than seek for a synonym that is only an elegant variation.

The writer should avoid slang and jargon, but should not hesitate to use colloquial words.

The news writer has more freedom in the use of the cliché than the writer who addresses an audience all of whose members are sophisticated.

The writer can improve the efficiency of his news communication by a careful choice of verbs.

DESCRIPTIVE NEWS WRITING

UP TO THIS point we have discussed only the conventional news story whose main characteristic is its objectivity. Now we are ready to discuss news stories that contain affective elements—stories in which the writer deliberately chooses expressions of intensional [1] meaning and inserts his own sense impressions into the pattern of objective discourse. The writer does these things to achieve vividness; that is, to cause the reader to perceive the object or scene with an intense awareness of reality.

Vividness: The writer achieves vividness in several ways. One of these is to cause the central figure to stand out from the background; as for example, this paragraph in Meyer Berger's description in the *New York Times* of the arrival of the first World War II dead from Europe:

> ... The transport "Joseph V. Connolly" broke through the haze outside the Narrows at 9 A.M., a shadowy hulk all gray and tan, with a funeral wreath at her forepeak. Nothing moved on her decks. The coffin picked out for the service, guarded by men at attention, was out on the boat deck....

To cause the central figure to stand out from the background it is sometimes necessary first to describe the background, as

---

1 This term is explained on p. 126.

in this description by Relman Morin, of the Associated Press, of the execution of Julius and Ethel Rosenberg:

> ... The party of official witnesses entered the death chamber a few moments before 7 P.M. It is a square room. Behind the electric chair was a white, wheeled table. In front were four rows of benches like pews in a church.
>
> The room was heavy with silence. From overhead the lights beamed on the electric chair.

Another way to achieve vividness is to present the events in the order in which they happened and, in the case of moving objects, their order of appearance before the observer. Meyer Berger's story also illustrates how this was done effectively:

> ... The curbs were crowded, but here, as at sea, the silence was awesome. ...
>
> Mounted police led the procession. Their horses' hooves pattered lightly on the soft pavement. Far down the line came the music—the slow, soft tones of the dirges—and the measured cadence of slow-marching boots. No other sounds broke in, except an occasional plane, or the voice of an officer chanting the step.
>
> The procession stopped at the Eternal Light. ...
>
> Then came the long march up Fifth Avenue's pavement. The crowds at the curb were moved. Some let the tears run freely. Some wiped them away. Some made the sign of the cross as the caisson rolled past them. In Fifth Avenue's canyons muted brass played "Onward, Christian Soldiers."
>
> The marchers were grim. Behind the mounted police came the West Point cadets, then a battalion of middies. The boots of the Eighty-second Airborne beat out a steady step and the sun struck light from their helmets. There were Marines

and sailors, Waves and Spars and Wacs,
winding slowly up midtown hill, paced
by the drumbeat.

A third way the writer achieves vividness is by describing
objects or movements in terms familiar to the reader—usually
by a simile or metaphor. Relman Morin's execution story,
quoted above, uses that device:

> The guards stepped back. A signal was
> given to the executioner, Joseph Francell,
> in an alcove to the left of the room.
> A metallic rattle *sounded like marbles
> rolling along a metal washboard.* Then it
> stopped. The room was filled with a hum-
> ming buzz.

In some instances, when the writer is describing movement,
he manipulates his sentence rhythm to imitate that movement. An example is Richard Lockridge's description of
Lindbergh's takeoff on his Atlantic flight:

Lindbergh Takes Off On Atlantic Flight

> ... Lindbergh got into the plane at
> 7:40 o'clock and the crowd cheered. His
> motor was started at once and for ten
> minutes droned as it tuned. At 7:50 the
> blocks were knocked from the wheels
> and, slowly, heavily, the plane started. It
> sank into the soft turf of the field, bear-
> ing down with its weight of 5,150 pounds.
> It started very slowly....
> The plane's speed increased—but not
> rapidly. It lunged and swayed. It hit a
> bump and staggered into the air a few
> feet. The watchers could see light under
> its wheels. Then it went down again,
> solidly, sulkily, into the mud. The motor's
> drone increased.
> It jumped out again a little further on.

It lunged and swayed in the air—now he'd
done it! The crowd yelled, and the plane
slumped down again into the mud. Behind it lay most of the course it had on
land—ahead lay a cornfield, some buildings and an ambulance. Its speed increased, but not fast enough. It lunged
up again; it clung to the air, ten feet
above the soggy earth which fought to
hold it. Now he'd done it! And now, indeed, he had.

He rose very slowly in the air. He
cleared the cornfield. He cleared the telegraph wires. He cleared the trees. They
could trundle the ambulance away, then;
Lindbergh was on his way to Paris.

Choice of expression: In addition to these devices, the
writer achieves vividness by inserting his own sense impressions—by having feelings and by translating them into words
that stimulate the same feelings in the reader. That means
using words with an "intensional" meaning, as distinguished
from words with an "extensional" meaning. The latter are
expressions that denote—that merely point to—an object, for
example, a ship. Expressions of intensional meaning connote,
that is, suggest. The meaning of such expressions is in the
user's mind.

The writer also chooses adjectives and verbs and sometimes
nouns to help the reader perceive an image. We have already
mentioned in an earlier chapter one instance of the use of
adjectives and a verb in a conventional news story and here
repeat it: "The *slashing* blades of a *giant* cement mixer *ripped*
Harley Ashburn to death today after he had gone inside it
to make repairs." A similar use of an adjective is in this lead
of a fire story: "Roaring flames and *syrup-thick* smoke killed
14 women and children last night at the State Mental Hospital." In Meyer Berger's story, quoted above, an effect was
achieved by the expression, "Their horses' hooves *pattered
lightly* on the *soft* pavement." The writer should bear in

mind, however, that adjectives and color are not necessarily synonymous. An unskillful use of adjectives results in sentimentality and exaggeration. The following news story in the New York *World-Telegram* is excusable because it was written that way to save the lives of auto drivers, but it contains the kinds of details that most editors think are in bad taste.

> Sudden death, with heads mashed to pulp and bones snapped like toothpicks, came to two men today.... The men and an attractive girl were hurled over the railing to the street 30 feet below....
>
> The men's heads were split open. One man's skull was mashed down almost to his ears. Blood was spattered five or six feet around them. Blood spurted from their wounds, too.
>
> The girl, only 18, struck a few feet from the men. Most of her teeth were knocked out. Chunks of flesh were torn from her face. Her pelvis was shattered. The sharp end of a broken bone stuck out of her thigh.
>
> But she wasn't dead. She lay weakly spitting out teeth and blood. Doctors think she will live. Her face may be twisted with scars despite the surgeon's work. A policeman said she looked as though someone had hit her in the face with a sledge-hammer.

The importance of details: The writer cannot achieve vividness unless he has closely observed the relevant details. It is the details that cause the reader to perceive the reality of the event. Before Sinclair Lewis wrote a novel he went to great pains to map the imaginary settings he intended to use. For *Babbitt,* for example, he constructed a map of the city of "Zenith" and drew fairly exact plans of homes and offices. The result was that when he began to write he was familiar with his setting even to the names of imaginary streets that he did not include in the story. The reader, therefore, per-

ceived the images that the author wanted him to see. *Time*
news-magazine goes to great pains and spends considerable
money to get details; the following is an extreme example of
that practice:

> In the Washington suburb of Chevy
> Chase, the modest neighborhood of
> Barnaby, is inhabited by citizens whose
> salaries mostly range from $5,000 to $10,-
> 000 a year. Nonetheless, the substantial
> redbrick house at 3122 Tennyson N.W.,
> home of R.F.C. Counsel Claude E. Hamil-
> ton, Jr., with its green shuttered windows
> and cement walk much like its neighbors,
> was one evening last week the scene of
> history in the making. A Diamond Taxi
> drove up to 3122 Tennyson, and stopped.
> Out of the taxi stepped Lawyer Hamilton
> and Associate Justice Hugo Lafayette
> Black of the U. S. Supreme Court. With
> his hat pulled over his eyes and two
> packages of Chesterfield cigarets in his
> hand, Hugo Black marched through the
> garage and into the house by the cellar
> door in order to broadcast to the U. S.
> people his reply to the accusation that he
> belonged to the Ku Klux Klan.
>
> In the street four newsreel cars and 250
> people—reporters, cameramen, and bare-
> headed neighbors—were lined up. At the
> house next door Mrs. Margaret H. Cox
> was giving a "Black radio party" with 18
> guests, obligingly sent out her maid with
> coffee for the press. . . .

The importance that editors attach to details in newspaper
writing is illustrated in this story about the late O. K. Bovard, managing editor of the St. Louis *Post-Dispatch*:[2]

Mr. Bovard ran a one-man school of journalism throughout 40
years of news planning and editing on the *Post-Dispatch*. His
course of instruction was particularly severe and intense when he

[2] Irving Dilliard, "O. K. Bovard, A Great Managing Editor—Complex Man,"
Nieman Reports (July, 1949), p. 12.

was city editor, from 1900 to 1908. One of the cubs in that period
was Charles G. Ross. Not long after Ross came to the staff, Mr.
Bovard sent the freshman reporter to get the facts about the fall
of a painter from a high smoke-stack in the extreme southwestern
part of St. Louis.

It was a hot summer day and a trip to the scene of the accident
was a long one. Not only was transportation slow and involved,
but it ended much too soon and when the youthful news gatherer
alighted from the last street car, he had a lengthy walk. At last
he found the factory, where he proceeded to collect information—
name, address, and age of the painter, the place, how he happened
to fall, the extent of his injuries and so on. The reporter then
reversed the weary transportation process, returned to the office
and wrote the short item which was indicated. Thinking he had
done a good job, he turned the item in to the city editor.

Mr. Bovard glanced over the few lines and called his cub to the
desk. "Ross," he asked, "how tall is this smoke-stack?"

The new reporter could not say. He gave an "about so-and-so"
estimate and repeated that it was quite "tall."

The one-man school of journalism said firmly: "Ross, 'tall' is
a relative term. I want you to go back and find out the exact
height of that smoke-stack."

Young Ross retraced the long, hot trip to the factory. When he
at last returned to the office, his weary day had passed into night.
But he had the precise height of the smoke-stack in feet and
inches.

The writer-reporter gets his details by close observation
and advance planning. In the case of certain ceremonial
events—such as parades and funeral processions for the distinguished dead—the persons who officially direct the cere-
monies supply reporters in advance with mimeographed
sheets that set forth the order of march and of ritual. But the
reporter is generally on his own. This sometimes means that,
in advance of the happening, he interviews certain persons
and makes certain observations; for example, how many steps
there are on the gallows, exactly which foods were given the
condemned person for breakfast and which foods he did and
did not eat. The writer also must find out in advance, when

he does not already know, the appropriate terms he should use to describe certain unfamiliar objects; as for example, the "catafalque" at a state funeral or the "forepeak" of the ship and the "caisson" mentioned by Meyer Berger on pages 123 and 124.

Summary: The descriptive news writer achieves vividness by these methods: causing the central figure to stand out from the background, presenting the events in the order in which they happened, describing objects or movements in familiar terms, and manipulating his sentence rhythm to imitate the movement he is describing. Since it is details that make for vividness, the writer, as spectator and reporter, must observe closely the objects and movements he will afterwards describe.

Chapter X

EXPLANATORY NEWS WRITING

THE DISCUSSION in previous chapters of efficiency in communicating news has related to news as if all news were unidimensional. We have hinted at a few places, however, that news sometimes has more than one dimension. We shall call that type of writing "explanatory." It means that the writer, trying to make the news meaningful, supplements his chronicle of the essential facts with other facts that he has to look up or dig up by reporting. Explanatory writing must be discussed on several levels. We shall note first the lowest levels.

Simple types of explanation: The writer should help the reader understand the *location* of an event. Most readers are very ignorant of geography. Dr. George Gallup has found this to be true after asking cross-sections of the public to identify countries on an outline map; his findings indicate that many readers of news stories about events outside the United States have only a vague notion as to their location. The reporter can often make news more meaningful by identifying obscure places—even in his own region—by referring their location to some widely-known place; as for example, "thirty miles east of Indianapolis," and "between Fresno and Bakersfield on Highway 99."

In reporting the data of public finance, the writer can sometimes *translate* it into terms that apply to the individual reader. Thus: "The 10-cent increase in the tax rate will mean about a $3 increase in the actual tax on a small house, which is carried on the assessment rolls at $3000." Any taxpayer with real property worth more than $3000 could easily tell from this illustration the amount of his own tax increase.

Since *magnitude* is a measure of significance, the writer should help the reader's understanding, in some situations, by a comparison with a similar event that the reader presumably remembers. For example, in reporting a nation-wide strike in France, the Associated Press said: "This was France's worst strike since the 1936 days of Socialist Leon Blum's popular front government." Other examples: "The drought is the longest in the history of Texas," and "Yesterday was the coldest January eighth since 1918."

The meaning of some events can be understood only in terms of some *past event.* Since the usual reader of a daily newspaper does not immediately recall the past, the writer can assist his memory by building in parenthetically a memory cue. For example, when the Communist rulers of Hungary, in 1953, were forced to promise economic and religious concessions to the people, the Associated Press included this paragraph: "[Premier Nagy] said the government, *which has imprisoned Roman Catholic prelate Josef Cardinal Mindszenty for nearly four years on charges of treason,* must be 'patient in respect to religion.' " Because of this memory cue, readers were better able to devaluate the Communists' promises.

Because a great many readers are ignorant of legal and legislative procedures they cannot evaluate adequately many of the events they read about. Examine, for instance, this lead: "The [U. S.] House [of Representatives] today passed a bill which gives the states title to oil-rich submerged coastal lands." Actually, the sentence may mean: "The House today passed [and sent to the Senate] a bill which. . . ." But it could also mean: "The House today passed a bill which. . . [Since the Senate had already passed a similar bill which varies in several important ways from the House bill, a conference committee of the two chambers will agree on a compromise version and submit it to both houses for approval]." A similar illustration could be presented here about procedures in the United Nations, the state legislatures, the city council, and the law courts. The news writer, of course, cannot write a section of a textbook on legislative procedure every time he reports a vote in a legislative body. Often, however, he can add an explanatory sentence to indicate that the action is not final—as for example, when a proposed ordinance passes "second reading" in the city council, he could add, "The bill will come up for final action in two weeks."

Explanation belongs where? At what place in the news story in the newspaper should the writer place explanatory matter? When the explanation is very brief the writer can simply put the explanatory matter in a parenthesis adjacent to the term that needs definition; as for example, in quoting a television station manager: "When we took to the air we had signed fewer advertisers than most VHF stations had when they first started (VHF, which means very high frequency, is that section of the broadcast band where all television stations were located until the ultra high frequency portion of the band was opened to TV)."

When the explanatory matter is longer than the brief parenthesis, however, the writer risks destroying the continuity of the story if he includes very much of it in the body. Perhaps this is a practical rule: When the explanation is no longer than one paragraph, place it high in the story and adjacent to the matter that needs explanation; when the explanation is two or three paragraphs long, use it as "shirt-tail" or "dash matter," that is, at the bottom of the whole story; never include an explanation longer than two or three paragraphs. There is no practicable answer to this question because one must choose between conserving continuity and presenting explanation near the point at which it is required. One type of explanation, however, certainly should be placed high in the story, viz., the "why" explanation: the reader should not be kept waiting too long to get the answer to a natural question that comes to his mind.

Writing the explanatory story: We have been discussing explanatory matter that is inserted in the news story about an event or is added to the story. Some news stories, however, are wholly explanatory in their purpose, even though they may hang on a "news-peg." An example of clear explanation of a complex subject is this news story in the *Wall Street Journal* explaining why interest rates on bank loans had increased and why business men were finding it harder to borrow:

> ... To understand how these funds are being limited, it's necessary to understand something of the complex workings of the Federal Reserve and its relationship with member banks.
>
> By law, member banks of the Federal Reserve System are required to keep funds in a reserve bank which are equal to a fixed percentage of the deposits on their own books. If the latter deposits increase, the funds in the reserve bank may have to be increased; if such deposits decrease, the reserve can be decreased.
>
> Since reserves limit deposits, they also limit loans because of the manner in which banks make loans. If you borrow money from a bank, it doesn't give you the cash, but rather sets up for you a deposit against which you can draw checks.
>
> The machinery works the other way around, too. For example, if the member bank's funds in the reserve bank are reduced, it can loan less money. And that's what's been happening.
>
> The Reserve System has been reducing the member banks' reserves as part of its credit-restraining program. Since the end of last year, the system has sold $891 million of its holdings of Government securities. Here's how this reduces the bank's reserves:

The Reserve System sells securities to a dealer. The dealer pays for them with a check drawn on his bank. The system then cashes the check by docking the reserve account of the dealer's bank by that amount. If the bank's reserves were just equal to the legal percentage of its deposits, it then must either cut its deposits or dig up additional reserves.

A good example of how a small daily newspaper can supply explanatory news that is highly appreciated by many of its readers is the following story by John Hubbard, of the Palo Alto (Calif.) *Times:*

Is Home-buying Boom Over? Yes, Say Local Realtors

It was wonderful . . . while it lasted.

The profit came in easily, automatically; it seemed almost unbelievable. And yet— as hundreds of Peninsulans happily discovered—it was true.

Take Mr. and Mrs. John Doe. Seven years ago they bought a home in the Palo Alto area for $10,000. Two years later they sold it for about $13,000, used the profit to buy a more expensive home, then sold again two years later—and again at a tidy profit.

Now they're living in a home in the $20,000 class. Just like that—without having to use hardly any, if any at all, extra capital of their own along the way.

As the Does jumped painlessly up the residential ladder, they let their apartment-dwelling friends, the Richard Roes, in on the "secret."

They're Still Waiting

So the Roes, too, climbed aboard. They

got on the bottom rung two years ago by buying a $12,500 home.

Then late this spring they decided it was time to take a step up. They tacked a "for sale" sign on their front fence, set the price at what they figured would be an ungreedy $15,000 and sat back confidently to wait for the customers to arrive, money in hand.

They're still waiting.

And they're sadly beginning to realize that today's buyers aren't buying ... not at that price.

What's the matter? What's happened?

Simply this: the "boom" is over.

That's the opinion of realtors interviewed within the past few days by the Times.

Why the Change?

And it's true throughout this area—in Menlo Park and Palo Alto, in Mountain View and Los Altos.

"The profit-taking days for the average home seller are gone," said William P. Neville, president of the Palo Alto Board of Realtors. . . .

"Prices are getting more realistic," said Mark Gregg, president of the Los Altos Board of Realtors. "Supply is catching up with demand. Buyers are not having to bid against each other now. . . ."

Why the change?

There are many factors which have come into play, some of them purely local in nature, others with nation-wide roots.

The two most common reasons advanced by the realtors were the economic law of supply and demand, as mentioned by Gregg, and the "tightening up" of available financing.

Credit Gets Tighter

"The fact that so many homes are being offered for sale indicates that there is a greater supply than before," said G. E.

Cary, Palo Alto realtor. "Developers, I think, are going to be quite cautious with new projects.

"They're going to be more careful to analyze the prospects of a given area before they start building.

"The Los Gatos market is an example. The home market there is saturated. Builders are having great difficulty selling."

A local banker supplied the facts on financing. Even though a short time ago the government raised the interest rates on GI and FHA homes, he said, most banks already have "lent up to what they consider to be a safe margin" and are not eager to extend their operations further.

"Banks in general are now trying to take care of their own customers," he said. "They're not going out to get the business of large subdivisions and people not known to them."

A Difference of $9500

What effect does the financing setup have on selling prices?

In the first place, obviously, the "tightness" of bank money means that loans are not so easy to obtain as they used to be. And that means fewer potential buyers.

In the second place, the bankers said, lending institutions feel that "all real estate has been greatly inflated in price" and they do not appraise many homes anywhere nearly as high as the owners would like.

"Say an owner wants $20,000," the banker said. "And say the lending institution says it's worth only $17,000. That would mean the maximum loan that could be made would be about $10,500.

"That leaves a difference of $9500 between the selling price and the loan coverage. It means the buyer has to come up with $9500. That's a lot of money.

"People who have it have been housed. Those who can't meet the spread haven't."

A Home Is Not an Investment

Reynolds Camp, Mountain View realtor, put it another way.

"The man with the money," he said, "is pretty well dictating the terms. As a result, he's getting the seller to come down on his price.

"Some sellers, to get around that, are resorting to second mortgages or second deeds of trust to help ease the down payment burden. That way, perhaps, they can come closer to the price they'd like to get. But, at the same time, they have to be content with getting repaid in installments instead of a lump sum for the amount of the 'second.' "

Does all this mean that a homeowner will be faced with a loss in selling?

The realtors agreed that it does not.

"I don't think very many people are taking losses," said Floyd Lowe, Palo Alto realtor. "And if they charge themselves a reasonable rental for the time they've spent in the house and figure the price on that basis, I think loss situations will be rare" . . . .

Neville offered these words of advice:

"Nobody should expect to make a profit out of his home. A man's profit should come only on real estate he buys merely as an investment, not from his home. A home is a place to enjoy and to raise one's family in; it should not be considered as a source of income."

The explanation of science: The discovery and exposition of universal phenomena by scientists are called "explanation." Broad organic theories that account for or appear to account for all of the relations of phenomena may even merit the appellation of "laws." Some of these are Darwin's explanation of evolution, Pasteur's explanation of bacteria, Joule's kinetic theory of heat, and Einstein's theory of relativity. Few such broad explanations are ever reported as news—because there are so few of them. Nearly every important science story, however, is a type of explanation. The following news story by Dr. Milton Silverman, science writer for the *San Francisco Chronicle,* is an excellent model of a science story:

Photosynthesis: How Plants Make Food From Light

A solution to one of the major mysteries of life—the harnessing of the sun's energy by a green plant—was presented here last night by a world famous University of California chemist.

The reaction is known as photosynthesis.

It is the apparently simple yet tantalizingly complex process which traps energy from the sun, and makes possible existence of life on this planet.

It is the fundamental reaction in which a green plant takes simple starting materials, adds the energy from sunlight, and yields sugar—the basic food eaten by plants and animals.

A Great Discovery

Scientists have long known the starting materials—water and carbon dioxide. They have known the end products—sugar and oxygen.

But, for more than a century, they have failed in all attempts to duplicate this reaction in their test tubes, and they have been unable to explain how it works in a growing green plant.

In particular, they could find no way to explain how the plant transforms the light energy from the sun into the chemical energy in the end-product sugar.

Last night, in an address before the meeting of the Society of American Bacteriologists at the Palace Hotel, Dr. Melvin Calvin presented an explanation which jibes with all available evidence. To many of the experts in his audience, his report marked one of the most significant advances yet achieved in man's attempt to understand nature.

The Four Steps

Dr. Calvin, who has spent many years in explaining other parts of the photosynthesis mystery, describes this reaction as "the fundamental driving force of living nature."

According to his proposals, here is what goes on—step by step—in a green plant:

1—A unit, or quantum, of sunlight strikes one of the active cells in a plant, and is absorbed by the complex green pigment.

2—The sunlight-activated chlorophyll—then passes its energy to a relatively simple fatty material, thioctic acid, a yellow, sulfur-containing compound recently found to exist in all green plants.

3—Up to this point, the energy from sunlight is only temporarily bound. It has not yet been converted into useful chemical energy. But in the next act, the thioctic acid reacts with a molecule of water, splits it, and combines with the split portions to form an energy-rich intermediate.

Alcohol for Water

Here is where the sunlight becomes transformed into chemical energy—a form of energy which can then be stored and eventually used to maintain plant or animal life.

It is this vital step in the photosynthesis process which was worked out only during the past few months by Dr. Calvin and his associates.

Because of technical difficulties, it cannot be proved by direct experiments. The thioctic acid-water combination changes so rapidly that it cannot be detected by any known test. Instead, it was checked with "model experiments," in which other substances—such as alcohol—were substituted for the water.

The new theory also seems to explain all the findings previously made by plant scientists on what goes on in nature.

Further Research Needed

4—In succeeding steps, the thioctic acid plus the fragments of water changes again to yield three products. One of these is the normal, unactivated thioctic acid, which is free to go to work again in the reaction. The second is oxygen, which is eventually liberated into the air as a gas. The third is hydrogen—which is combined with carbon dioxide to form a series of complex compounds and eventually to form sugar.

Details of these last reactions—the transformation of hydrogen and carbon dioxide into sugar—have been explained by earlier work of the UC scientists.

Dr. Calvin emphasized that many of the fine points are yet to be satisfactorily clarified. For example, the details of precisely how the oxygen and the hydrogen are divorced from their combination with thioctic acid are not completely understood.

But for the first time, he suggested, a logical and reasonable explanation has been presented for this age-old mystery— the trapping of energy from the sun.

"Interpretive" reporting: The trend in newspapers is toward more explanatory writing. Editors realize that radio (and to some degree television) supplies most people with spot news. They recognize, too, that since the early nineteen-thirties people have been striving to understand their complex environment in which they feel insecure. To fulfill that human need, radio commentators and syndicated newspaper columnists have multiplied and the weekly news magazines have developed. All of these "explain" events by supplying a context for the spot news that readers and listeners are presumed not to have.

In addition to this twentieth-century demand for help in the individual's pursuit of meaning, there developed in the nineteen-fifties a great fear of Communism. Dramatic exposures of some persons in high places, such as Alger Hiss, led to criminations by politicians and others which the newspapers naturally reported. Since some persons were unfairly accused, this caused some thoughtful persons to criticize deadpan reporting and to assert that "sticking to the facts" was inadequate journalism. The demand for "interpretive" reporting increased.[1] A thorough analysis of this debate is beyond the scope of a book of this kind, but a few considerations will be mentioned.

Some editors argue that, since fewer people read editorials and editorial page columnists than read news, interpretation should be built into the news itself. They point to the example of the news magazines that supply context along with

[1] See, for example, Elmer Davis, "News and the Whole Truth," *The Atlantic* (August, 1952), pp. 32-38; and various issues of *The Bulletin of the American Society of Newspaper Editors* in 1953. Palmer Hoyt, publisher of *The Denver Post,* in the same year, issued the following directive to his managing editor:

"1. Instruct the news staff always to evaluate the source of the charge.

"2. Ask the news staff to weigh the story and to see what they would do with it if official immunity were lacking.

"3. Discuss with the news staff the general proposition of whether or not *The Denver Post* can withhold publication of this particular moot story until proper proof or a qualifying answer can be obtained from the person, organization, or group accused.

"4. Ask the news staff whether they themselves know a doubtful charge to be false, and ask them to apply any reasonable doubt they may have to the treatment of the story.

"5. In connection with banner lines or other headlines on this type of story, ask the news staff to determine whether wording is used as shock treatment or to summarize the facts."

the essential facts of the news.[2] A certain proportion of these editors assert that news is subjective anyway; and they are correct in one sense.[3] The reporter, for example, may learn 30 facts, decide to use only 10 of them, and to put 1 of them in the lead. His editors use one of these major facts (usually the one in the lead) in the headline and decide whether to publish the story on page 1 or on an inside page. It should be pointed out, however, that these selections and decisions almost always refer to the reporters' and editors' appraisal of the readers' interest in the various facts and not to their own opinions and prejudices.

These editors, however, do not favor mixing opinions with the facts in the news story, as do some of the news magazines and radio news specialists. What these editors demand is more reporting, or "reporting in depth." That may mean several things. Here is one example: A man formerly in the federal government and now holding a high position commits suicide. Since his name had been mentioned in connection with a senatorial investigation of Communists in government, it is proper for the news writer to state that fact. But it is also only fair for the news writer to add that the man had been exonerated by his former superiors' evaluation of the FBI's data.[4]

Some reporting in depth—with a good motive, of course—is begun when the editor knows in advance what the additional facts will prove. This is an example: An employee who had worked in a large bank for 27 years defalcated in the amount of $4000. Instead of reporting only that fact, the editor in-

[2] See the discussion of "objectivity" on pages 41-44.

[3] An excellent demonstration of the subjectivity of news in British newspapers is that of Robert Sinclair (a London editor) in his *The British Press* (London, 1949), Ch. 39.

[4] Contrast that practice with the following incident: An irresponsible radio news commentator, competing with variety shows for a Nielsen audience rating, made an unsubstantiated and sensational accusation against a high official on a Sunday evening program. A news agency reported it deadpan without any qualification or any response by the person accused.

structed a reporter to ask the bank what salary was paid the employee. The bank refused. The reporter then found out from the employee's wife that his salary was only $250 a month (in 1946). The bank had to confirm this, and that fact was added to the news story. After the publication, the officers of the bank received a large number of criticisms from depositors.[5] The point made here is not that the editor was not justified: the point is that the editor was certain in advance of his depth reporting that low salaries were paid by most banks. Thus, depth reporting may be a form of subjective reporting.

How much context? Some persons argue, as we have already said, that it is not possible to report important news objectively. The news writer, they say, cannot give meaning to the event unless he evaluates the event. There is considerable truth in this assertion because the evaluation supplies a frame of reference that assists the reader to understand the facts of the event. There are, however, two other considerations. One is that the reader is deprived of any alternative frame of reference to that presented by the medium. Another consideration is that the news medium that explains every major event must pose as being omniscient. When the writer is omniscient (his medium cannot ignore any major event) he is compelled to invent an explanatory context when he doesn't have an accurate one.

This book argues that, except for news that reports an accusation, it is better to let some of the news go unexplained *on the day it is published* than it is to risk a departure from the traditionally-established attitude of keeping news and opinion separate. Certainly the news agencies cannot afford to tilt the lid of Pandora's box.

The fact remains, however, that the media of news communication have not realized all of the possibilities for mak-

---

[5] The employee restored the money and was not prosecuted. Most banks are insured against defalcation.

ing the news more meaningful. Various techniques are being used. One is to publish a weekly review of the news; this can be effective when the analyst-writer is expert and has enough space. Most small daily newspapers, however, must rely on the news agencies for such a service. It is also possible in some situations—even in politics—to "wrap up" some events that signify potential approval or disapproval of a party's policies and acts—provided the report is in a balanced form. By a skillful arrangement of the details it is possible to present readers with evaluations. The following excerpt from an Associated Press dispatch by Joe Hall is an example:

> WASHINGTON—Democrats displayed quiet confidence today that they have found an issue which may win them the 1954 elections and perhaps lay the basis for a return to national power in 1956. Many Republicans take issue with that appraisal.
>
> The issue is falling farm prices and the views of Republican Secretary of Agriculture Benson, which Democratic lawmakers assert are opposed to high-level, mandatory price supports.
>
> GOP Senate Leader Taft conceded yesterday that "if the Republicans don't do better than the Democrats did in the last two years" in checking farm price drops, "we probably will lose the next election."
>
> But Taft scornfully added that it should not be a hard task because. . . .

Several of the technical possibilities for making the news meaningful will be realized in the future because most daily newspaper editors are not satisfied with their performance in that respect.

So that the student may differentiate the various ways of supplying interpretive context, the following example is presented. *Time* published an article about the natives' violent disobedience of British rule in Nyasaland. This happened more than a year after the murderous attacks of the Mau Mau in Kenya. The writer of the article, realizing that readers would wonder whether the disobedience would subside or increase, stated that the British Colonial Office was not worried. The writer then added this sentence: "But British planters, who evacuated their woman & children to the market town of Blantyre, remember that London once classified Kenya's Mau Mau as a 'minor incident.' " The writer, of course, did not know what British planters "remember," but he inferred it from their action of evacuating women and children. Is that the same as *Time* expressing its own opinion? Would you defend the news agency or daily newspaper using this device?

TYPES OF NEWS STORIES

THERE ARE NUMEROUS types of news stories classified according to their subject-matter. Those that require a technical knowledge to write (such as news about courts and governmental administration and legislation) are best studied in the advanced textbooks which treat of them at considerable length.

The following types are presented in this chapter: (1) the speech report (including coverage of conventions); (2) the interview; (3) the obituary; (4) the human interest story; and (5) the picture caption. Stories about science were examined in the chapter on explanatory writing.

The speech report: When an advance copy of a speech is available, the task of the news writer is merely to select the most significant points and quotations and to organize them so that the reader who was not present will be supplied with as much understanding as the limiting circumstances permit. The competent writer can do this reasonably well because he can read the entire speech and then reread parts of it. When an advance copy is not available, the writer must take notes during the course of the speech without knowing what the speaker is going to say further on.

In both instances, context is a factor. The writer's selection of quotations may be influenced both by the context of the speaker himself and by the writer's perception of the broader context. As an example of the latter, a statement by a speaker during a presidential election campaign may not have the same meaning to readers as would the same statement made in a different context. (Excellent examples of relating communication content to the broader context were the decisions of many advertisers during World War II to present their advertising themes and of most film producers to present their story plots in the broad context of the war effort; they assumed that since the American people were so engrossed with the war they had hardly any other frame of reference and would not be responsive to a theme outside the war frame of reference.)

The speaker himself is sometimes context, and the writer may have this fact in mind when making his selection of quotations. An example of that situation was the reporting, in 1953, while an anti-Communist fear gripped the minds of many people, of two speeches by a distinguished Jesuit editor. His talks were about academic freedom, but during the question period he expressed a mildly adverse opinion of Senator Joseph McCarthy that was featured in two speech reports in a New York newspaper. The newspaper admitted that its report was not a balanced account, although disclaiming any intent to use the speech to support its anti-McCarthy editorial policy.[1] This instance is cited here as an example of how a reporter, in striving to relate news content both to the broader context of the time and to the context of the speaker himself, presented the speaker's utterances in a way that the speaker did not intend.

Reporters vary in the standards they apply to the selection of the most significant parts of a speech. In some instances, one newspaper has selected one set of quotations and a second newspaper has selected an entirely different set. The speaker himself has sometimes assumed that the newspaper's editorial policy about the subject-matter of his speech was the standard applied, whereas the differences were actually to be accounted

[1] See *Time* (Aug. 3, 1953), p. 52.

for by the variations in intelligence and information of the two reporters.

Writing the speech report: The lead of a speech report—unless the speech is one of several delivered on the same day at a meeting of some kind—should usually be a summary statement. When the speech is hortatory, this amounts to the writer telling the readers what it is that the speaker wants his audience to do or to think. Usually the lead can be an indirect quotation or, if it is short, a direct quotation. Sometimes, however, the writer, for lack of an appropriate quotation, must use his own words, as in the following example:

> District Attorney Paul Forsyth called yesterday for a "complete reappraisal" of the way the city is meeting its alcoholic problems.

At some early place in the story, the writer should tell where and when the talk was made and sometimes the circumstances. He should, of course, identify the speaker adequately. In the body of the story he should *alternate direct and indirect quotations* so as to break up the speaker's direct discourse into units of one to three paragraphs and sometimes also to provide transition. The indirect quotations must sometimes be paraphrases of the speaker's actual words, as for example:

> Referring to the "bewildering world" that Americans are now living in, he declared that the only way to understand it is by way of the "Great Acquaintance" which the newspaper supplies.

The following speech report illustrates how the writer alternates direct and indirect quotation:

Only a Profitable Press Can Be Free, Editor Tells Ad Men

A newspaper must be profitable to be free, Grove Patterson, editor-in-chief of the "Toledo Blade," told the Advertising Club yesterday.

"Free enterprise is completely united with free expression," he warned. "If the day comes when there is removed, in any considerable degree, the advertising from the American newspaper, it will start down the short, dark road to failure."

The editor summarized the current criticism of the press and presented what he called "four simple conclusions":

"1. Newspaper publishers will have freedom of the press so long as they deserve it through devotion to the public welfare.

"2. A newspaper can rise no higher than the intelligence and character of its owner.

"3. With conscientious, public-serving newspaper owners, we shall not lose the value of the press in America.

"4. If we do not lose the value, we shall not lose the freedom."

Two Major Responsibilities

Referring to the "bewildering world" that Americans are now living in, he declared that the only way to understand it is by way of the "Great Acquaintance" which the newspaper supplies.

"Today, through the window of your newspaper," he said, "you see the drama of a changing world. The great acquaintanceship even includes the shape of things to come.

"Never in the more than 150 years since America became a united nation, have its newspapers been called upon for so vital a task of interpretation and leadership.

"What the people think of their government, how they act toward their government, toward their ideals and freedoms, is heavily determined by what they read in their newspapers."

The speaker listed two major responsibilities of the newspaper:

"First," he said, "is the responsibility to make certain that the people shall know. This responsibility calls for complete objectivity in the news columns.

"Second—the most profound of all responsibilities—is that of publishers to feel that their first and continuing duty is to be honestly representative of the people as a whole and not of special interests."

Conventions: Since a good many different persons speak at conventions, the writer reports several speeches in the same news story. His lead usually features the most important or most interesting speaker of the particular day (although he tries not to feature the speaker who was reported in the previous news cycle). Some convention speakers arrive with texts of their speeches. The reporter can usually obtain them in advance either from him or from the secretary of the association; in those instances in which the speech seems to be very newsy, the reporter can also interview the speaker to get more explanation. In writing the story that includes several speeches, the reporter should begin the first sentence in which he quotes a succeeding speaker with that speaker's name so as to signal the reader that the writer has finished quoting the last speaker and is now presenting another. An example of a convention news story in an afternoon newspaper follows:

AFL Hears of Senate Probe of Fund 'Misuse'

State labor organizations are facing a State Senate committee interim investigation to determine if legislation is necessary to "protect" members from misuse of their funds "or other activities" by their union officials.

Delegates to the State Federation of Labor's 51st convention in Civic Auditorium were alerted by Paul Scharrenberg, state director of industrial relations, at yesterday afternoon's session to this unpublicized, far-reaching move.

Scharrenberg said the Senate Committee on rules the last day the Legislature was in session empowered the current standing Senate committee on labor to make the investigation and gave it a $20,000 appropriation for its assignment.

He pointed out that a majority of the committee members have a record unfavorable to labor.

The convention today went into its second day with only a morning session scheduled. The 2000 delegates heard talks by Lloyd C. Murdock, AFL representative in the Treasury Department; Deputy Attorney General Emmet Daly; Edward P. Park, state labor commissioner; and George Sehlmeyer, master of the State Grange.

Nine Million Members

Harry O'Reilly, AFL director of organization, yesterday told the convention the AFL "in the main" dominates the organization of atomic energy workers. Despite the Taft-Hartley Act and restrictive state laws, the AFL is winning new members, he said, and predicted it would have a

nine million membership before the end
of the year.

W. Wayne Kenaston, Federal Concilia-
tion Service regional director, said that although substantial budget cuts were
made, the service will use every effort "to
maintain our standards of acceptability
and effectiveness."

William F. Patterson, director of the
bureau of apprenticeship of the Department of Labor, praised the federation for
its support of training programs.

Undersecretary of Labor Lloyd A. Mash-
burn reported substantial progress by a
committee of representatives of the White
House, the departments of Labor and
Commerce, and chairmen of the Senate
and House labor committees in preparing
proposed amendments to the Taft-Hartley
Act to make it "more equitable" to all.

The resolutions that are passed in the business session of a
convention are frequently of news interest, as are also the
names of the new officers. The following news story shows how
such matters are reported:

Cut Out Gadgetry,
Contractor Warns

The American home is in danger of
"over-gadgetitis," members of the Heating,
Piping and Air Conditioning Contractors
National Association were told at the
close of their 61st annual convention at
the St. Francis Hotel yesterday.

Wray M. Scott, newly elected president,
said the future needs for home construction call for fewer and simpler controls
for heating and air conditioning installa-
tions. . . .

The delegates passed a resolution calling for greater public attention to urban
redevelopment and slum clearance and

asked for the encouragement of private
capital to participate in rebuilding programs.

The convention closed with the elec-
tion of officers: Wray M. Scott, of Omaha,
president; H. E. McGregor, Cambridge,
Mass., vice-president; William W. Murray,
Jr., New York, treasurer; and Joseph C.
Fitts, New York, secretary.

The interview: Most of us read about or hear about certain
personalities and feel that we would enjoy talking with them
—finding out what they are really like as persons and what
they are thinking about certain matters. The purpose of the
interview type of news story is to satisfy this desire of the
reader or listener. Radio and television news directors often
present these persons in "live" interviews. The newspaper
reporter talks with the person as an agent of the reader.

Such personalities are important or interesting persons
who are visiting in the city or who are returning from a trip,
or persons—local or otherwise—who have had interesting
experiences or whose opinions are highly respected. They may
be American or foreign statesmen, authors, soldiers, come-
dians, animal trainers, the man and woman who have just
crossed the ocean in a small boat, widely-known and well-
known persons who are retiring from public activity, or some
other type.

The best interview is one in which the reporter substitutes
successfully for the reader. That is, he reports on the personality of the subject or quotes his opinions on subjects in
which the reader is interested. Hence, the role of the reporter
is not to inject his own personality into the story, but to focus
on the personality and conversation of the subject of the
interview.

The interview can seldom succeed unless the reporter
makes adequate preparation. He should find out in advance
all he can about the subject and especially about his achieve-

ments and public activities and sometimes about his opinions and prejudices. Some writers who specialize in writing personality sketches and "profiles" even make inquiries of the subjects' opponents, rivals, critics, or enemies. For the usual newspaper interview, for which the reporter has only a brief time for preparation, he certainly must know, for example, the books the author has written or the films in which the actor has appeared. When the reporter prepares a list of possible questions and memorizes them, he at least is better prepared for beginning the interview.

During the interview the reporter should try to remember that, as the representative of his readers, he should talk about the matters that will probably interest his readers. In some instances, however, the reporter has difficulty until he has mentioned something that the subject is interested in. A good interviewer succeeds in getting the subject to talking without having to put words into the subject's mouth. There is no rule about how this can be done except that it has reference to the interests of the subject himself.

The interviewer generally should take notes. At the beginning of the interview, it may be best not to produce one's copy paper conspicuously as if the subject is going to be cross-examined. The taking of notes, however, gives the subject some assurance that he will be quoted accurately. The reporter, generally, should not interrupt the speaker but should wait until the appropriate moment and then ask the subject to repeat a statement, a figure, or a name.

Since as many examples of interviews could be presented here as there are different kinds of subjects, a single example will suffice. The interview is with an American prisoner of war just returned from Korea. It was written by Michael Harris, of the *San Francisco Chronicle* (with the name of the subject changed).

Returned P.O.W. Tells Why He Was A 'Progressive'

A 23-year-old blond soldier from Meyers Grove in upper New York State, who became something of a political celebrity among his fellow-prisoners, said yesterday:

"I was a 'progressive' in the prison camp. I realize now that I was wrong."

The soldier, Corporal Malcolm Morgan, said he became disillusioned with the Communist line almost immediately after his release from prison camp. He never became a Communist during his 33 months of captivity, he added, but he did become convinced that the Reds were right and the United Nations were wrong in Korea.

Once he was released, he said he found that much of the information given him by his Communist teachers was untrue.

Lied About Segregation

"The Communists told me that Syngman Rhee freed the anti-Communist North Korean prisoners because the United States told him to," Morgan said. "That seemed reasonable to me. After all, Rhee doesn't have much of an army and he depends on America.

"When I got out, I learned that was a lie."

The Reds also told him that the racial problem in the United States was getting worse and worse, Morgan said.

"Now I see they used the racial problem to help themselves," he continued. "In 1947, when I got into the Army, you didn't see whites and Negroes together. Now they even have Negro WACs with white ones."

Segregation bothered him a great deal when he went into the service at 17 six years ago, Morgan continued. Many of his playmates had been Negroes and his father, he said, was a man completely without racial prejudice.

Wounded, Then Captured

"My real problem was that I was politically ignorant," Morgan continued. "I knew nothing about the setup of the Government, hardly anything about the Constitution and nothing about social problems.

"Nobody ever told me why I was in Korea, and though I realize now it's right for us to be there, I didn't think so then."

Although he is obviously above average in intelligence, Morgan had only eight years of schooling. His father, a truck driver, died in 1941, and the corporal supports his mother out of his Army pay.

"I studied for one reason—I wanted to learn," Morgan went on. "I still do. What I'm planning to do now is to talk to more Army officers and to other people at home.

"I've heard one side. Now I'd like to hear the other."

Morgan was wounded in both legs in mid-1950 and was captured after he was unable to walk.

"They just put bandages and mercurochrome on the legs and let them heal themselves," Morgan said. "The nerves are still dislocated. If I touch my leg at one place, I feel the touch somewhere else."

Was Not an Informer

While in prison camp, he got pellagra, a form of dietary deficiency, and he received even less medication for this.

"I got no special favors," Morgan said. "I got the same details and ate the same chow. If I missed a detail because I went to class, I had to make it up afterward."

Some of Morgan's fellow prisoners had promised earlier that they would get their

revenge on "progressives." It was suggested
that some of them might not survive the
trip home.

Morgan was well known as a "progressive" by his fellow prisoners.

"I studied Communism openly," he said,
"but there's a lot of difference between a
'Progressive' and an informer, and I was
no informer."

The group interview at a press conference, attended by reporters from several newspapers, news agencies, and radio
stations, presents a certain problem for the interviewer. Although he can share in the information that the questions of
others develop, he cannot conduct the interview in the atmos-
phere he would wish, especially when some of the questions
are inane. Some reporters have adopted the practice, when
they think it is worthwhile, of remaining after the group
interview has ended to ask certain questions of their own
choosing, especially questions that elaborate the subject's
previous answers.

The obituary: Few news stories in the newspaper have
higher interest than the obituary of a person the reader has
heard about or who was related to some event the reader had
known about. Many readers, in the first place, are interested
in knowing who has just died; in the second place, they like
to read about personalities—whether they are living or deceased. The beginning reporter often does not realize the high
reader interest in obituaries because every day he has to
collect and write a few commonplace details about the death
of relatively obscure persons.

Newspapers supply blank forms to undertakers, who have
them filled out by members of the deceased person's family
and returned to the newspaper. These forms list the time,
place, and cause of death; length of illness; primary bio-
graphical facts; occupation; church and lodge membership
and activities in organizations; names of survivors; place and

time of funeral; place of interment (when there is not inurnment); and, sometimes, the list of pallbearers.

Deceased persons can often be identified in a way that causes them to be thought of as unique personalities. For example, "the man responsible for the burial of Buffalo Bill on Lookout Mountain," or "the last of the direct descendants of the Spanish don who once owned much of the lands in this country," or "the man who fathered the direct primary law in this state."

The following is an example of an obituary of a distinguished foreign author that was written by a news agency:

Hilaire Belloc, Critic, Author, Dies at 82

GUILDFORD, England—Hilaire Belloc, 82, poet, novelist and historian, died today from burns received when he fell into a fireplace at his home Sunday.

Belloc was one of the literary giants who dominated the decades at the turn of the century. Through two generations, beginning in 1896, Belloc's facile pen poured out a seemingly endless cascade of brilliant essays, novels, histories, poetry and light verse. Altogether he wrote 153 books.

He was born in France, but became a British citizen in 1902.

Always a fervent Roman Catholic, Belloc was once described as a "genially pugnacious protagonist of the Catholic faith in English literature." He supported the thesis that Latin culture was superior to Nordic and believed in the continuity of Roman influence in Great Britain.

"Controversialist"

Belloc was widely known as a controversialist. He not only debated religion and politics, but also set himself up as a

military critic, and throughout World
War I and four years thereafter analyzed
the various battles. A favorite antagonist
was H. G. Wells.

He was born at La Celle, St. Cloud,
France, July 27, 1870, the son of a French
barrister, Louis Belloc, and an Irish
mother, Bessie Rayner Parkes. The latter,
who lived until 1925, when she was 96,
was prominent in the early days of the
suffrage movement. A daughter, Marie
Adelaide Belloc, became a successful
novelist.

Visit to America

His first volume, "Verses and Sonnets,"
appeared in 1896 and in that year too he
visited America where he gained wide publicity as a walker, one account being that
he walked right across the United States
to meet Elodie Agnes Hogan in Napa,
Calif., whom he married in 1896.

They had two sons and two daughters.
Mrs. Belloc died in 1941.

Politics attracted him and in 1906 he
was elected a Liberal member of the
House of Commons for the South Stafford
constituency. He held this seat for four
years.

This was Belloc's own epitaph:

"When I am dead I hope it may
 be said,
 His sins were scarlet but his
 books were read."

The obituary should be written in a restrained style. When
the subject is widely-known and respected or beloved, the
reader often feels some personal loss on reading of the death.
The writer, however, can do an affective type of writing
merely by reciting facts and by quoting the deceased person's
associates; he does not need to write a tear-jerker that slops
over with sentimentality, as did the writer of the following
obituary:

AIKEN, S. C.—A full dozen dull-feath-
ered Carolina mocking birds, perched in a
tree just outside his sick-room, sang for
Nicholas Longworth today at dawn.

And they were still singing—a requiem—
as one of the most fascinating figures in
American statesmanship passed on. . . .

Newspaper men stood with bowed heads
in the flowered portico of the Curtis man-
sion as Dr. R. H. Wilds, one of Mr. Longworth's physicians, told them he would
live but a few hours.

Then the doctor stepped out of the
house and told newspapermen the end
had come. Throughout the world the news
of his death flashed. Thousands of words
described his career.

The vigil was over.

Our task done.

The writer is sometimes called upon to do a thorough reporting job for an obituary about an interesting personality.
The data in the form mentioned on page 158 and one or two
telephone inquiries will not be enough. The writer may have
to dig into the newspaper's files and library, make long-
distance telephone calls, and get direct quotations from the
former associates of the deceased person. For the very prominent, the news agencies write obituaries in advance, keeping
them up to date; these are mimeographed and sent to client
newspapers to be released at the time of death.

The human interest story: Editors try to present, along with
the important news, affectively written news stories that are
of minor significance as news yet are entertaining. They are
more a form of popular literature than they are news. They
relate to humorous or pathetic aspects of life or to the pictur-
esque. They are about such subjects as children, animals, a
happening on the bus, and an incident in a railroad station.

They pretty much organize themselves and are in a style
that fits the subject-matter. To present them effectively, the

writer has to be precise about the details, has to report the conversation realistically, and has to achieve enough unity to cause the story to make a single impression; the latter is often achieved by the repetition of some expression or idea. Of the numerous types of human interest story, the following story from the San Francisco *News* is one example:

The Dirty Snake Is All Dishwashed Up

Mrs. Grant Payne scraped the dinner dishes over the week-end while her husband read a book at their home, 2759 Edwards Avenue, in a new wooded subdivision.

The house is new and equipped with a lot of time-saving devices—which are fine as long as nothing goes wrong.

But when Mrs. Payne opened up the dishwasher, the mechanism apparently had gone haywire. A thick coil had sprung up towards the lid.

She reached in to put it back in place, but it moved.

She quickly slammed the lid and shouted into the living room, "There's a snake in the dishwashing machine."

"Yeah, yeah," said her husband, chuckling. "What else is new?"

And suddenly he realized she wasn't kidding.

He looked into the dishwasher and found he would need help to remove the snake because it was coiled in the mechanism.

He phoned a neighbor to ask for help but the neighbor said, "Yeah, yeah," and hung up laughing.

Then he called the police, and the desk sergeant said, "Yeah, yeah," the way he often does to cranks, pranksters and drunks.

But Payne convinced the sergeant that he wasn't kidding, and the sergeant dispatched Policemen Norman Saunders and J. D. Drury.

The three of them managed to uncoil the snake from the mechanism, but then it escaped underneath a kitchen cabinet.

"Finally, after just about tearing up the place, we caught it," Payne said. He said it was a two-foot long rattler, and the policemen killed it in the yard.

But the police said, "Yeah, yeah, it was a gartersnake."

A somewhat different type of human interest story is this one:

Lucky Housewives Grow 4-Leaf Clover

Two local housewives, Mrs. Luke Westlake and Mrs. Wallace Kiesel, are toying with the idea of going into the four-leaf clover "business"—if they're lucky.

And, so far, they couldn't have been luckier.

It all started on June 16 when Mrs. Westlake discovered one of the rare four-leafers in her backyard at 1819 Marshall Street, and decided to pick it to insert in a birthday card for her friend, Mrs. Kiesel, of 1714 Woodward Street.

Mrs. Westlake, who has found many of the good luck omens before, suggested that Mrs. Kiesel immerse the stem in a glass of water.

"I told her it would keep a week or so that way," Mrs. Westlake said. "So she put it in just plain water, naturally expecting it would start wilting in a few days.

"But, lo and behold, it didn't. It started growing. I've never heard of such a thing before. With some other kinds of plants, yes, but with clover, never."

Mrs. Westlake, measuring the miracle today, found that it has progressed by leaps and bounds. It had a tiny stem when she picked it, and a leaf-span of only about three-quarters of an inch.

Now, however, the stem has stretched to five inches, the roots dangle down another four and the leaves are almost three inches across.

She and Mrs. Kiesel plan to plant the roots in rich soil sometime soon. Then they'll sit back and wait to see what happens.

"You never know," Mrs. Westlake said. "Maybe it will produce nothing but four-leafs."

Her husband already is looking forward to that possibility. She said he told her, with a gleam in his eye: "If that thing sends out shoots, I want one of them."

For an analysis of the human interest story as sociology as well as literature, one should read Helen M. Hughes' *News and the Human Interest Story* (Chicago, 1940).

The picture caption: The action picture caption in the newspaper is different from the news story in these ways: (1) it is shorter than most news stories, (2) it usually begins with a short "legend" instead of a headline, and (3) the picture itself is the lead for the caption. Because the reader looks at the picture before he reads the caption, the picture orients the reader to a considerable degree and presents an image. The purposes of the caption, therefore, are to (1) give more meaning to the picture by telling the reader what to look at—*what the people in the picture are doing;* and (2) give more explanation as to *who the people are* plus a few other facts that the reader needs to know to understand the picture.

Picture captions, in many newspapers, do not communicate as efficiently as do the news stories. That is because the editors do not analyze adequately the function of the caption. One major fault in picture captions is the long sentences. Because of its typography the picture caption is harder to read quickly than is the news story. Sentences in picture captions should be even shorter on the average than in news stories.

EXERCISES

_____

CHAPTER I

1. This is not a test of your memory.

After the rewrite man on the *Daily Beagle* had finished making his early telephone calls, the city editor asked, "What have you got?" The rewrite man said:

A woman burned to death on the East side. Her husband woke up about daylight choking from smoke and saw flames in the ceiling.

He ran out of the house to call a neighbor. He and the neighbor couldn't get back through the front door. The husband got in a window but couldn't stand the smoke and flames. He was badly burned about the face and arms.

A neighbor gave the alarm and firemen put out the fire after the fire had gutted the house.

The newspaper operates a radio station. The city editor told the rewrite man to run up to the studio on the top floor and talk the story into a tape recorder so as to have it ready for the next newscast.

After the rewrite man got to the studio, he found he had left part of his notes behind. But fortunately he remembered the other facts well enough to make an adequate cast.

You are the rewrite man.

Here are the notes you take with you. Talk your story into a tape (or wire) recorder, using your memory for all of the facts that are not mentioned below.

Her address is 3514 Polk Street.

The dead woman was Mrs. Alice Warner, 30.

Her husband is Ben Warner, a garage mechanic.

The neighbor who rushed to Warner's assistance was Worth Martin, of 3512 Polk Street.

The time was 5:15 A.M.
The Warners had a five-room house.
Fire Chief Henry Hogan said electric wiring in the attic was defective.

At the end of your newscast get your name on the tape by saying, "This newscast was by (your name)."

Note to instructor: The performance of individual students may be influenced by some of these factors: (*a*) had or did not have a course in speech; (*b*) had or did not have a high school course in journalistic writing, and (*c*) had or did not have some kind of newswriting experience.

2. Next week play back your newscast and transcribe it. Then write a news story for a newspaper using the same facts. Do you think there should be any difference between the two forms of communication in so far as this type of news story is concerned?

3. After a friend has finished reading the newspaper, have him draw a vertical line through the center of each item he has read on the front page. What is the percentage of items he has read? How does this compare with the average percentages mentioned on page 16.

4. Have the friend indicate how far down he read into four of the longer items he read on the front page (if he read that many).

5. Have the friend mark in the same way as in Exercise 3 all of the items in the newspaper that he read. Did he seem to reject many items that he "ought" to have read in order to be well informed?

6. When do you usually read the morning newspaper? the evening newspaper? the Sunday newspaper?

7. What types of channel noise interfere with your news reading? Your radio listening?

8. In your newspaper reading today, did you note any factors inherent in the news stories or in the makeup of the newspaper that retarded or interfered with easy reading?

9. How many things did you find in your newspaper that you did not understand very well?

10. In the language of chess, *Pd4xBc5* means "the pawn on square 4d moves onto and captures the bishop on square c5." Taking *x* as the verb in chess language and considering the most elementary rule about *capture*, which words are redundant in the English language quoted above?

Are there any other verbs than *x* in the language of chess? (For a discussion of redundancy in connection with chess language, see G. A. Miller, *Language and Communication*, pp. 106-109.)

11. In the Journalism Library you will find copies of the New York *Herald Tribune,* the New York *Daily News,* and the Minneapolis *Tribune.* Examine a copy of each carefully. Then compare and contrast them. Your analysis should cover the following points:

    a. Differences in format and typography.
    b. Use of graphic material.
    c. General differences in content.
    d. Differences in news writing style.
    e. Kinds of advertising.

Describe briefly in general terms the audience to which each seems to be directed (e.g., economic status, education).

12. Circle the usage that is in accord with the style guide (pp. 239-241).

    a. M. J. Cox, Jr.   M. J. Cox Jr.   M. J. Cox, jr.
       M. J. Cox jr.
    b. West High school   West High School
       West high school
    c. 11 p.m.   11:00 p.m.   11:00 P.M.   11 P.M.
    d. Mississippi River   Mississippi river
    e. William McKinley was President.   William McKinley was president.

13. Here is a news agency story for publication in a newspaper and below it the same story as written for the radio wire of the same news agency. What are the characteristic differences in the lead, the sentence structure, the sentence length, the tense of verbs, and the handling of quotations?

The newspaper story:

> PITTSBURGH—Firms which make nearly half the nation's paints, varnishes and lacquers, and the men who run them were under indictment today—charged with a conspiracy to fix the prices of their products.
>
> A federal grand jury, acting on complaints of the U. S. government, handed

down the indictments in the U. S. District
Court yesterday, naming 14 major paint
companies and 20 officials.

These companies, the indictments said,
handled more than 45 per cent of the
nation's billion dollar yearly paint business.

Attorney General Tom Clark said the
cases were a part of the government's
antitrust program aimed at "illegal conspiracies" in the housing fields.

He said Commerce Department records "indicate that prices in the paint
industry rose more rapidly after the removal of OPA ceilings than in any other
industry."

The indictments specifically accused the
firms of engaging in "a combination and
conspiracy to fix, stabilize, maintain and
control the prices, discounts, allowances
and terms of sale" of their products.

The firms, the indictment said, agreed
"to exchange with each other information
about prices charged . . . and other factors
affecting prices."

In Cleveland, spokesmen for two of the
companies under indictment protested
there was no basis for the charges.

Adrian D. Joyce, chairman of the board
of Glidden Co., said:

"There's nothing to it. We never met
with any other paint concern to discuss
prices and costs. Our prices are very much
the same as other firms' due to competition."

Luther H. Schroeder, treasurer of the
Sherwin-Williams Co., declared:

"We don't see any basis for it (the
charges) whatsoever."

One indictment listed these firms. . . .

The radio story:

Indictments have been returned against
the firms which make nearly half the nation's paints, varnishes and lacquers. These

firms and the men who run them have been charged with a conspiracy to fix the prices of their products. But in Cleveland, spokesmen for two of the companies are protesting that there is no basis for the charges.

A federal grand jury handed down the indictments yesterday, naming 14 major paint companies and twenty officials. According to the indictments, these companies handle more than 45 per cent of the nation's billion-dollar yearly paint business.

Attorney General Tom Clark says the cases are a part of the government's anti-trust program aimed at what he calls "illegal conspiracies" in the housing fields.

Clark adds that Commerce Department records "indicate that prices in the paint industry rose more rapidly after the removal of O-P-A ceilings than in any other industry."

The indictments charge that the firms agreed "to exchange with each other information about prices charged and other factors affecting prices."

The chairman of the Glidden Co., Adrian Joyce, has replied to it. "We never met with any other paint concern to discuss prices and costs. Our prices are very much the same as other firms' due to competition."

And the treasurer of Sherwin-Williams Co. says: "We don't see any basis for the charges whatsoever."

14. How does your dictionary define *semantic?*

CHAPTER II

1. Using the terminology of this chapter, write a short explanation of the following news story, analyzing it as a stimulus to the reader:

The slashing blades of a giant cement mixer ripped Harley Ashburn to death today after he had gone inside it to make repairs.

A detective, who examined the mixer, said he could find no accidental way to start it. Two of Ashburn's fellow workers are being questioned by police at the request of Coroner Sam Jorgenson.

2. In the same way, analyze this supposititious news story:

YELLOWSTONE NATIONAL PARK —"Old Faithful" geyser ceased to spout at 3:05 P.M. today.

3. How much do you agree with this statement: "The newspaper seeks to reach everybody, and hence deals with those subjects that relate to everybody's experience."

4. A George Lichty ("Grin and Bear It") cartoon shows one of his characters sitting on a sofa near a radio and a globe, surrounded by newspapers carrying headlines about international conflicts, and mopping his brow perplexedly. His wife is saying to her caller, "Sometimes I think the reason Fignewton is so confused is because he's so well informed. . . ." What is the meaning of this cartoon, if any, as it could be expressed in the terminology of this chapter?

5. Which of these news stories would interest the most readers? Rank them in 1, 2, 3 order. Defend your rankings.

An 18-year-old youth was executed today for a murder shot he did not fire—despite a dramatic eleventh-hour appeal for his life to the Governor.

The Defense Department today made public a special feature of the new atomic artillery shell.

An architect, who asserted he never drove a car in his life, today started to serve a six-month jail sentence for manslaughter arising from a traffic accident.

Mrs. Edward Sampson filed a petition for divorce in Superior Court today. She and her husband celebrated their golden wedding anniversary five years ago.

> The number of Roman Catholics in the
> United States topped the 30-million mark
> last year, the Official Catholic Directory
> reported yesterday. This is a net increase
> of 1,017,495 over last year.

6. In the Journalism Library you will find copies of *The Times* (London) and *The Daily Express* (London). Examine a copy of each carefully. Then compare and contrast them. Your analysis should cover the following points:

  a. Differences in format and typography.
  b. Use of graphic material.
  c. General differences in content.
  d. Differences in news writing style.

Describe briefly in general terms the audience to which each seems to be directed.

What seem to be the main differences between these and the American newspapers you previously analyzed?

7. Circle the usage that is in accord with the style guide:

  a. 25%   25 per cent   25 percent
  b. A room 9 x 12   a room nine by twelve   a room nine x 12
  c. Tuesday Tues.
  d. Governor Mark Garver Gov. Mark Garver
  e. Professor Clarence Green Prof. Clarence Green

8. Discuss this anecdotal news story in the terminology of this chapter:

> City Coroner Patrick Taylor was ques-
> tioning a witness at a murder inquest.
> "Where were you when the first shot
> was fired?" he asked.
> "Down at the end of the bar," the man
> replied.
> "Where were you when the second shot
> was fired?"
> "What second shot?"

Why would some readers *start to read* this story? Why is it humorous?

9. Find in today's newspaper one example of episodic news. Does the news story mention any institution (such as a committee of the United States Senate) or a procedure that you feel you do not understand thoroughly? How do the facts in this story relate to something that has been reported previously? After you finished reading the story, did you feel that you don't care to read anything in the future about the matter, or do you feel you would like to continue an interest in it until something definitive has happened?

10. Count the number of items in your newspaper that are general news (i.e., not sports or other specialized types of news). What percentage of the items can be classified as episodic and what percentage as news about completed actions?

11. Listen to a radio newscast, noting the subject-matter of each item mentioned. Check these against the items in your daily newspaper of the corresponding date. What kinds of news does the radio omit? As to the items that are reported in both media, do you find any differences as to the details of the individual news stories as reported in one medium but not in the other?

12. Locate a news story in your newspaper in which there seems to be a personality with which the usual reader identifies.

13. Locate a news story which you think has an instrumental value for many readers. What kind of readers would they be?

14. Locate a news story of which the salient element (of subject-matter) seems to present the reader with a threat to his peace of mind.

15. Locate a similar news story of a second order of threat value.

CHAPTERS III-IV

1. Write a sentence that is a directive type of communication.

2. Write a sentence that is an affective type of communication.

3. What is the dictionary definition of *chronicle?*

4. What is meant by the statement on pages 42-43 that "the context was *the author* of a statement"?

5. What is meant by the statement in the footnote on page 41 that the "kind of man the Governor is" is the context?

6. What is meant by the statement on page 43 that "the newspaper or its writer" is the context?

7. To what extent is the dateline on a wire news story context?

8. Debate the question: "The reader is better off to get his news from *Time,* which always supplies some frame of reference, than to get it from the daily newspaper, which nearly always assumes the reader will supply his own context."

9. Which is the better lead on page 27? Why?

10. Circle the usage which is in accord with the style guide:

    a. The Reverend John Black   Reverend John Black
       The Rev. John Black

    b. The thermometer dropped to five degrees. The thermometer dropped to 5 degrees.

    c. He is three years old. He is 3 years old.

    d. 2100 pounds 2,100 pounds

    e. February 21 Feb. 21st February 21st Feb. 21

11. Mark out enough of the details in this news story to reduce it to about 200 words. Defend your deletions.

Ramon Flores, wealthy bar operator, was kidnapped, robbed of $11,500 cash and dumped on his face in the weeds near the airport road yesterday morning.

The daring kidnap was witnessed by a passing motorist.

He said one of the gunmen threatened to shoot him if he interfered.

Flores, who is 67, was met as he left the rear door of the Fidelity Bank & Trust Co. at Morris avenue and East 14th street, at 9:35 A.M.

He was forced into the back seat of an old model Chevrolet at gunpoint and made to lie face down.

The robbers bound his eyes and mouth and tied his arms behind him, Flores said.

Four miles from the scene of the kidnapping, the men carried Flores from the car and laid him in the weeds 15 feet off the airport road.

He was able to free himself and report the robbery to his bar at 1800 East 14th street, two blocks from the bank.

Flores carried the money in cash; $7000 in $20 bills, $3000 in $10 bills, $1100 in $5 bills, and the rest in rolls of silver. It was loose in his pocket, he told police.

In addition to the cash he had just

drawn from the bank—to cash paychecks at his saloon—Flores also lost $100 in his wallet.

The robbers took his 44-40 Colt pistol, too. They left him with two watches and two diamond stickpins valued at $1500 and a $5200 diamond ring.

Flores said he was insured against robbery.

Clark Marder, a passing motorist, saw the whole thing. His way was blocked by the kidnap car, he said.

"Turn around or we'll drill you," the gunman who forced Flores into the kidnap car told him.

The gunman who forced Flores to submit was described as between 40 and 45. He is a dark-complexioned white man, 5 feet 9 inches in height and weighs between 180 and 200 pounds. He wore a light gray business suit.

Police were checking airport dispatchers on the theory the two kidnappers may have boarded a plane to escape.

They are searching also for the kidnap car.

Police said the car carried stolen license plates numbered 43-G-749. Earlier the car mistakenly had been reported registered to a San Francisco man.

Meanwhile, Manuel Gonzales, night floorman at the Club Montez, told police three men had robbed him of $400 early yesterday.

He said they carried a knife, shotgun, and pistol.

12. Write a news story based on the following facts:

N-25338, a Bellanca plane, belongs to Carl Peterson, a crop duster.

Peterson, who was born April 18, 1930, used to fly planes in Saudi Arabia.

The Bellanca has cream-colored numbers on it, but is painted a red color.

Hamilton Field has an air rescue squadron, and its members are hunting for the plane belonging to Peterson, who lives in San Carlos.

It seems that Peterson left the San Mateo flying field at 4:45 o'clock in the afternoon yesterday, and he has not been heard of since.

Peterson, whose address is 465 Oak Street, had four hours of fuel when he left. He was on his way to Bakersfield.

The air rescue squadron is commanded by Capt. Stephen Winters.

Peterson was actually headed for Fresno, where he was to stop en route to his destination.

Winters ordered the search. Peterson did not land at Chandler field, Fresno, as he was expected to.

13. Is there too much attribution or the right amount in this lead?

> KARACHI, Pakistan—The office of Hyderabad's agent general in Pakistan tonight quoted the Hyderabad radio as saying that Indian troops are reported to have entered Hyderabad territory.

14. Rewrite the following news story to eliminate any attribution which you believe is not justified, considering the context of race relations issues:

> MOUNT VERNON, Ga.—A Negro father of six children was shot and killed because he insisted on voting in the Georgia Democratic primary election on Wednesday, Sheriff R. M. McCrimmon said today.
>
> The slain man was identified as Isaiah Nixon, 28, of Alston, Ga. Sheriff McCrimmon said he died in a hospital at Dublin from three gunshot wounds received Wednesday night.
>
> Sheriff McCrimmon said he was holding Johnnie Johnson, 22, an Alston logger, on a charge of accessory to murder and is seeking to arrest his brother, M. A. Johnson, on a charge of murder. They are white men.
>
> The sheriff said he was told that Mr. Nixon went to a polling place in Alston and asked if he could vote. He was told, Sheriff McCrimmon said, that he had the right to vote but was advised not to do so. He insisted, however, according to the

sheriff, and was allowed to cast his ballot.

The sheriff said the two Johnson brothers went to the Nixon home that night and that M. A. Johnson fired the fatal shots in front of Mr. Nixon's wife and children.

According to the sheriff, Johnnie Johnson said he and his brother went to the house to get Mr. Nixon to work for them and that his brother fired in self defense....

15. Are the italicized adjectival phrases justified in this news story?

CHICAGO—A *fast-thinking* socialite thwarted the abduction of himself and a young woman concert singer early Saturday by breaking the speed laws and talking sassy to the cop who stopped him.

The move delivered a *gun-toting* stowaway in the car into police custody and scotched the kidnapping of Spencer Newton and his girl friend, Willina Garrett....

They were talking in Newton's parked car when Davis thrust a pistol through the window....

He slipped into the front seat, keeping his gun on Newton.

Newton gunned the car up to 40 miles an hour in a 25-mile zone on Lake Shore Drive, steering a weaving course.

A squad car spotted him and pulled alongside. Patrolman Rizer demanded his driving license.

"I don't have one," Newton said. "I don't have a car registration, either..."

Rizer order Newton out of the car to explain and Newton whispered that Davis was armed and abducting them....

16. Write a news story based on these facts:

Man reported struck by automobile—Sixth and Market streets.
Accident reported to police 10:15 A.M.
General Hospital ambulance called.

Patrolman John Clancy took injured man to hospital.

Henry Swenk, witness, 4416 Vallejo Street, an accountant, says victim was crossing street with green light when car approached at high speed.

Driver failed to stop after accident. Car is green coupe. Witnesses failed to get license number. Broken headlight glass in street.

Receiving room at hospital says victim probably has fractured skull. Condition serious. Card found in pocket gives name of Vincent Furi, 2214 Porter Street.

Victim identified by brother, Anthony Furi, of same address. Vincent is 45, father of two children, an electrical appliance salesman.

Hour after accident motorist arrested at Union Square garage. Attendant John Smith, who heard police broadcast, noticed broken headlight on car and called patrolman on beat. Driver gives name of James Masterson, 21, 3510 Plymouth Avenue, junior college student. No previous arrests.

Masterson signs confession admitting accident. "I became frightened and I guess I lost my head," he tells police. Released on bond on charges of reckless driving and leaving scene of an accident.

CHAPTER V

1. Organize these facts in a descending order of their importance and interest:

Mr. and Mrs. Oliver Cortesi, owner of Oliver's Restaurant, met instant death last night when their automobile was struck at the Linden Avenue crossing by a C. X. & Y. passenger train.

Both were 56 years old.

The accident happened at 10:20 P.M. at the same point where four other motorists had met death this year.

There were no witnesses other than the train crew.

The train, a southbound local, struck the Cortesi car broadside, carrying it a distance of 216 feet, Police Chief Louis Belloni said.

The Cortesis had just left a Burlingame mortuary, where they had paid respects at the bier of a friend.

The bodies remained in the car after the car was struck.

Mr. Cortesi was a brother of Mayor Emilio Cortesi.

2. Organize these facts in a descending order of their importance and interest:

Two robbers held up the "Jolly Tavern."

The address was 693 King Street.

They stole $6000.

The robbers fled to a waiting car.

The robbery was in daylight (3:30 P.M.).

Three patrons were held at bay for twenty minutes while the safe and the premises were searched and robbed.

Police Chief William Peterson said it was the largest hold-up for years in this community.

When the men entered the place they both drew guns. The leader was a six foot, heavy set, round-faced man. His partner was tall, slender, and mustached.

The leader said, "This is it. Climb from behind the bar."

The bartender's name was Harold Weinstein, of 987 Middlefield Road.

The three patrons were lined up and marched into a booth.

The leader forced the bartender to open the locked safe. He had just put away $6000 in cash.

The patrons' names and addresses were: Harry Wyatt, 108 Fremont Street; Eddie Morrison, 418 Spruce Street; and Lorraine Wacker, 2100 Westgate Road.

After the robbers had taken the money from the safe, the leader told his accomplice, "You get in the car."

He then told the victims in the booth: "Lie on the floor on your faces and keep your arms outstretched. Stay there. The first guy that moves— I'll kill him dead."

3. Mark out the three transitional phrases in the Gandhi assassination story on pages 50-52. How do these deletions affect the reader's understanding of the events?

4. Analyze ten news stories in yesterday's newspaper to determine whether the blocks of subject-matter are adequately tied together by transitional devices.

5. In yesterday's newspaper, can you find any news story that would be more easily understood if it were organized climactically?

6. Circle the usage that is in accord with the style guide:

    a. ten cents 10 cents ten ¢ 10¢ .10¢
    b. one dollar 1 dollar $1.00 $1
    c. sixty-five dollars 65 dollars $65.00 $65
    d. "South Pacific" is a fine show. South Pacific is a fine show.

7. The following news story is organized according to the inverted pyramid structure. Rewrite it in a climactic structure.

> A 19-year-old girl and a young sailor were killed on the Bayshore Highway in Burlingame last night when the car in which they were riding crashed into a power pole.

The girl, Warrena Deming, a junior college student employed as a "mother's helper" by a Hillsborough family, and the sailor, Martin Shea, 21, of Macon, Ga., were both pronounced dead on arrival at Community Hospital.

The driver of the car, Alvin Williams, 22, who served with the dead sailor at Thompson Field Naval Air Station, suffered internal injuries.

The fourth occupant of the vehicle, Jack Ennis, 21, a seaman on the military transport President Jackson, suffered shock and back injuries. Both were treated at Community Hospital and then transferred to Johnson Field Hospital.

The accident happened on 19th avenue between the C. Y. & X. Railroad tracks and the Bayshore Highway. Highway police said the sailors were driving Miss Deming home from a roller-skating rink on the Bayshore Highway.

The young woman often skated there to pass the time during the long evenings until her fiance, William Anderson, returned from an aircraft carrier in Pacific waters. Williams was a good friend of Warrena's fiance. It was he who offered her a ride home.

Williams, at the wheel, failed to negotiate a slight jog in the road, and the right side of his vehicle was sheared off when he hit the pole. Miss Deming and Shea, passengers on the right side of the car, were thrown out and apparently killed instantly.

Mrs. Gilbert Cox, who employed Miss Deming, said the girl's mother was killed in an automobile accident several years ago. The girl's father is Warren Deming, an upholsterer.

Highway police reported the survivors of the crash said they had bought a pint of whiskey yesterday afternoon. A half-empty pint bottle was found in the car.

> Mrs. Cox described Miss Deming as "a
> wonderful girl, popular, pretty, and
> friendly." She was "marvelous with chil-
> dren," she added.

8. On page 53, the statement is made that it is not always
necessary for the news writer to report certain details in a
chronological order. Why is it not necessary in the specific instances mentioned there? In what situations would it be necessary?

9. This exercise has two parts:

- *a.* Write a chronicle (inverted pyramid) type of news story
  based on the following facts for a morning newspaper.
- *b.* Do you consider this the most effective way of telling
  this particular story? If so, then you have completed the
  exercise. If not, rewrite the story in a more effective form
  and submit both versions.

The Facts

(1) Dorothy Talbot, 18, 35 Powell Street, died at St. Francis hospital
tonight.

(2) It was "Bingo Night" tonight at the Rivoli Theater. Mrs. Talbot
went to the theater with her husband. His name is David Talbot. He
has been unemployed for months, but he got a job two days ago and was
to report for work tomorrow. The Talbots were feeling pretty cheerful
about this.

(3) The bingo wheel was on the stage of the theater. It had been spun
26 times, and 26 players had collected cash prizes. The prizes were
hidden behind large silver stars on the stage. The stars were shiny.
There was one star left on the stage. Behind it was $3. The wheel spun
a final time and a number flashed on the screen.

(4) The Talbots were nearly broke. They hoped they might win some
money at the theater—that's why they went. Their little boy, 2, won a
baby contest at the Rivoli last year.

(5) Mrs. Talbot, seated in the balcony, saw the number on the screen.
She held the number. "It's my number," she gasped.

(6) Mrs. Talbot had been suffering from a thyroid condition for
several years. But lately she had been feeling fine.

(7) When she saw that she had won, she laughed. Then she slipped
past her husband and ran down the stairs to collect the prize which was
hidden behind the star. When she reached the lobby, she stumbled a bit
and then collapsed.

(8) At St. Francis hospital a few minutes later doctors said that she
was dead. They said she probably had a heart attack as the result of the
thyroid condition.

10. Rewrite the facts in Exercise 7 in a form that is appropriate for a radio broadcast.

CHAPTER VI

1. Which of the two leads on page 68 is the better? Why?
2. Which of the two leads on page 69 is the better? Why?
3. In the following news story, should the first word be "because" or "after"? Is the difference an important one?

> Because of an argument about where she and her husband would spend their vacation, the wife of a psychiatrist committed suicide today, according to police.
>
> Mrs. Mary Fox, 30, wife of Dr. Robert Fox, was found dead on an empty lot on Elliott Avenue. Beside her body were some bottles and a box which had contained drugs.
>
> The doctor told Police Inspector William Maxwell that he and his wife quarreled last night about where they would spend their vacation and she walked out of their home at 918 Stevens Street at about 10 P.M.

4. As an editor, would you accept this lead or would you require a shorter one?

> A slip of the foot yesterday resulted in: (1) extensive damage to an automobile; (2) the ripping off of a corner of a garage; (3) snapping of a gas main and damaging of an electricity meter; and (4) sending of members of the police and fire departments and a gas and electric company repairman to the scene.
>
> A garage at the home of Mrs. Elmer Richmond, 511 Johns Street, was the scene of the accident. Mrs. Richmond reported her foot slipped from the brake to the gas pedal while backing her car out of the driveway. . . .

5. Rewrite this lead:

> A circuit court judge today upheld the validity of Mrs. Ben Eagelson's previous marriage to Actor Kenneth Ashbaugh and her present one to Hollywood producer Max Linit and awarded her increased custody of the daughter she and Eagelson adopted five years ago.

6. Delete the quotation marks in this lead. Have you altered the meaning in any way?

> Harold E. Stassen, Minnesota aspirant for the Republican presidential nomination, in a speech recorded for radio release tonight, urged that a "courteous welcome" and "friendly hearing" be given leaders of the Republican party who visit his home state.

7. The following AP lead was for publication throughout the United States. Why did the writer decide to write it this way? Is it the best way?

> LOS ANGELES—Where else besides Los Angeles do you see things such as this right out on the sidewalk? Twelve long-haired women spread their tresses on the walk for a Buddhist priest to walk across. . . .

8. The following lead presents several points for discussion:

> Are women being denied rights they ought to have?
> The answer may surprise men. It's "yes," say the women.

Can the gist of the event be presented in question form? To what extent do readers of this lead *identify*? Do they read it for an instrumental reason?

9. In the lead on page 79 ("financially-well-off couple") would you justify inserting the word *attractive* with reference to the wife if you thought she was attractive?

10. Some editors say, "No name, no story," meaning they never write news about anonymous persons (except juvenile delinquents and victims of rape). Here is a story from *Time* about an anonymous person. As an editor, would you use it without the name or omit it if you did not believe you should use the name?

> When Mrs. McK., 25, gave a pint of blood for Britain's National Blood Transfusion Service in Sheffield last March, the doctor and nurses who checked her saw nothing unusual. But when technicians typed the blood, they did a double take, and with good reason: Mrs. McK. was the first human being in medical history with a double set of blood groups. Her red cells were 61% type O and 39% type A.
>
> Puzzled, the researchers asked Mrs. McK. whether she was a twin. No less puzzled by their apparent second sight, Mrs. McK. replied that she had had a twin brother, who died when three months old. That explained it, they figured: in the womb there had been a connection between the arteries of the fraternal twins, and Mrs. McK. had picked up some of her brother's blood-making cells.
>
> In cattle, a female twin born with a male is a freemartin, intersexed and usually sterile. Said the *British Medical Journal:* Mrs. McK. has had a child and is clearly feminine—no human freemartin.

11. Why was this lead written in this way?

> Three men in a top-down convertible breezed over the Golden Gate bridge yesterday morning, sped up the hill, through the tunnel and down Waldo Grade, weaving in and out of traffic, speeding up, then slowing down, enjoying the day.
>
> A short time later, all were dead.
>
> The convertible had suddenly swerved into the guard rail over the underpass to Marin City, at the foot of the grade.
>
> It ripped out a section of the 6-by-8 timbered guard rail, knocked out a 12-by-12 post and hurtled 30 feet to the pavement of the Marin City side road below.

12. Why was this lead written this way? Do you like it this way?

Under the showcase in the jewelry shop belonging to Harland Shane at 312 Nansen Street is a small cubbyhole.

The space has never been used for anything, except that Shane—perhaps out of whimsy, perhaps for lack of any other place to put it—had got down on his knees and tacked on the wall of the cubbyhole, where only a dog would be able to see it, the sign, "Time Is Precious."

Yesterday morning for some time—nobody knows for how long—a middle-aged woman lay crouched in that niche holding a loaded .45 automatic and a Luger type .38 automatic pistol.

The woman was Miriam Roark, 57. For the past seven years she was the next-door neighbor of the Shanes, whose home was at 4344 Manchester Boulevard.

Shane, a man of 47, opened his jewelry store at the usual time yesterday, about 8:45 A.M. He found the store as he had left it and it did not occur to him to look under the showcase.

The mailman came a moment later, chatted with Shane a minute and gave him a card telling him there was a package at the post office down the street. Shane went to get it, and on the way back stopped to talk to two men on the sidewalk waiting for the barber shop next door to open. [Their names.]

The men saw Shane go into his shop. Then they heard shots. They found Shane near his work bench with a bullet in his head and another in his abdomen. He was dead. They went for help. It was not until about 20 minutes later, as police were searching the place, that they found Mrs. Roark's body.

She was dead also, huddled in the niche, the Luger in her hand and the .45 under

her body. She too had a bullet in her head
and one in her abdomen.

In her purse police found a key to
Shane's jewelry shop. They also found a
long, rambling note addressed to Shane's
wife, Helen. . . .

Mrs. Shane said she and her husband
had known Mrs. Roark casually for seven
years but they had not been friends, never
visited with each other, and she was sure
her husband had not been intimate with
Mrs. Roark.

13. Improve this second day lead:

Robert Wright, president of the Pacific
Biscuit Company, was dead today following an operation. Funeral services will be
held tomorrow afternoon.

14. Anything wrong in this sentence? "For the second time
in four years, Fairfax voters defeated a school bond issue while
voters in the county voted 3 to 2 for highway improvement bonds,
County Clerk Franklin Nelson revealed today."

15. With which of these rules about style do you agree?

a. "The traditional practice of placing 'the' before 'reverend' . . . is too formal for newspaper usage"—Fort
Worth *Star-Telegram.* "Use of the definite article preceding the word 'reverend' in the title is essential."—
Tacoma *News Tribune.*

b. "Do not say 'the' police."—Cincinnati *Enquirer.* " 'The
police arrested the man,' not 'police arrested the man.' "
—Fresno *Bee.*

c. "After introduction of name, refer thereafter to the
person as 'Mr.' except when the context of the story . . .
suggests dropping the title."—Washington *Star.* "Nobody rates a 'Mr.' in front of his name in the *Daily
News,* directly quoted matter excepted."—Los Angeles
Daily News.

d. "A widow, not a wife, survives."—Portland (Me.) *Press
Herald.* "A man is survived by his wife, but leaves a
widow."—New York *Journal-American.*

16. Why did the news writer use this kind of lead?

> Senator Clinton P. Anderson, who was secretary of agriculture in the Truman administration, testified yesterday in a trial in federal District Court.
>
> The Senator, who testified for the Government, explained the Truman administration's farm price support programs.
>
> He was a witness in the suit in Judge George Harris' court brought against the Commodity Credit Corporation by Rosenberg Brothers and Company, Inc. The firm alleges it lost $400,000 in its raisin merchandizing because the CCC forced the price of raisins up through competitive bidding.

17. Is any essential or desirable element missing from this lead?

> John Jones shot and killed James Smith today at the corner of 8th Street and 10th Avenue.

CHAPTER VII

1. Retype the following story supplying the necessary paragraphing and quotation marks. Make the story conform to the style guide. Do not make any other changes in the copy.

Serenely the good ferry Golden Shore steamed halfspeed through the fog, San Francisco bound from Sausalito today. Suddenly a wild-eyed man dashed past the Passengers Keep Out sign into the wheel house. Captain, he panted. Captain! My wife is about to become a mother. Congratulations, said Capt. Edward Hallin calmly. Congratulations be darned! cried breathless George Babcock. I don't want congratulations. I want help! She's going to have the baby here, now. Below on the decks, startled passengers heard the jangle of engine room bells, felt the ferry leap full speed ahead. But the sturdy Golden Shore, tearing recklessly through the fog, was no match for the stork, who swooped down on the boat like a hungry seagull right smack between Alcatraz Penitentiary and the Hyde street ferry slip. Deckhands dashed through the ship crying: Is there a doctor aboard? Dr. Dohrmann K. Pischel pushed his corn flakes aside in the restaurant. I'm a doctor, he said, gulping the last of his morning coffee. We have a case for you, explained the deckhand. What kind of a case? A—a baby ... That is, a baby any minute ... I mean a lady who's going to have one! Heavens! I'm an eye specialist. Notwithstanding, Dr. Pischel, who hadn't delivered a baby since he left medical

school in 1923, rolled up his sleeves and he and the captain helped Mrs.
Fay Babcock, 34, to bring into the world an eight-pound sea-going girl,
her fourth, and the ferry service's first in memory. The boat docked in
record time; an ambulance was waiting, and Mrs. Babcock and the baby
were taken to the University of California Hospital. John P. Tibbett,
U.S. Hull inspector, receiving the report, grinned: Government regula-
tions. In all out-of-the-ordinary events on the boats we have to determine
if the captain is to blame. We were on our way from our home in Sausalito to the hospital and we had ordered an ambulance to meet us at the
dock, explained the father. But we didn't expect the baby that soon. I
was sitting in the car with the Missus when she said she was beginning
to feel kind of funny. So we climbed upstairs to the ladies' lounge. I was
waiting outside when a woman came out and said, Are you Mr. Babcock? Yes, I said. Well, she says, your wife is having a baby. We're going
to call the baby Goldie (after the ferry) Ruth. I must notify the United
States inspector of hulls and boilers, said the captain. What's he got to
do with babies? he was asked. Oh, it's rules. I have to. The law prescribes
you've got to report any unusual occurrence on your ship.

2. Rewrite this sentence: "Adamic's body was found lying on
a couch with his head on a pillow in an upstairs bedroom."

3. Improve the following sentences:

    a. Alderman Jones pointed out that he thought all milk
    plants should be forced to submit to inspection.

    b. The council voted approval of Alderman Jones' move
    that passage of the resolution be approved.

    c. Partitions between departments will be semimovable in
    order that, if needed, floor space for a new department
    may be expanded.

4. Rewrite this story to eliminate 10 to 15 words.

        The Athletic Club has offered to pay
    the expenses of one of the foremost golf
    course architects in the country to ap-
    praise the possibilities for the proposed
    municipal golf course.

        It was revealed in the city council last
    night that William Bell, president of the
    Golf Course Architects of America, will
    undertake the job.

        The council unanimously voted to ac-
    cept Club President Marvin Thompson's
    offer, which was made known in a letter
    to the council, read by the mayor.

5. What point does this sentence emphasize by its construction? Rewrite it to emphasize a different point. "As proposed on a county-wide basis, the United Charity Fund drive would seek in one campaign donations for all agencies concerned."

6. Improve slightly the emphasis in this sentence: "Some 60 per cent of county tax bills never reach the home owner, but are sent to banks and other lending institutions instead."

7. What is the term that describes the fault in these sentences?

  a. A Rhodes scholar and graduate of Montana State University, Streit will probably arrive on campus this afternoon.

  b. ... Chief of Detectives Ray Humphreys said the bad check charge was admitted by Bell, 28, merchant seaman, who asserted that a leg infection incapacitated him from work.

8. Compute the average length of sentences in the story about Gandhi's assassination on pages 50-52. How does it compare with (a) the average in the chart on page 94, and (b) the average in the last news story that you wrote?

9. Improve these sentences:

  a. When five years old, Helen's father died.
  b. He sustained severe injuries.
  c. He was well acquainted with the best literature, thus helping him to become an able critic.
  d. The accident occurred last Monday.

10. What is wrong with this expression: "He was shot with a 38 calibre pistol"?

11. Rewrite these passages to make them more acceptable for broadcasting:

> Starting in the basement, the fire spread through the shafts. . . .
> Two firemen suffered fractured skulls and one a painful skin abrasion. . . .
> Fire Chief Sheehan estimated that five-sixths of the structure was destroyed.

12. Circle the usage that is in accord with the style guide.

  a. He entered the U. S. in 1939.
     He entered the United States in 1939.

    b.   R. R. Doe, president of Cox College

         R. R. Doe, President of Cox College

    c.   The major praised the Negro soldier.

         The major praised the negro soldier.

CHAPTER VIII

1. A cub reporter (female), reporting an arrest, wrote this lead: "An alert policeman *put the finger on* a suspected murderer last night." What term, used in this chapter, characterizes this erroneous choice of expression?

2. For each of these instances, write a sentence or paragraph in which you define the meaning of the expression by building in context. Use your imagination to supply details when necessary. First, look up the expressions in a dictionary. Test your ability to make the expressions comprehensible by trying the sentences out on some of your friends who do not already know the meaning of the expressions.

Example: The vice president today denounced filibustering. The way you write it:

> The vice president today denounced filibustering.
>
> The Senate must change its rules, he said, to prevent a few senators from talking to death a bill they don't like. A few senators can thwart the will of an overwhelming majority, he added.

    a.   She was a *termagant* witness.

    b.   A *bizarre* robbery trial. Suggested beginning: "The Judge said: . . ."

    c.   Senator Wilson, the majority leader, said tonight a *cloture* petition has been drafted but he thought the Administration lacked the 64 votes necessary to shut off debate on the immigration bill.

    d.   He explained that tennis and golf are *epicene* games.

    e.   The speaker described the admiral as a man *obsidian*.

3. The first lead read:

> WASHINGTON—The Communist-controlled government in Czechoslovakia re-

vealed its *chagrin* at the resignation yesterday of the Czech ambassador to Washington, Dr. Juraj Slavik, by an angry telephone call to him.

The rewrite read:

WASHINGTON—Dr. Juraj Slavik reports he got an angry bawling out by telephone from Prague yesterday because of
his resignation as Czech ambassador to
Washington.

Test the first lead on two or three unsophisticated persons you
know to determine whether or not it was necessary to rewrite the
lead without the word *chagrin*.

4. Substitute a stronger verb in each of these sentences and,
when desirable, change the other words in the sentence to accord
with the improved substitution of verb:

    a. The defendant looked at her with wide open eyes.
    b. The witness' response was low and indistinct, and Judge
        Murphy asked her to speak louder.

5. Improve these sentences:

    a. The auto workers' union today struck the Ford Motor
        Co. plant.
    b. The city council voted to give the gasoline contract to
        the Shell Oil Co.
    c. Councilman Willis Jerome commented that he did not
        feel the houses should all be of one design.

6. Are the following pairs of words synonymous?

sewage/sewerage	revolver/pistol
anxious/eager	half-staff/half-mast
another/additional	engine/motor (aeronautic)
less/fewer	substitute/substitution
amateur/novice	realtor/real estate broker

7. Most news writers use the expressions *gubernatorial election* and *mayoralty election,* but never *gubernatorality election*
and seldom *mayoral election*. Analyze this inconsistency and state
a rule to govern the situation.

8. In an election in which 5000 votes were cast, Jones received 2000 votes, Smith 1800, and Brown 1200. Which, if any, of the candidates received a *majority* of the votes? What is the technically correct term that describes Jones' votes?

9. What is a *shambles?* a *clash?*

10. Which of these clichés would you use and which would you shun?

sit on the fence	ultimate goal
steer clear of	cursory examination
turned the tide	accepted a position
weather the storm	rang the gong
won hands down	in the bag
blaze was brought under control	gay Lothario
with telling effect	nip in the bud
by leaps and bounds	under a cloud

11. To which of the following ages would you apply the adjective (a) *old,* (b) *middle-aged,* and (c) *elderly:*

$$46 \quad 56 \quad 66 \quad 76$$

12. In what age bracket would you include the terms *girl* and *youth?*

13. Is *streamline* an acceptable word in this context?

> A new plan to streamline Jonesboro's history-rooted business district was proposed last night to the city council.

14. Substitute the proper word in this sentence: "An unnamed man was killed last night by a hit-and-run driver."

15. Write an additional paragraph for the following lead that you believe is sure to supply adequate context:

> WASHINGTON—The attorney general said before he left for the California-Mexico border that he will study the "wetback" problem on the spot.

16. Distinguish *inurnment, interment,* and *internment.*

17. What word can you substitute in the following sentence for the cliché, "up in arms"?

> Growers in the Santa Clara Valley were up in arms today as they desperately watched ripening fruit rot on the ground

while striking cannery workers and their
employers continued wage negotiations.

18. How do you reconcile these conflicting statements?

The newspaper is not a textbook: it does not have an obligation to
increase the reader's vocabulary.

For most people—since more than one-half of the population of 25
years and older did not finish high school—the newspaper is a textbook
in adult education.

Although few adults ever look up a word in a dictionary, they learn
new words from their newspaper because of the context in which the
words appear.

19. The word *run* appears in two different contexts in Chapter
III (pp. 29 and 30). One dictionary reports 104 meanings for it.
How many meanings can you think of?

20. Correct this sentence: "The plane staggered along the run-
way for 100 feet and then zoomed up above the fog."

21. Which two words are misspelled in this sentence: "The
appelate court ordered a new trial on the ground that no opportunity was permitted for peremptory challenges of jurors before
Murphy plead guilty"?

22. Distinguish *sanitarium* and *sanatorium*.

23. Which of these words are misspelled:

accomodate	embarrased	liaison
commitment	guage	playright
consensus	harassed	neice
dietitian	homicide	seized
dissension	innocuous	siege
ecstasy	inoculate	supersede
exercize	kidnaped	withold

24. Improve this sentence: At 11 A.M. the patrolman ordered
such signs, posted by the Highway Improvement Association, as
"If you think this curve is bad, wait till you see the next one,"
taken down.

25. Compute the Flesch reading ease formula and human
interest formula for the story about Gandhi's assassination on
pages 50-52.

26. Compute the same formulas for the last news story you
wrote.

27. Suppose you wrote a chronicle type news story with inverted pyramid organization that yielded a "fairly easy" score by

the Flesch reading ease formula and a score of "interesting" by the Flesch human interest formula. If the subject-matter permitted of a climactic organization, do you suppose that this change in organization would make the story more readable even though it did not change the Flesch scores?

28. Substitute a stronger verb in these sentences:

a. He looked at her with wide-open eyes.

b. The officer said that after the woman got out of the car her movements indicated she was drunk.

29. Is this expression redundant: *new recruit?*

30. Improve the following sentences:

a. The option is for a short space of time.

b. They left him in a dying condition wrapped in a brown colored cloth in close proximity to the cage of the canary bird.

c. During the winter months the widow woman lived in Florida, always returning on Easter Sunday.

d. He told the large size man he was asking only for the purpose of checking all alibis.

31. Write a news story of 300 words based on the following press release:

DEPARTMENT OF DEFENSE
OFFICE OF PUBLIC INFORMATION
Washington 25, D. C.

HOLD FOR RELEASE
UNTIL 7:00 A.M. (EST)
WEDNESDAY, NOVEMBER 1

FOR THE PRESS:

The attached is a statement of the Navy plans regarding recall and release of Naval Reservists.

STATEMENT ON RESERVE RECALLS

In order to implement the rapid expansion of the Navy to meet the current international situation it has been necessary to call to active duty relatively large numbers of trained Reserves, officer and enlisted, to supplement the regular personnel strength. At the same time, the recruitment of Regular Navy enlisted personnel has been accelerated to the greatest possible extent. (It is regretted that the requirement for a rapid expansion has in the past necessitated the issuance of recall orders with a relatively short period of delay in reporting for active duty.) It is planned to implement immediately a policy requiring that a Reservist called to active duty will be allowed at least 30 days between the time he is called and the date on which he must report for active duty. It is further planned to institute at the earliest practicable date a program which will provide that Reservists selected for recall will received a four months' notice of such recall. By such a method, all Reservists, not so selected, will be notified through press and radio releases that recall to active duty is at least four months remote unless a material change in military requirements otherwise dictates. It must be realized that probable deferments of some individuals with the necessity for replacements by other individuals will cause a certain number of exceptions to the complete success of such a program. It is felt that this program can be made effective for all Reserve personnel to be recalled after July 1st. That date will be anticipated to the maximum possible extent, and while it may well apply to numerous individuals recalled during April, May, and June 1951, it cannot be guaranteed to apply to all individuals during this period.

In addition to the Reserve officer and enlisted personnel requirements for the expansion of the Navy during this fiscal year, it will be necessary for the Navy to continue the recall of Reserve personnel, officer and enlisted, for the forseeable future in order to maintain its personnel strength. The number of Reserve officers so recalled involuntarily in future years will depend on many factors, the major one being the number of Reserve officers who choose to volunteer for active duty or to remain on active duty after recall. It is expected that only a relatively small number of Reserve enlisted personnel will be involuntarily recalled to active duty after the completion of the initial expansion during the current fiscal year. It is also anticipated that in the main those Reserve enlisted personnel recalled in the next fiscal year and in future years will be relatively untrained personnel without prior active service who will be sent through recruit training prior to assignment to regular billets. By such means the mobilization potential of our Naval Reserve will be increased and the year by year manpower requirements of the Regular Navy will be met.

Both Organized and Volunteer Reserve personnel, officer and enlisted, are subject to involuntary recall, but the Navy effects recall on a priority basis, Organized Reserve personnel first and Volunteer Reserve personnel second, to the extent necessary to meet the needs of the service. In this connection, it is considered pertinent to call attention to the fact that enlisted quotas issued to date have, in the main, depleted the recall potential of the Organized Reserve in the ratings needed. It is also anticipated that by next January it will be necessary to call some officers in the categories required from the Volunteer Reserve since the

Organized Reserve potential for these categories will be largely depleted by that date.

In calling Reserves to active duty their qualifications to fill Navy billets on the basis of their records are the controlling factor. It may well be that an individual has other special qualifications as a civilian which might be considered more important to him in civilian employment, but for which the Navy has no need under the conditions prevailing on his recall. The Navy Department encourages all members of the Reserve to report new skills or specialties acquired while in inactive status and which can be converted to classifications or job codes for Navy record purposes. Such reports are important to insure to the maximum practicable extent that members of the Reserve called to active duty are given assignments which utilize their primary skills for which the Navy has need.

Present law which authorizes the involuntary recall of Reserve personnel specifies that the maximum period of involuntary duty is limited to 21 months. This does not preclude such personnel from volunteering for additional active duty. Reserve personnel released to inactive duty after completion of 21 months active duty will be replaced by newly procured Regular personnel and the remainder, as necessary, by other Reserve personnel who have had no postwar active duty.

The Secretary of Defense has established a policy with regard to delay in calling of Reserves who are filling key billets in essential industries or positions essential to community welfare. In addition, the Navy Department considers elements of extreme personal hardship as justifying delay or deferment. In this connection the Navy Department is not knowingly ordering Naval Reserve personnel to active duty on an involuntary basis if they have four or more dependents. Such personnel who had previously been recalled are permitted to request release or discharge at the option of the individual. The procedures for requesting delay or deferment by an individual member of the Reserve or his employer have been well publicized. Prompt request, addressed to the Commandant of the Naval District or River Command through whom orders to active duty are issued, is necessary.

Since the need exists for personnel fully qualified for sea duty the age of the individual will be a dominant factor in determining whether or not recall orders are issued.

The needs of the fleet for junior line officers will be met by supplementing the regular personnel by Reserve officers who have completed their college education since V-J Day and have had no active duty.

The recall of medical and dental officers will be in accordance with priorities recently enunciated by the Secretary of Defense.

The Navy Department does not contemplate the necessity of resorting to Selective Service to meet personnel requirements for enlisted personnel since USN recruitment augmented by untrained Naval Reserve personnel will be sufficient to meet anticipated needs for the for-seeable future.

The future recalls of Naval Reserve personnel discussed above is pred-icated on the extension of the Selective Service Act of 1948 as amended by recent congressional action.

Since members of the Naval Reserve who have been commissioned or enlisted since June 24, 1948, the date of enactment of the present Selec-tive Service Act, are not thereby exempt from the draft, the Navy De-partment does not intend to commission or enlist in the Naval Reserve draft eligible personnel unless their services can be immediately utilized on active duty.

CHAPTER IX

1. Write a "sidebar" descriptive story of an important football game, concentrating on the behavior of the spectators.

2. Which of these nouns are intensional?

carrot	razor
tavern	democracy
chagrin	saloon
common	gentleman

3. In the news story from *Time* on page 128, underline those details that the reporter observed that he thought would give reality to his description. In your opinion, which, if any, of them are not necessary for his purpose?

4. Locate in a newspaper a well-written descriptive article about some special occasion and list those devices that make for vividness.

5. From the Gloom Funeral Home, the General Hospital, the office of the State Highway Patrol, and your own newspaper library, you collect the following information:

The Gloom Funeral Home telephones to say that its ambulance was called a short time ago to the Springer Road junction on the Bayshore Highway, three miles south of town. There they found an automobile overturned and two women lying unconscious beside the road. The call was sent in by Dino Tisierra, who operates a filling station about 100 yards up the road. Sorry, the ambulance driver didn't find out for sure what caused the accident, but he thinks it was from a blown-out tire. No, we don't have the names of the women yet. They were taken to General Hospital.

From the General Hospital: Miss Patty Carter and Miss Mildred Carter admitted as emergency patients at 1:20 P.M. Both women are still unconscious and the extent of their injuries has not yet been determined. No other information.

From the office of the State Highway Patrol: Patrolman Edward Murphy investigated the accident. A Buick sedan, driven by Miss Patty Carter, overturned about 12:45 P.M. when the driver lost control after a front tire had blown out and the car skidded on the shoulder of the highway, which was slick from a brief shower that had fallen about noon. Miss Patty Carter was accompanied by her sister, Mildred. Both are teachers in McKinley High School and were on the way to a meeting of the State Teachers' Association at Belleville. Dino Tisierra, the filling station operator, said the car was not going more than 35 miles an hour when he saw it pass his place of business.

From the newspaper library: Miss Patty Carter is 44 and her sister 46 years old. Both have been teaching at McKinley High School for more than 20 years. They have no living relatives. They live together at 126 Bowdoin Street.

Write a news story for the *Times*. It is 1:45 o'clock and you have a 2:00 P.M. deadline for this afternoon's paper.

6. While he was speaking at a public meeting, the speaker interrupted his talk to say that he does not wish to be quoted on the matter he is about to discuss. Will you quote him or not?

7. A university dean whose office is on your college newspaper beat tells you in confidence that he will recommend a drastic change in the final examination schedule for next semester. But he asks you not to publish it until after he has talked to the president who will return in two weeks. The local newspaper has a reporter who also has the dean's office on his beat. What will you do?

8. After an interview has begun, the subject of the interview announces that everything he has told you has been said "in confidence." What are your ethical obligations?

9. Define the following ecclesiastic terms: *altar, chancel, pulpit, rector, canon, dean, deacon, chapel.*

CHAPTERS X-XI

1. A prominent newspaper that nearly always had supported the Democratic candidate for president announces in an editorial in the course of the campaign that it will support the Republican candidate. The news agencies report this fact throughout the country. Is that objective reporting? Why?

2. In reporting a burglary, a newspaper identifies the accused person as a Negro. Is that objective reporting? Why?

3. The quotation marks have been omitted from the following speech report. Put them in where you think they belong.

NEW YORK—President Truman said today that America is building up its strength to discourage Soviet Russia from marching against us and the free world.

Addressing 3300 student editors at Columbia University, the President said the Soviet government is a menace both to the United States and to all the free world.

Mr. Truman told the young editors that he once was a school editor in his home town of Independence, Mo.

From then on I kept going, and you know the trouble that I'm in today, he said. So you see if you are not very careful you may end up by living in the White House. And I'll say to you that it's a wonderful experience indeed in spite of all its troubles.

Mr. Truman lauded Woodrow Wilson as one of our very greatest Presidents.

I sincerely believe that if we had followed him in what he wanted to do we would certainly have avoided the second World War, he said. I hope that we will not make that same mistake after this last world war.

The President said he had come up here from Florida to talk to the convention because the future of this great republic of ours depends upon young people like you.

The policy of the Fair Deal, Mr. Truman said, is to reduce inequality in the U.S. Not by pulling down those at the top but by lifting up those at the bottom and that same program applies to foreign policy.

The President said he and Charles G. Ross, his late press secretary, helped get out the first number of the Independence, Mo. high school paper, the Gleam.

Mr. Truman recalled that the name of
the publication was taken from the Ten-
nyson poem which ends Follow the gleam.

I've been trying to follow it ever since,
he added.

Mr. Truman said it was a very great
responsibility to be the editor of a newspaper or periodical.

4. United Press asked one of the student editors at the convention mentioned in Exercise 3 to report President Truman's speech.
The 10-year-old reporter wrote in part as follows:

... Then the President made a speech
about the press and being a newspaper
man. Then he talked about a convention
they had when he was a little boy at the
age of 16. Then he told about what he
had done when he was young. He told
about how he had voted for Wilson and
thought that Wilson was one of the greatest presidents of all time.

Then he told about why he had come
from Florida. The reason was very simple.
He had come to talk to us so we would
grow up to be good men like him.

Then he talked about being on a newspaper when he was a little boy. Then he
told us that we might end up in the White
House just like him.

Then he said that being in the Government was tiresome but very nice and also
that every nation needs a government.

He also talked about the increase in
rich people.

He also said that if Wilson had been
able to have his own wishes there wouldn't
have been a World War II.

I thought the whole thing was pretty
good.

Compare the two versions of the speech where they refer to the
same subject-matter. What differences in context are involved?

5. Report in 300 words the speech of a prominent person
delivered on your campus and then compare it with the version

of a fellow student who also reported the speech in the same number of words. Do you find any differences between the two reports as to (*a*) the words used in the same quotations, and (*b*) as to the quotation used in the lead?

6. In connection with an assignment to report a speech (at a meeting at which there is only one featured speaker), compare your selection of quotations with the selection made by a classmate. Did either of you have in mind, when you chose specific quotations, any particular context?

7. Compare the obituary of Hilaire Belloc, on pages 159-160, with the obituary of Belloc in the "Books" section of *Time,* July 27, 1953.

8. How does the repetition of "yeah" in the human interest story quoted on page 162 contribute to the effectiveness of the story?

9. Write an interview based on the following transcribed verbatim report of an interview with Dr. R. C. Arnold, acting director of the National Heart Institute, a federal government research institution.* The recent deaths of several congressmen from heart disease is your "newspeg."

Q We've been hearing of a number of Senators and Representatives who have died of heart disease the last couple of years, Dr. Arnold. Do you think there has been an unusual number?

A No, I don't think that it was an unusual number, although it may seem to be at the time when you consider that possibly 13 men in Congress died from a cardiovascular disease [disease of the heart or circulation]. We see heart disease in other walks of life, other professions, and the rate may vary some with different professions. Yet I believe that this is not an unusual number among that many men.

Q You mean that you would expect about the same number of deaths at that age level among men in the general population as has occurred in the Senate and the House in the last couple of years?

A Yes.

Q Would you say that political careers have anything in particular to do with heart trouble—in the sense that pressures and tensions put a strain on an individual that would make him more susceptible to a heart condition?

A Well, I suppose you could find some individuals who are expert in the field of cardiology who might say that being under the stress and

* Reprinted from "U.S. News & World Report," an independent weekly magazine published at Washington (August 14, 1953). Copyright 1953, United States News Publishing Corporation.

strains of an active public life might cause them to have cardiovascular diseases more frequently. But you will find other physicians who would not agree with that.

Q   Don't some people think that because you are under pressure and tension in political and business life you are more likely to have heart trouble?

A   You can have a certain type of heart disease—say, hypertensive— and if you are under considerable stress and strain, then your longevity is probably not as great as it would be if you lived a more quiet life.

Q   Does that mean these emotional strains cause hypertension? And that from hypertension you develop heart trouble?

A   I don't believe that you can say that emotional strains cause hypertensive heart disease, but they do aggravate it.

Q   Is the individual who is high-strung, nervous, and always working under pressure more likely to be subject to heart diseases?

A   I hardly think so, although sometimes you will find people in public life who have this drive which is frequently noted in individuals who have, say, hypertension. But hypertension is not caused by that; neither is this personality type caused by hypertension.

Q   So that, let's say, debating in the Senate wouldn't necessarily cause a Senator to become a victim of high blood pressure?

A   I don't think so.

Q   But if he already has a heart condition of some kind, would the tension that arises between two men who oppose each other in debate bring about a sudden attack that would cause death?

A   Yes, that might be a contributory factor.

Q   But that doesn't happen very often, does it?

A   No, and it may not happen at the moment.

Q   When a man gets angry and someone advises him "Don't raise your blood pressure too much," is it probably good advice?

A   Yes.

Q   Don't the records show that about as many coronary attacks occur while a person is asleep or at rest as when he is under violent excitement?

A   When a person has an attack in public view, it does receive a good deal of publicity. Many attacks do occur when people are in bed, even asleep.

Q   Do you think it is wise for a person when he gets into his 60s and 70s to lead a strenuous life and carry on activities under a lot of pressure and drive?

A   I think there would be a lot of unhappy—and perhaps even unhealthier—people if they were not allowed to do the things that they felt were necessary.

Q   So that your age and the way you live doesn't necessarily mean that you are going to have a heart condition?

A No, because many individuals lead a very active life in their 60s and 70s and just go merrily on their way without developing an acute cardiovascular condition.

Q Then is that why there can be so many men in the Senate and the House who are getting along in their 60s and 70s and still are active?

A Yes. Of course, our research has not yet given us the answers as to why certain individuals develop cardiovascular diseases earlier or later in life. Certain individuals may develop a coronary disease that will be fatal in their 40s. Others may live to be in their 60s or 70s or even 80s and never have a coronary attack.

Q We don't know the reasons for that?

A We do not know all the reasons. But research is bringing us to a better and better understanding of the causative factors.

Q Sometimes you hear of the "hypertensive personality," the individual who is constantly bucking his emotions, who becomes a victim of hypertension. Is there any such thing?

A Research to date has not given us a definite answer along those lines.

Q Studies are being carried out, however?

A Yes, and it is always the question as to whether the individual is hypertensive because he has this great emotional drive or whether he has this emotional drive because he is hypertensive.

Q And that is true whether you are a Senator, a businessman or a housewife?

A Yes.

Q Would you say that it is better from a general standpoint to lead a calm sort of life unbroken by flare-ups, temper and so on? Would it add years to your life?

A If it adds years to your life, they might be unhappy ones. However, I don't think one can make a blanket diagnosis about all people of a given age because obviously it's necessary for a man's own doctor to study the specific factors in his situation.

Q Would a thorough physical examination before a man runs for public office show whether he might be susceptible to a heart attack after he gets elected?

A Some kinds of heart disease can be detected early by such an examination.

On the other hand, an individual's general health may be good and he may not have clinical evidence of heart disease which could be detected at the time of the examination. Yet in a month, or years later, he may develop cardiovascular disease. We need additional research so that we will know more about the causative factors and will have ways and means of determining whether individuals are going to be susceptible to cardiovascular disease at a later time.

For instance, all of us at a certain age have physical examinations and may apparently be in good health, yet within a year some individuals will develop a coronary attack and others will not. We have no methods of detecting those individuals who are going to develop a coronary attack.

Q   You can't predict it, then? All you can do is detect it after it arrives?

A   Yes. But there is real hope for the future that we shall be able to.

Q   Is there some work going on to develop diagnostic tests to predict a thing like that?

A   A great deal of research is being conducted for earlier diagnosis and for causative factors. The type of hardening of the arteries that leads to coronary attacks is an insidious disease that develops over a period of many years. It's most difficult because we haven't studied the causative factors of the chronic heart diseases very long.

Q   If a person has a physical exam that shows he has a heart condition, would that mean he should quit all the activities that have put him under pressures?

A   The answer to that question would depend upon the disease that the individual had and the recommendations by his doctor. Some individuals may have a cardiovascular disease which does not prevent them from going about their work.

Q   In other words, you can learn to live with your heart disease?

A   Yes.

Q   What about fellows getting along in their 60s and 70s? Is exercise like golf too strenuous for them?

A   It depends upon the individual and upon his physical condition as determined by his doctor.

As a matter of fact, many individuals play golf because it gives them a great deal of pleasure, physical exercise and mental relaxation. There are those, of course, who play golf very seriously—and that might not be very relaxing.

Q   A lot of people worry about high blood pressure. But just what is it—and what is high for an individual?

A   Blood pressure varies with age, and between people of similar ages. In the same person, it may vary from day to day, and may even vary at different times in the same day.

Q   And that would be perfectly normal?

A   Yes. You might even go to the doctor and just the fact that he is taking your blood pressure might send it up.

Q   Then do people worry too much about having high blood pressure?

A   Yes, they do. I don't know, though, that there is a way to keep people from worrying about something if they want to.

Q   Should they worry about it?

A   I think that if anyone has had a diagnosis made by a physician which shows he has hypertension he should take the advice of his physician as to what he should do and the treatment he should take, because it will vary with each individual.

As a matter of fact, in some cases the blood pressure may be elevated only slightly and there is no need to do anything. Other individuals do need to be careful and to take treatment and to lead a more restricted life.

Q If a person has a regular physical examination, say once a year, so that his blood pressure is checked and recorded, could a rise in blood pressure then serve more clearly as a danger signal?

A Yes, blood pressure readings from regular, repeated examinations would be significant. More than a single blood-pressure reading is necessary to determine whether or not a person has hypertension.

You may go to a physician and have your blood pressure taken, but the strain of going there, or the emotional upset, may cause your reading at that one time to be high—but that is not hypertension. If a person has a blood pressure that is above normal continuously—over a sustained period—then it is significant.

10. With reference to the speech report incident referred to at page 148, one editor commented as follows: "Father Hartnett makes a couple of speeches.... After the first speech a reporter asks him what he thinks about Senator McCarthy. He criticizes the Senator's methods. And, in the name of the man who bit the dog, what would a newspaper be expected to play up? To the considerable extent that the Catholic church is identified with the battle against Communism and its spokesmen generally sympathetic with Senator McCarthy, Father Hartnett was saying the unexpected, the unpredictable thing. *And that's news!*" Do you agree or disagree with this editor's definition of news as applied in this instance?

11. "Discrepancies and contradictions [in the talk and acts of politicians] are news, news to which the public is entitled; and in so far as reporters don't call attention to them, we are falling down on our job." Do you agree or disagree with this statement by Elmer Davis?

12. What did Elmer Davis mean by this statement: "One *Chicago Tribune* is enough"?

13. This exercise tests, among other things, your ability to (*a*) select the appropriate lead, (*b*) take advantage of the drama in the situation, and (*c*) to be fair to both sides.

The material is a part of one day's testimony before the Commission on Industrial Relations in 1914. On this day (May 27) the Commission was investigating the Colorado coal miners' strike, and some of the testimony related specifically to an incident (on April 20) which had been referred to in a part of the press as "the Ludlow massacre" because 40 miners were killed, including some women and children.

Witnesses on this day were Mrs. Pearl Jolly, wife of one of the striking miners; Ben B. Lindsey, a judge of the Denver juvenile court, who had acquired a national reputation as a pioneer in the administration of justice for juvenile delinquents; and Lt. Col. Edward J. Boughton, judge advocate of the Colorado National Guard.

Chairman of the Commission was Frank P. Walsh. William O. Thompson was counsel for the Commission. Other commissioners who participated on this day were: John B. Lennon, Florence J. Harriman, and S. Thruston Ballard.

You are to write a news story of 700 words as if the hearing were held today and your story is for a morning newspaper. The dateline is NEW YORK, May 27—.

TESTIMONY OF MRS. PEARL JOLLY

MR. THOMPSON. Will you please give us your name?

MRS. JOLLY. Mrs. Pearl Jolly.

MR. THOMPSON. Where do you reside?

MRS. JOLLY. At Ludlow, Colo.

MR. THOMPSON. And you are married, of course?

MRS. JOLLY. Yes, sir.

MR. THOMPSON. Your husband living?

MRS. JOLLY. Yes, sir.

MR. THOMPSON. A miner?

MRS. JOLLY. Yes, sir.

MR. THOMPSON. What is your age?

MRS. JOLLY. Twenty-one. . . .

MR. THOMPSON. You may proceed with your story.

MRS. JOLLY. I want to take up just as little time as I can, so I will tell this story of the strike.

CHAIRMAN WALSH. Tell it in your own way, taking up as little time, but giving all the details that you think are pertinent.

MRS. JOLLY. Yes, sir. Well, a week previous to the strike my husband went to Trinidad to do a little shopping down there. When he came back from Trinidad he put on his clothes and went to the mine on the following morning. They asked him where he had been. He told them to Trinidad.

CHAIRMAN WALSH. Who asked him?

MRS. JOLLY. The superintendent. They wanted to know his business in Trinidad. He told them he was down there on private business. They asked him if he was a delegate to the convention at Trinidad that the United Mine Workers had held before there. He said no. They told him that they did not need him there any more; that he was to get out of camp. I think it was 15 minutes that they gave him to move his furniture and everything and get out of camp. He moved. I went down to a farmhouse below and spent the week there, until the Ludlow tent colony. On the 23d day of September the strike was called and we all moved into the tent colony. From my first experience in the Ludlow tent colony the gunmen would come there and would try in every way to provoke trouble. They were trying to cause a battle between the miners and the gunmen, but we knew that and we did not want to have any trouble. At one time the gunmen came to the Ludlow tent colony, just as near as they could get, fired two shots into the tent colony. Our men took their rifles and went to the hills, thinking that by so doing they would lead the fire that way and keep them from firing on the colony, where the women and children were. There was no way to protect the women and children. After that our men took and dug pits under the tents, so that if the same thing should happen again there would be some means of escape for those women and children. Following that, the militia came into the field. When the militia came in there we made them welcome; we thought they were going to treat us right. They were escorted into the camp with a brass band. They attended all of our dances. They came down and took dinner with us two or three different evenings, but when they were in there two or three days they turned, and we could see that, but we did not want to have any trouble with them. One of the women, I believe, told them that they could not be on two sides at once. So following that they would come into our tent colony and searched about one a week or more. When they came there our arms were all turned over to the militia.

CHAIRMAN WALSH. What is that?

MRS. JOLLY. Our arms and ammunition. They told us they would disarm the others, but instead they took the arms and ammunition that the strikers had and turned them over to the mine guards. Then we were searched; our tent colony was searched about once a week or more. When they came they would bring axes, picks, shovels, and such things with them. They would search in all the little drawers about this big [indicating] looking for things. Anything they could get hold of to carry away without being seen they would take it. They would take the axes and cut up the floors so that the union would have to buy new lumber in order to rebuild the floors. Our men had to stand for that....

On April 19 we had a baseball game. The militia had always been in the habit of attending the baseball games, but never before had they attended with their rifles. On April 9 was a Greek holiday, Easter Sunday, and they thought perhaps that they would be drinking, and those men, if they were to go down there with their rifles, would be able to stir up some trouble. They stood right in the diamond with their rifles. One of the men asked them if they would please get out of the diamond. He told them if he wanted to watch the baseball game it was not necessary to guard them, to put their guns to their side. They became indignant and made their threats what they could do and what they would not do. One of the women said to them, in a joke, "Don't you know if a woman would start toward you with a BB gun you would all throw away your guns and run?" He says, "That is all right, girlie, you have your big Sunday today, but we will have the roast tomorrow. It would only take me and three or four men out there to clean out all the bunch." And they cleaned out the bunch on the following day. They tried every way they could before they left the baseball ground to create trouble. They would call the different players and want them to come over and talk and when they refused they said, "Come on, we will take you to the guardhouse and talk to you." They left the baseball game. Sunday night they came into the tent colony, but they would not go up to speak to any of our leaders in the camp at all. When the leaders would start toward them they would go right away, so they concluded they were trying to blow up the camp. They had made their threat and told about how they had previously torn down the Forbes tent colony.

They put guards in our camps Sunday night to take care of the camp, but nothing happened. On the following Monday morning, about 9 o'clock, the same five militiamen who had been at the baseball game on Sunday came to the Ludlow grounds. They had a paper and they sent in for Louis Tikas, a Greek and the leader; they handed him this slip of paper, and it had some foreign name on it of some man that was not in the tent colony. They told him they wanted to take the man out of the colony; they asked him if they had a warrant or had been sent there by the civil authorities. They said no, they had been sent there by the military authorities. They said, "I understand the military commission is out now." He says, "I would like to talk to Manager Hemrock," who was in command. So they left the Ludlow tent colony with a threat that they would be back again. When they met Louis Tikas they went and called up Manager Hemrock and asked him if he would see him and talk to him. He said he would. They met at the C. & S. depot. I don't know what the conversation was at the depot, but I know when Louis Tikas came back he told us the machine guns and everything were set ready to wipe the tent colony. The next thing we observed was Louis Tikas coming from the depot waving a white handkerchief. There was about 200 tents in the tent colony and about 1,000 inhabitants, about 500 women and 500 children. We were all in front in large groups. He was waving this white handkerchief, I suppose, for us to get back. While he was running toward us and waving the white handkerchief, they fired two bombs. Following that they turned the machine gun into the tent colony and started to firing with rifles. Our men decided if they could take the hills, take their rifles and go into the hills, that they would lead fire from the tent colony into the hills and thus protect the women and children in the tent colony. There was just 40 rifles in the Ludlow camp. They will tell you there was 500 or so. There was 40 in there, and I would swear to that before any jury in the United States. The men who had rifles went to the hills, and the others, too, so that there would not be any men in the camp, thinking in that way they would attract the fire away from the women and children. Then if no men were there they would not fire. They did not follow the men into the hills; they were too cowardly; they wanted to fight with the women. They kept the machine guns turned on the camp all day, more or less. The women and children, too, could run out of the camp, but there were so many women there expecting to become mothers, and also many that had such a large family of small children that they could not possibly get out. I had been the nurse in the tent colony. Louis Tikas came to me and told me if I was not afraid he wanted me to stay in the camp and take care of the wounded and the women and children. . . .

They got the machine gun set better and at better range, for it was terrible how those bullets came in there; it does not seem possible to tell how they were coming in. They would say if the bullets were coming in like that, why were there not more shot? Simply because the caves were there and the dogs and chickens and everything else that moved were shot. Between 5 and 6 o'clock they set fire to our tents. When they set fire to our tents we decided that we would go from cave to cave as fast as we could. They could see us going through, and we had to dodge their bullets. We were going from cave to cave, getting the women and children together, and let them out, and took chances on being shot. We had about 50 together when we saw one little Italian woman, and who came with us to Washington, but she was simply grieving herself to death. She is not sane, I don't think. She is killed, they say. Her three children were killed out there. We knew and her three children were in the cave. We could not understand how they got the three and herself there, but we afterwards moved into the hills. So Louis Tikas told me that if we would get them together and lead them down the aroyo—we didn't know that there was any men there—we thought it was she and her children. While he was on his way—the screams; I believe you could hear them for a mile. The screams of the women and children—they were simply awful. When he was on his way to the cave they captured him and took him prisoner. After they took him prisoner, they couldn't decide for a little while how they wanted to kill him. Some contended to shoot him; some contended that he should be hanged. Finally, Lieut. Linderfeldt went up and hit him over the head with a rifle, broke the butt of the gun over his head, and then made the remark he had spoiled a good gun on him.

They stepped on his face. We have a photograph. I don't believe we have it here, but it shows plain the prints of the heel in his face. After he fell, he was shot four times in the back. . . .

On Wednesday they told me that they found 700 guns—and it is just such outrageous stories as that they tell on the miners in this case, and you have simply got to judge them yourselves. They told me they had 700 guns and 10,000 rounds of ammunition in John R. Lawson's tent. And one of the first tents to burn down on Monday was the Lawson's. Now, that is the story told. Now, if there had been 700 guns in that tent, gentlemen, I tell you here, there would not have been quite so many have come through that day—that is, the militia. If our men had had 100 guns they could have protected us and there would not have been so many women and children slaughtered. But they did not have nothing, and they couldn't get anything. The militia had taken up all our guns and given them to the mine guards. They had, every one of their men—we speak of the guards as scabs—with their guns and revolvers two weeks before, and had them at the mines there. And this corporation there, they were taking these men out, these strike breakers, and taking them to Trinidad and giving them commissions allowing them to carry a revolver; and at the time of this battle these men all had commissions and were armed, and our men didn't have anything and couldn't get anything. I think that is about all my experience; but Mrs. Thomas can tell just a little bit more...

COMMISSIONER HARRIMAN. Mrs. Jolly, do you know how many of the strikers are Greek? That is one statement made, that they were nearly all Greeks and that a great many of the men had been soldiers in the war.

MRS. JOLLY. Why, I think if I was giving my own judgment about it, I should say probably about one-fourth of them were Greeks. We had 21 different nationalities in the Ludlow tent colony. Now, you can imagine how many Greeks out of those; and there was about 1,000 inhabitants, I should say, probably one-fourth of them Greeks.

COMMISSIONER BALLARD. You spoke of Louis Tikas as leader of the strikers?

MRS. JOLLY. Yes, sir.

COMMISSIONER BALLARD. Was he a Greek also?

MRS. JOLLY. Yes, sir....

COMMISSIONER BALLARD. Was Louis Tikas himself a miner?

MRS. JOLLY. Yes, sir.

COMMISSIONER BALLARD. Had he been working in the mines up to the time of the strike?

MRS. JOLLY. He came in there from Denver. Up to the time of the strike he had been working for the mines at Louisville—Louisville, not working in our vicinity, but in the northern mines.

COMMISSIONER BALLARD. And he came down from Denver to help the strikers?

MRS. JOLLY. Yes, sir.

COMMISSIONER BALLARD. What did he do in Denver?

MRS. JOLLY. He had previously worked in the mines, and at one time was, I know, in the insurance company; but just before the strike he had worked in the mines there.

COMMISSIONER BALLARD. Well, just before he came down to the strike colony, what had he been doing in Denver? What was his business in Denver?

MRS. JOLLY. I couldn't tell you. I think he came from one of the mining camps, just the other side of Denver—Louisville—no; Frederick.

COMMISSIONER BALLARD. Did he and his brother have a saloon in Denver?

MRS. JOLLY. I don't think so. I never heard of it if they did. I don't know.

COMMISSIONER BALLARD. You were in the tent colony the day of the battle, and what day was that; do you remember?

MRS. JOLLY. That was the 20th of April.

COMMISSIONER BALLARD. You were in the colony at the time of the fire?

MRS. JOLLY. Yes, sir. . . .

COMMISSIONER BALLARD. You say the financial secretary was an old man?

MRS. JOLLY. Yes, sir.

COMMISSIONER BALLARD. He was killed that day?

MRS. JOLLY. Yes, sir.

COMMISSIONER BALLARD. What was his name?

MRS. JOLLY. James Feiler.

COMMISSIONER BALLARD. You said he came back to the tent to get about $300?

MRS. JOLLY. Yes, sir.

COMMISSIONER BALLARD. Where did that three-hundred dollars come from?

MRS. JOLLY. It was the money they allowed them in the camp. Saturdays were pay day in the camp, and this money had been left there, and as the railroad had been sent back, he had not had any chance to send back any Monday morning; and it was money that was left there in the tent, because Saturday was pay day.

COMMISSIONER BALLARD. They paid every Saturday, then?

MRS. JOLLY. Yes.

COMMISSIONER BALLARD. Did he pay all the striking miners that were there?

MRS. JOLLY. Yes, sir.

COMMISSIONER BALLARD. What did he give every miner, if you know?

MRS. JOLLY. Yes. The men got $3, each woman $1, and for every child 50 cents.

COMMISSIONER BALLARD. Where did he get the money to pay them if they were not working?

MRS. JOLLY. Why, it was sent in by the United Mine Workers of America.

CHAIRMAN WALSH. That is all. Thank you, Mrs. Jolly.

TESTIMONY OF JUDGE BEN B. LINDSEY

MR. THOMPSON. Now, just for the purpose of making our record, I will ask you a few preliminary questions. Your name?

JUDGE LINDSEY. My name is Ben. B. Lindsey.

MR. THOMPSON. Your address?

JUDGE LINDSEY. Denver, Colo.

MR. THOMPSON. And your profession or——

JUDGE LINDSEY. I am a lawyer, a judge on the bench, and have been for 15 years or thereabouts, in the city of Denver.

MR. THOMPSON. Now, you may go on with your story....

JUDGE LINDSEY. I would like to state, or make some general statements about the situation down there, or about my mission here. I came to Colorado when I was a small boy about 10 or 11 years of age. I have lived there for 30 years. I know the politics of our State. I know something of the industrial conditions of our State. I know the struggles in the legislature in our State, and I want to say this question in Colorado is a bigger question than a mere question of a strike. It has got beyond that. It is a great political and industrial struggle. It is not local; it is national. The symptoms may be local, like a boil which comes from the humor of the blood, working out that poison. It has broken out in Colorado at one time; it has broken out in Michigan at another time; in West Virginia at another time; in Pennsylvania at another time. It is going to keep on breaking out as long as we continue to put salve on the sore and do nothing to cure the humor in the blood. By that I mean you have got to go deeply into fundamental questions concerning rights of property and the rights of humanity. And I would like to give a few concrete illustrations, if I may with your permission, to explain to you why I am interested as a citizen in these questions and why I think I have a right to come to this commission from the people of Colorado and to the President of the United States and the people of the East.

In the first place, I have been judge of the children's court anyway 15 years. I have helped to establish those courts in this city and in nearly every city in this country. But I know how futile and absurd that sort of work is if it stopped there. For an example, this court deals with dependent children as well as delinquent children. Numbers of dependent children come to those courts every year—increasing numbers—and we are not going to help them by sitting on a bench and trying these cases. For instance, in Colorado the official report issued by the secretary of the board of charities and corrections, taken from the coal-mine inspectors' reports, showing that in the space of about four years, limited to three or four counties in the State of Colorado where coal is mined, nearly 700 little children were made orphans or fatherless and dependents because of explosions in these coal mines, a large number of which, if indeed not the greater number of which, might have been avoided had the ordinary safety appliances been employed that are employed in other countries, where such accidents are as 1 to 3 as compared with the number in this country. The testimony seems to be undisputed. As I understand, and there is much evidence to prove it if it is disputed, that about three times as many men are blown up in the coal mines of Colorado as are blown up in the coal mines in other States, and the claim of the men is that it is due largely to incompetence; that it is due largely to carelessness; that it is due largely to unwillingness to use the dividends, or rather to use the money, to purchase and install the safety appliances that ought to be installed and to the control of public officials or the refusal to permit public officials to inspect these mines. . . .

Now Mr. Chairman and gentlemen and Mrs. Harriman of this committee, this thing is deep down, and this sore is the result of long years of lawlessness and oppression on the part of the utility corporations. I know whereof I speak, when I say to you that they have owned judges on the bench as they have owned their office boys; that they have owned judges on the supreme bench as they have owned their office boys; that they have controlled those judges; that they have controlled district attorneys; that they have controlled governors; that they have been in the most perfidious deals to control the agencies and officers of the law time and time again, so that they not only make the law to suit their own wishes, primarily—though it does not always do it—to protect property and stand against the rights of humanity; but when occasionally, as happens after a long struggle against every step of the way—for there is terrific opposition to get a law through for the protection of human rights—they control through the bipartisan machine in Colorado the agencies of the law and prevent the enforcement of those laws.

And now, members of this commission, what is that? It is violence. It is the most terrific violence in the world. It is the kind of action that raises the coal dust all over this country, and that thing is going to be exploded, if we don't correct it. That is our contention. Now we don't want it to be, but they are doing the thing, as much as the other people. And I am not saying that there is not fault on both sides, but my contention is this, that violence produces violence every time. That is the law of nature —as hate produces hate; and when through these conditions—not so bad, I am glad to say as they have been in the past, but I would not have you understand that our officers are all controlled by these forces.

There are honorable men on the bench; there are honorable district attorneys; there are fearless district attorneys; there have been some fearless governors as there have been fearless judges. But those men have been fearless at terrific sacrifices as a rule, knowing all the time that they were doomed for slaughter, political or otherwise, if they attempted to call their souls their own. This has been the condition of terror which the industrial government of Colorado, backed by the industrial government of this country with its seat in New York City, has ever shown against the political government in Colorado, and, for that matter in this Nation, in a measure. . . .

Now, Mr. Chairman, I have talked to many witnesses of the Ludlow horror, to come back to that, as one of the moving causes that produces hate. I have read the affidavits and I have the testimony here before the coroner's jury. I have affidavits here that I have read and pored over and gone over, and in those affidavits and in that testimony, it is shown here, an indifference, with a brutality, with a cruelty, the like of which I never heard of outside of savage warfare, militiamen, officers or men, gave the orders to destroy and burn up this tent colony. And I am here on the strength of this testimony, assuming it to be true, and assuming also there may be testimony to the contrary, to say that a case to that effect, a prima facie case, has been made out, that certainly demands some very strong testimony to refute.

There is the testimony of the stenographer before the military commission, who says that he heard the order given to burn up this tent colony, and it was given by one or two—one or two of these officers whom he knows, and here is the testimony of an unbiased, unprejudiced man who drove an automobile, who was held up on the road by the soldiers and compelled to deliver over his automobile, in which there was a machine gun that mounted a hill overlooking Ludlow, and that machine gun, with a brutality and cruelty, the like of which has never been equaled, so far as I know, was turned on these defenseless women and children, their tents, that are their houses and their habitations—residence, if you please—so that it was either an alternative of these women and children going into these pits that had been prepared for them through a foresight for which I think they are to be commended, or else being stricken down by the bullets of these men who could not have been responsible, for it is not an act of civilized warfare, if you please, to turn machine guns and rifles upon a tent colony in which it is known by those who are responsible and those who do the deeds that there are defenseless women and children. . . .

My point is, and I wish to make it clear, that that is not a matter merely of the present strife. It is bigger than the question of the present strife. For, however important it is, Mr. Chairman, to settle that strike, and it is important, and I was sent here by a great number of citizens of Colorado to help bring about the set-tlement—it is only temporary; it is only one of the lulls to the storm that is ahead in this country, unless the men who benefit through these laws of property and who are gradually gaining to themselves the natural resources of this country, are willing to see that they have certain duties and responsibilities that are not altogether impersonal, and are willing to share with these men. But that they have not done. They have recurrently refused to treat with them. They have said there was not anything to arbi-trate; but in saying there wasn't anything to arbitrate, they are falsifying, for there is much to arbitrate, and I think that will be shown by the congressional investigation that has been going on in our State for some time. . . .

My plea is for a better understanding of these questions. There-fore, I thought if I came over to New York after the President of the United States had given us a most courteous hearing, that

Mr. Rockefeller himself would be willing to see me and permit me to present this phase of the situation. But after a courteous request for that privilege he has refused, not only to see me, but while I am of no particular consequence perhaps, I think it is of great consequence that he should have heard the miners' wives whom you courteously and kindly and considerately heard here yesterday, whom the President of the United States heard, because, I contend that when men receive profits or have possessions that promise profits, they haven't any right to take the impersonal view that he takes, and deny any responsibility. Kings have gone down among their people, even in the days of the old feudalists, or even in modern conditions, we have known of kings going among their people and lending them succor and help and not being so impersonal and above them that they would not listen to their woes and troubles and miseries, and be willing to lend something of themselves to really find the cause of these things, and help to solve them, and surely Mr. Rockefeller is no bigger than the President of the United States. He isn't any bigger than kings, who have done it. But in the new feudalism that exists in Colorado, where towns are built up and owned by private corporations, if you please, these men refuse any present relation to conditions like these, refuse—those at the top—to listen to the wails and pleas and explanations and the facts which might be presented by these women. And I say that that attitude of such men is doing more to produce lawlessness and talk about confiscation and what they call anarchy than all the anarchists I know, and the men who stand for that sort of thing in the opinion of some of us who have studied these industrial conditions, if they are ever injured and harmed, and I pray God they never will be, they can damn nobody but themselves, because it is simply a new and novel method of committing suicide, and the President ought to grab men like that and save them from jumping into the river, like the policeman would grab the poor devil on the street who attempted to jump in the river, because that is the way they are going, and I think he ought to do it. . . .

COMMISSIONER O'CONNELL. Judge, the law creating this commission instructs them to seek and find the underlying causes of industrial unrest and report a remedy. What do you think the commission should do with reference to that situation in Colorado or that it should report to Congress as a result of your instruction?

JUDGE LINDSEY. It is a mighty big question, Mr. Commissioner, to go into details. Still, I think you will have to report to Congress that there has got to be some great big changes made in the laws of property in this country, or the possession of property, or the private ownership in coal mines or other great public necessities must be changed entirely, because there must be some power that can settle disputes that are going to continue right along. Now, just what the detail of that might be would take us into all sorts of sociological discussions.

COMMISSIONER O'CONNELL. Would it mean compulsory arbitration, or would you ——

JUDGE LINDSEY. No; I don't say that. But I do believe that in the case of the Erdman Act, recently amended providing for voluntary arbitration, and the working of that came through one of your commission, Mrs. Harriman, largely, and the work we appreciate, and I feel that the public sentiment is so powerful that in a case like this, that if we have a law in Colorado such as you have in the Erdman Act, with reference to transportation companies, that if we had a law in Colorado in reference to our coal-mining property, or with reference to any of the other natural resources that provided for voluntary arbitration, sir, in a case like this right now, the high degree of public sentiment and public opinion in our State is so strong that neither party would dare to refuse to submit their side of this controversy to such a board.

COMMISSIONER O'CONNELL. Would you extend the authority of that law, then, to cover mines and mining?

JUDGE LINDSEY. Yes, sir; I think it should be, and the Government, Federal Government, should pass a law refusing to give title to any more lands that contain natural resources like coal, but should provide a leasing system, if you please, where the title remains in the Government, and with the right of the Government, if you please, always to settle disputes of this kind when they menace the peace and happiness of a whole State or any part of the Nation. . . .

COMMISSIONER GARRETSON. Is there any difference of interest or action between the different classes of mine owners of the State of Colorado; that is, metalliferous or coal?

JUDGE LINDSEY. No; but with unions and possessions, they represent a solidarity when it comes to these questions.

COMMISSIONER GARRETSON. Applies equally to the time when they had a universal association?

JUDGE LINDSEY. Absolutely; just as strong as ever.

COMMISSIONER LENNON. Judge, what has been the power of political domination in Huerfano and Las Animas Counties by the coal companies as to the election of sheriffs, coroners, prosecuting attorneys, and the other officers?

JUDGE LINDSEY. As a rule, with a possible few exceptions, and I can recall no exceptions now, they have been absolutely the State, absolutely the State. The sheriffs and officers of that kind were, with a few exceptions, at different times when they broke through the lines, no more than their office boys. Not as much so, because an office boy can quit, and there is difficulty even if they could quit if they wanted to.

CHAIRMAN WALSH. That is all, Judge. You will be excused. Thank you.

JUDGE LINDSEY. I wish to thank the commission for the privilege of appearing before you.

TESTIMONY OF LT. COL. EDWARD J. BOUGHTON

MR. THOMPSON. Mr. Boughton, will you please give us your full name and spell it?

MR. BOUGHTON. Edward J. Boughton.

MR. THOMPSON. And your address?

MR. BOUGHTON. Denver, Colo.

MR. THOMPSON. Your occupation or profession?

MR. BOUGHTON. Attorney at law.

MR. THOMPSON. Do you have some position with the Militia of the State of Colorado?

MR. BOUGHTON. I hold a Commission in the National Guard of Colorado.

MR. THOMPSON. What is that commission?

MR. BOUGHTON. Major of infantry.

MR. THOMPSON. In regard to the late trouble in the State of Colorado, did you serve with the militia in any districts where trouble had occurred, for instance, at Ludlow?

MR. BOUGHTON. Yes, sir.

MR. THOMPSON. How long did you stay there, and when did the service end, and in what capacity did you serve?

MR. BOUGHTON. On the 26th of October, 1913, his excellency the Governor of Colorado issued an executive order calling out all troops of the National Guard to the occupation of the disturbed regions of the State. That order was executed on the 28th of October by the sending of an incomplete brigade of the State troops to the southern fields where they occupied a line of about 120 miles long through the counties of Las Animas and Huerfano, with expeditions into other and remote fields of the State. That occupation continued until the 14th of April, 1914. During all of that time I served in the field with my command, and later I detached from my command as judge advocate of the military district, which the commanding general established by order of the governor.

MR. THOMPSON. Where first did you take the field when you were called out in October?

MR. BOUGHTON. I entrained at Denver and proceeded to Trinidad in Las Animas County, where I arrived on the 29th of October early in the morning. I remained in Trinidad until the 20th of November, at which time I was detailed as judge advocate, when the judge advocate's department was created. From that time, with headquarters at Trinidad, I moved about the whole district in the discharge of my work, in the conduct of my investigations and accumulation and accretion of evidence and information to be submitted to the military commission, or for the compilation of the reports to the governor. That was the work of the judge advocate.

MR. THOMPSON. What would these investigations that you would make, as judge advocate, cover? What kind of trouble? What manner of trouble?

MR. BOUGHTON. At first, in factions, interfering with a solution of the peace problem. I can illustrate that perhaps vividly in this way: It would be reported that at one of the detached posts, of which there were 32 over that line of 120 miles, an incipient riot had occurred, which was produced by a speech, we will say, of some individual connected with one side or the other of the industrial conflict. The evidence concerning that episode would be taken. The utterances of the man in question would be ascertained, all of that would be submitted to the commission, by whose collective judgment it would then be determined whether it was wise or necessary to detail that individual for a while as a peace measure. Afterwards, of course, we had assignments from the governor, where we were required to investigate and report to him the facts of particular assigned instances.

MR. THOMPSON. Were you requested by the governor to examine into the causes of the battle at Ludlow?

Mr. Boughton. Yes, sir.

Mr. Thompson. On Monday, April 20th?

Mr. Boughton. Yes, sir.

Mr. Thompson. Of this year?

Mr. Boughton. Yes, sir.

Mr. Thompson. In what capacity did you act there? In the same capacity?

Mr. Boughton. In the same capacity.

Mr. Thompson. Did you have with you a board?

Mr. Boughton. Yes, sir; a board of officers.

Chairman Walsh. As briefly and concisely as you can, give us the facts in connection with the Ludlow matter.

Mr. Boughton. Yes, sir. May I ask leave to use a drawing which I have which will expedite, perhaps, the explanation I can make of the incident?

Chairman Walsh. Just give it to the stenographer and he will mark it.

You might pass one to the commission for them to examine.

Mr. Boughton. Only one-half of the drawing is the map of that vicinity. At the point Ludlow, on the point of the Colorado Southern Railroad, which is the artery of commerce north and south between Trinidad and Denver, the two canyons converge at that point and enter the plains or prairies. That is where the hills end and plains begin. Up those two canyons are the largest coal mines of the State. At the point where the canyons converge and the wagon roads from each cross the railroad tracks was located the Ludlow tent colony. That point is commonly called in that vicinity the "crossroads." Across the railroad track and to the west about 550 yards away from the tent colony was established a detached post of the militia where there had been in the field a couple of companies of infantry and a troop of so-called mounted infantry.

On the 14th of April all of these militiamen were withdrawn, together with all other militiamen all over the State, except that there were left to do police duty merely at that immediate point of Ludlow 34 men. Of that 34 men there were 12 who occupied the tents that I speak of across the railroad track from the tent colonies, the other 22 occupying a detached camp about a mile and a half away and out of sight of the two groups of tents. The tent colony was inhabited by a good many hundred people among whom there were 22 languages used, indistinguishable and not understood one of another.

Sunday, April 19, was, according to the Greek Church, the Greek Easter; it did not come when our Easter comes. It had been anticipated that so soon as the troops were withdrawn some sort of disturbance would occur by reason of a clash between the remaining militiamen and the occupants of some tent colony, not particularly this one. The clash occurred within one week after the withdrawal of the troops. We learned from certain prisoners of war, using that term for want of another one, who were inhabitants of the tent colony, that the attack had been planned for Sunday, the Greek Easter. It was postponed, however, until the next morning. This tent colony had been searched by direction of the governor for concealed arms four different times, each time with increasingly angry resentment of the inhabitants of the colony, quite emphatically expressed.

It was not supposed, Mr. Thompson, it was not known to contain any arms whatever at the time the troops were withdrawn. On the morning of April 20, a Monday morning, there came to the tents of the commander of the National Guard a woman who claimed that her husband was detained against his will in the tent colony and asked help to obtain his release. At that time there were occupying the five remaining tents of the militiamen only the 12 men of whom I spoke, of whom 10 were absent on ordinary camp duty; some were quartering their horses at a considerable distance from the camp, almost a mile, and others were upon the train detail. The train detail is a detail of three or four men who are kept constantly at the depot to protect incoming and outgoing passengers upon the trains against a police infraction by the inhabitants of the tent colony. There were only two men, the commanding officer, Maj. Hamrock, and a cripple, in the tent at the time the woman called and for some considerable time afterwards and until after the battle, so called, started. The commanding officer telephoned to his train detail at the depot to go to the tent colony and ask for the woman's husband, which was done.

Each nationality in the tent colony had its own leader, but the Greeks of the colony were the force of that population. We learned that a considerable portion of them had returned from service in the Balkan wars; they were regarded, perhaps, by their fellows as men of experience and heroes. At any rate, the head of the Greek contingent was the head of the colony. His name was Tikas, commonly called Louie the Greek in that vicinity. He it was who was killed afterwards in the day. The Greek leader answered the train contingent that he understood the troops had been withdrawn from the field and asked him if he had a civil warrant calling for the production of any prisoner that they might have. There were some words passed, heated words between the soldiers, enlisted men, and Tikas, and I think it safe to say that the militiamen said to Tikas, "We will come back later in force and get that man. We know you have him."

The train detail returned to the depot and telephoned to the commanding officer of the tents that they were unable to get the man and that Tikas denied having him and denied the right of the militia to make a search for him. Maj. Hamrock then telephoned to Tikas himself and asked Mr. Tikas to come to his tent —that is, the tent of the National Guard, which Tikas, for the first time, flatly refused to do. It had been a matter of daily occurrence for Tikas to come to the tent of the commanding officer of the guard or the commanding officer to go over to his tent and discuss the peace problem.

I may say for this Tikas that his presence in the tent colony was for good. He was a restraining influence among his own people.

CHAIRMAN WALSH. How old a man was Mr. Tikas?

MR. BOUGHTON. That is hard to say. I should judge him to be about 40 or 45 years of age, but he was a man, rather dark, sallow complexion, and hard to judge his age.

CHAIRMAN WALSH. That is all right.

MR. BOUGHTON. He was not a coal miner. He lived in Denver and was at one time the head of a combination of bootblacks of that city.

CHAIRMAN WALSH. Had he never been a coal miner?

MR. BOUGHTON. He testified before the commission that he had done some coal mining at one time in the northern part of the State for a short interval, but at the time the strike broke out. After Tikas declined to come to Maj. Hamrock's tent, Maj. Hamrock telephoned to his detachment at Cedar Hill, the 22 men, and directed that they should proceed to a hill in plain view of the tent colonies and the military camp, and they drew there. That had been done a great many times before. It was a moral move, having troops in sight when we knew that we were going

to have to insist upon some determined position with the tent
colony people. The detachment, except four men, at once came
to this hill, marked on the map "Water Tank Hill." In the meantime, it seems, that, according to a preconceived design, the Greek
inhabitants of the tent colony to the number of 35 armed themselves inside the colony, with the avowed intention of attacking
the camp. The evening before at a near-by nonunion mine 2 of
those 35 Greeks, afterwards engaged in the battle, visited a cousin
of theirs who was at work, a nonunion man, and advised him con-
fidentially that this attack would be delivered the next morning
and that upon the wiping out of these soldiers, the attack would
proceed against the property where he was at work, and urging
him to be absent on that day. The information was at once communicated to the superintendent of the mine by the employee so
advised, and it was afterwards communicated to Maj. Hamrock.
It seemed that while Louis Tikas was talking with Maj. Hamrock
over the telephone, in the intervals of two conversations that he
had —

CHAIRMAN WALSH (interrupting). Did you ever meet Mr. Tikas
personally?

MR. BOUGHTON. Oh, yes; I knew him quite well. We had him
before the commission a number of times.

CHAIRMAN WALSH. Go ahead.

MR. BOUGHTON. It seems that he was arguing with his armed
Greeks, his armed compatriots, urging them to refrain from this
intended attack. He finally got so far that he said they promised
that they would refrain from any overt act until he had seen
Hamrock.

After the major had telephoned for his detachment to come
to the hill, Louis Tikas then called the major up a second time,
after having the promise of his Greeks to refrain until he could
call Maj. Hamrock. It is supposed that the conversation was over-
heard by somebody in the tent colony, for it is a known fact that
all the wires in that vicinity are so tapped as that conversations
over them are quite generally heard. I may pause to say here
that that accounts for the episode, perhaps related to you by one
of the tent colony inhabitants here, that she heard telephone conversations between other people. She, of course, has determined
for herself who those people were and what the conversation was.
But, at any rate, at the close of the conversation between the commanding officer and his detachment, Louis Tikas called up the

major and asked to see him at the depot, a neutral position, which was accepted; and Maj. Hamrock and Louis Tikas were in the depot talking; and Maj. Hamrock had with him a woman, who was complaining of the imprisonment of her husband, and Louis Tikas, upon seeing who the woman was, said that he recognized who she was and now knew who was meant by her husband; that he had been in the colony the day before but was not there then. About that time the commanding officer of the detachment coming from Cedar Hills rode up to report the arrival of his detachment on Water Tank Hill to the commanding officer at the depot. He was returned to his detachment. But he had gone but a very little ways when he hastily returned to the major inside of the depot, saying, "My God, Major! I wish you would look at these men" [indicating an easterly direction] and added, "We are in for it for sure." Thereupon Tikas and the major and the officer came out of the depot and discovered the rest of the Greeks whom Tikas had left in the tent colony crossing the open space between the colony in an easterly direction to the railroad cut indicated upon the map. [Here witness indicates.] The chief cover in that country for any infantry report. It was told to us, and I believe it to be true, that after Tikas left the tent colony to call upon Maj. Hamrock the appearance of the troops in plain view on Water Tank Hill so excited them that they forgot their promise to their leader to refrain until his return, and simply filed out. Tikas remarked to Maj. Hamrock as he left the depot, "I will call them back." As he ran toward the colony waving his arms to his Greeks to return, and saying with an oath, "What fools they are." He was unable to accomplish anything in that direction. The Greeks continued to cross the plains to the cut. Tikas evidently seeing that he could accomplish nothing further by way of restraint then went into the colony, where he was plainly seen shortly afterwards emerging with a gun in one hand and a field glass in the other. From that time forward he joined his compatriots and became a combatant in the day's events. During the crossing of the Greek contingent from the tent colony to the railroad cut, they were in plain view of the troops on Water Tank Hill. The troops there almost rebelled against their officers who were holding their fire. They vociferously urged that the Greeks, armed as they were, ought not to be permitted to take the cover of the railroad cut before the militiamen were permitted to open their fire upon them. However, they were successfully restrained.

We get that from all sources. In the interim, and while the de-
filing was being made into the railroad cut, Maj. Hamrock
called a second time to Cedar Hill, to the force that remained,
ordering that they change their command to Water Tank Hill
and bring along with them the machine gun that was kept at
Cedar Hill. There had been constructed a couple of crude dyna-
mite bombs. It had been arranged that these would be exploded if an attack of this kind was made as a signal to inhabitants
of the coal-mining towns up the canyons that the attack had
begun, in order that these might prepare themselves for what
would follow.

Those bombs were exploded as they signaled, and that was the
first explosion of the day. Almost at once, after the explosion of
the bombs, the Greeks having obtained cover, opened fire upon
the camp of the militia. During the crossing of the Greeks to the
railroad cut the women and children from the tent colony were
seen leaving the colony and hastening to an arroyo in the rear of
the colony indicated upon the map. In our country that word
means a dry creek, a dry deep creek. It is what ought to be a
creek, but never is; it has not any water in it at all at any time
of the year. This was from 10 to 20 feet deep at places, and 20
to 30 feet wide. Under the protection of the arroyo, the women
and children of the colony were able by following the arroyo out
to the plains to reach farmhouses and other places of safety at a
great distance away. Armed men in large numbers were seen at
the same time also seeking the cover of the arroyo. After the open-
ing of the attack by the Greeks in the railroad cut upon the
soldiers, at once the whole arroyo in sight delivered a fusillade of
shots. Those were answered by the 12 men in the tent and by
the 22 men on Water Tank Hill, together with the machine gun
at that place. From that time the history of the battle, so called,
is a history of the advance of the 22 men on Water Tank Hill
along the line of the railroad after dislodging the Greeks in the
cut, without which, of course, the advance could not be begun.
The advance of the 22 along the railroad passed the colony to
the capture of the steel bridge over the arroyo and the taking of
the arroyo. That was not accomplished until evening.

Early in the day three sorties were made by four men each
from Water Tank Hill, in an effort to dislodge the Greeks in the
cut. In one of the sorties a private soldier was wounded. When
a sortie retreated, as it had to do, they tried to carry with them

the wounded comrade. They had to abandon him under the cover of a bush. They were not able to retrieve that ground.

COMMISSIONER O'CONNELL. What do you mean by the private soldier?

MR. BOUGHTON. A private soldier of the National Guard, one of the troop on Water Tank Hill. They were not able to recover the ground until afternoon. In the meantime the Greeks from the country had themselves made sorties against Water Tank Hill, and had arrived on two different occasions at about the spot where the private soldier had been left, the wounded soldier had been left. In the afternoon when this soldier was discovered he was found dead, his arms broken, his face mashed, and otherwise horribly mutilated.

In the afternoon the Greeks were dislodged from the railroad cut and the advance on the arroyo was commenced. That advance was covered by the machine guns. The machine guns were not used against the tent colony. There is no fact better established than that. The tent colony has in front of it several wooden structures, a blacksmith shop, chicken coops, fences and posts, no one of which exhibits any shots from a machine gun, or from any other weapons, so far as that goes; whereas the fences along the railroad right of way, the water tanks, other buildings, are riddled with machine-gun bullets. The machine gun was used along the right of way of the railroad to cover the advance of the troops.

About 7 o'clock at night the advance had so far proceeded as to arrive at the crossroads, that is to say, at the tent colony itself. At that time, the impact of a bullet with some high-explosive material inside one of the tents caused the tent to catch fire. The first was accidental in its origin. I shall show you afterwards that it was deliberately spread by members of the National Guard. Three tents exploded high in the air. Afterwards we took several thousand rounds, 19,000 rounds of ammunition out of the tent marked "Headquarters, John R. Lawson." The fire being under way, and our men having arrived close to the tent colony, it was then discovered by the officers that the tent colony contained women and children; screams were heard from inside the colony. You must know, gentlemen, ladies and gentlemen, that in front of the colony on all sides were located carefully constructed earthworks, rifle pits, constructed in such a position as that any return of the fire from them was drawn right into the colony.

Having taken the children and women over to the arroyo early in the morning, and discovering these rifle pits being used against us and drawing the fire of all the troops into the tent colony itself, it could not be supposed that any women and children were in it, but upon our discovering that they were, and the tents having begun to burn, the officers of the National Guard made several passes into the colony for the purpose of removing them, in which they were successful. They removed in that way 36 women and children; reluctant in the doing of that rescue work, the officers were constantly under fire from the arroyo and from the rear of the tents. Notwithstanding which, and the reluctance of the women and children to come out, 36 of them were removed. A great part of these were removed from cellars or dugouts constructed beneath the tents. One dugout in particular, that is depicted on the map accurately, was not discovered until Wednesday morning. It was almost sealed, hermetically sealed, and the entrance to it was concealed by furniture in the room. In that place, on Wednesday morning, there were removed, with one exception to be presently noted, the only people who died in the colony, the 2 women and 11 children who were found suffocated. There was not a mark on their bodies. They were not shot; they were not burned, or even charred, and the position of the bodies in the remote corner of the dugout, and not in the entrance, evidenced that at the time they died they were not making any effort to crowd out into the air. Expert testimony before the board of officers is to the effect that the oxygen in this chamber was not sufficient to support the lives of 13 people, 2 of them adults, for more than two hours. They died probably early in the day. So later this morning in almost every paper in New York there appears reiterated the assertion that women and children were killed, were burned, were shot, using all of those words in the Ludlow tent colony. That is not a fact. It is common with some of those who have appeared before you, and whom I heard in Washington and in New York, at public gatherings, to use the word massacre, variously pronounced by the witnesses, and the impression that there was a massacre—

CHAIRMAN WALSH. I don't understand what you mean by variously pronounced massacre.

MR. BOUGHTON. I want to emphasize the particular word, because to me it seems important. There was no such thing as the Ludlow massacre. Nobody was massacred at Ludlow. Nobody was killed at Ludlow in the tent colony or burned, with the one exception of a small child by the name of Snyder, who during the day, according to the statement of his father, made at the time he was holding the body of the dead child in his arms to officers of the National Guard in large numbers, was that the child had gone out of his tent in the afternoon, had faced toward the arroyo for a private purpose and was shot in the forehead from the direction of the position of the tent colonist combatants; that he was not shot by the troops of the State. At that time the father's resentment seemed to run against the Greeks, who had precipitated the struggle in which his child was slain. A collection was taken up among the officers of the guard for this one man, who was destitute of all means of arriving at Trinidad, with a large family of children, and by that means he was enabled to take the train and go to Trinidad and not to walk over the hills as the other refugees did.

MR. THOMPSON. I would like to ask at that point, Major, from whom did you get the testimony at your hearings?

MR. BOUGHTON. I beg your pardon?

MR. THOMPSON. From what kind of people, from whom did you get your testimony?

MR. BOUGHTON. From all of the officers of the National Guard, from all of the enlisted men, privately examined. That is one out of the presence of the others, so that we could get all of the stories without there appearing any agreement or convention as to what should be told, and we discovered a great many things by that means. From the inhabitants of the town of Ludlow, who were in the main sympathizers with the colonists in their struggle industrially; from certain of the inhabitants of the tent colony; from the coroner and the transcript of the testimony adduced before his jury; from a physical examination of the field itself. I think that exhausts an enumeration of the means.

MR. THOMPSON. In other words, there were no strikers or union representatives appeared or were heard at those inquests—at those inquiries?

MR. BOUGHTON. As a matter of fact, there were none. We made every effort to obtain a number and that effort is progressing still. We urged the appearance of Mr. Lawson and Mr. McClinnon, in Denver, after our return to tell what they knew or they could obtain for us. We urged the cooperation of their head man in Trinidad, who promised us that we should have it, but reconsidered his determination. A personal interview with Mr. McClinnon and Mr. John R. Lawson in Denver by one of our number, Gov. Danks. A personal request made of them was answered by their attorney in their presence—Mr. Harris N. Hawkins—that the officials of the United Mine Workers must decline to supply us with any information they possessed, upon the ground that our hearings were not conducted in public.

CHAIRMAN WALSH. Are your hearings only adjourned now, Major?

MR. BOUGHTON. Upon this feature they are closed; but it was a part of the recommendation of the board of officers, who did not feel itself constituted to determine the guilt or innocence of individuals, that a court-martial be organized and try all of the officers involved for every crime of which they had been accused in the newspapers, and that court-martial is progressing, ordered by the governor under our recommendation.

To resume: After the rescue work had progressed, which was attended with a number of incidents displaying real heroism—I do not hesitate to make that assertion on the part of some of the officers of the National Guard—and the tents being on fire, the Greek leader, Louis Tikas, was taken personally, together with another officer of the local union by the name of Fyler about the same time. Then another person whose name I have not. These three prisoners were taken to the crossroads, where were a group of soldiers and unorganized enlisted men in civilian clothing, from the camp up Hastings Canyon. The cry went up from that group numbering 40 or 50.

The cry went up "We have got Louey." It was proposed to hang him up. And that proposition was so far carried into effect that a rope was obtained and thrown over a telegraph pole. At this point, at this time, a lieutenant of the guard, the one who is being particularly assailed, Lieut. K. E. Linderfelt, arrived. He said, "There will be no hanging here." He had to fight with his men in order to prevent, or to successfully prevent, the hanging of Tikas. He did not get into an altercation with Tikas himself. What they said is unimportant excepting—unless you would like to know it.

CHAIRMAN WALSH. Was anybody there except his own troop and Tikas?

MR. BOUGHTON. Oh, yes. It so transpired that there are a number of officers in the National Guard who do not like Linderfelt, who happened to be in this group and who were ready to tell from an anti-Linderfelt standpoint all the incidents that occurred.

CHAIRMAN WALSH. Were there any of the Greeks there, any of Tikas's companions, or was he alone with Linderfelt and his soldiers?

MR. BOUGHTON. No, sir. These three prisoners were there with their 40 or 50 captors; yes, sir.

CHAIRMAN WALSH. Then there were 3 prisoners and 40 or 50 soldiers?

MR. BOUGHTON. Yes, sir. I am going now to an incident which is quite indefensible on the part of any National Guardsman. In the altercation between Tikas and Linderfelt, Linderfelt hit Tikas over the head with a Springfield rifle. It is true that it broke the stock of the rifle. This was shortly after. I believe that I owe this to Lieut. Linderfelt, to add at this point, that this was shortly after Lieut. Linderfelt had repeatedly risked his life by exposing himself to the fire of the adversaries in the rescue of their women and children. He did more in that respect than any other officer.

CHAIRMAN WALSH. Well, you say that in justice to him or in justification for him hitting Mr. Tikas?

MR. BOUGHTON. That is all.

CHAIRMAN WALSH. Why do you mention it at that point? I just want to get your viewpoint.

MR. BOUGHTON. Because, I think, having made the assertion that Lieut. Linderfelt's act in striking a prisoner of war is wholly indefensible, and having emphasized that at that place I think that it is just to Linderfelt to make mention at the same time of something that redounds to his credit. After Tikas arose from the blow—he dropped to his knee and after he arose from the blow Lieut. Linderfelt then carried Tikas and Fyler, the other prisoner, over to a noncommissioned officer, giving him strict injunctions as to their safety, telling him that he would hold the noncommissioned officer responsible for Tikas's life.

CHAIRMAN WALSH. Where did Linderfelt get this rifle that he struck Mr. Tikas with?

MR. BOUGHTON. Using it all day long, sir.

CHAIRMAN WALSH. He had been using a rifle himself?

MR. BOUGHTON. Yes sir; we had so few men there that the officers had to get on the firing line. He then returned to the depot in the discharge of his duties, sir. After the departure of Lieut. Linderfelt you are to observe now that we are at the crossroads

opposite the tent colony. That is where the incident occurred that
I have just related. After the discharge of the lieutenant, Tikas
and Fyler, the other prisoner, were slain between the railroad
track and the beginning of the tents.The evidence is conflicting,
and we had so to report to the governor, as to how they came by
their death. According to some, Tikas attempted to escape after
a fire had been opened up from the rear of the tent colony upon
the group at the crossroads, the group falling to the protection of
the railroad bank; that when the fire started up there Tikas and
the other prisoner made a dash into the tents and were caught
between the fire of the troops and their adversaries and so killed.
Another statement is that Tikas at least was compelled to run
into that fire; that he was shoved over the embankment into the
crossfire between the National Guard and their adversaries and
so slain.

CHAIRMAN WALSH. Who testified to that?

MR. BOUGHTON. Some—one officer that I know of and two or
three enlisted men. —

CHAIRMAN WALSH. Of your own troops?

MR. BOUGHTON. Yes, sir.

CHAIRMAN WALSH. Those were the ones that were prejudiced
against Lieut. Linderfelt, were they?

MR. BOUGHTON. That had it in for him.

CHAIRMAN WALSH. Those were the ones prejudiced?

MR. BOUGHTON. No; I don't know that they are the same. I can
explain that conflict quite easily. One of the enlisted men said
that as he dropped to the ground behind the railroad bank——

CHAIRMAN WALSH [interrupting]. As who, Mr. Tikas?

MR. BOUGHTON. As he, the witness, dropped to the ground behind the railroad track he saw the man in charge of Tikas shove
him over the bank. Others testified that as they dropped, Tikas
ran over the bank and that his captor, his custodian, made a grab
for him to pull him back. That might easily be the same movement, but the evidence is so conflicting that we could not arrive
at what the real fact was.

CHAIRMAN WALSH. The theory, then, of the testimony of one
side, the witnesses's, was that Tikas was trying to escape under
those circumstances?

MR. BOUGHTON. Yes, sir; he was making a dash. It is only a
short way, some 50 yards at most.

CHAIRMAN WALSH. To where?

MR. BOUGHTON. Into the tents, to his own people.

CHAIRMAN WALSH. Was the fire going on at the time? Was it on fire?

MR. BOUGHTON. Yes, sir; among the first of the tents.

CHAIRMAN WALSH. At what time of day was it?

MR. BOUGHTON. Some time between 7 and 9 o'clock. We have great hardship in fixing the time.

CHAIRMAN WALSH. What date was it?

MR. BOUGHTON. The day of April the 20th. Continuing at any rate, the fact remains that these three men were killed between the railroad tracks and the beginning of the tents and that one of them was shot in the back and one was shot in front as they ran from the direction of the bank to the tent. Fyler was shot in front and Tikas was shot in the back. The only piece of ammunition that was discovered in Tikas's body was of a kind not used by the National Guard; but that is explainable, because there were in the group of National Guardsmen at that time civilians from the coal-mining villages up the canyon, who had come to their assistance.

You must remember, gentlemen, that at the time this fight began it was 350 to 34.

COMMISSIONER O'CONNELL. What was the total number of tents in the camp?

MR. BOUGHTON. Sir, I haven't that data.

COMMISSIONER O'CONNELL. Approximately?

MR. BOUGHTON. Oh, approximately, 100 tents; a large colony. It housed 1,200 people at one time; perhaps 800 there then.

CHAIRMAN WALSH. Proceed.

MR. BOUGHTON. If I may be permitted now to explain the attitude of the National Guard, which throws considerable light upon this episode—the National Guard is composed of the small farmers, tradesmen, professional men of all sorts, artisans, and craftsmen, for the most part—citizens of the State of long standing. It has served under the call of the governor since the 28th of October, the men and officers abandoning their professions and their trades—ruining them. The men and officers have served out of sheer citizenship at a tremendous sacrifice to themselves, incurring the dangers of a peculiar kind of combat. They have not been paid this year. In large numbers of instances their service has been attended with downright suffering at home in their own affairs. They are engaged in keeping the peace endangered by a quarrel that is not theirs—that is wholly impersonal to them; and the governor of the State, at least, feels it due to that body to assert now by whatever means he can find to do it that they did not deliberately burn or murder or kill women and children at Ludlow, or at any other place, but on the contrary their chief efforts were directed, so far as women and children are concerned, to the saving of them from the flames, under the fire of their own people.

CHAIRMAN WALSH. Is that all, Mr. Boughton?

MR. BOUGHTON. That is all, sir.

14. A Michigan mother gave birth in a local hospital to quadruplets. She had been divorced for more than nine years and had not remarried. How would you handle this story?

A GLOSSARY OF NEWSPAPER* TERMINOLOGY

Advance: A news story about a future event.

Banner: A headline that extends across the whole page; also called "streamer" and "line."

Boil: To condense news copy.

Box: A short news story inclosed in rules.

Bulletin: One kind of urgent wire news.

By-line: The writer's name at the top of a news story; sometimes called "signer."

Caption: The descriptive text that accompanies a piece of art.

Chase: A metal frame in which a page of type is assembled and secured by sliding wedges called "quoins"; the quoins "lock up" the page.

Copy cutter: The employee in the composing room who receives editorial copy and apportions it to the individual printers (line-casting machine operators).

Credit line: A line that designates the source of a picture.

Cut: A printing plate that reproduces a photograph or drawing.

Date line: Placed at the beginning of the story, it indicates the place at which an event happened (or from which the story was filed) and sometimes the date the story was filed.

---

* Almost none of radio's terminology refers to the news.

Dummy: A printed form filled in to indicate the placing of individual advertisements, editorial matter and art.

Dupe: Carbon copy of a news story.

Ears: The upper corners of the front page.

Edition: Newspapers printed during one press run and containing the same matter.

Feature: Noun. (1) Generally a news story of human interest that is not spot news; (2) any nonnews matter, such as columns and comic strips; (3) the chief aspect of importance or interest in a news story. Verb. To give prominence to a news story or to a specific element within the news story.

Filler: Standing matter used to fill space when needed.

Flag: The title (i.e., name) of the newspaper at the top of the front page; it is usually a logotype.

Flush left head: Each line of a headline begins at the left-hand margin. Contra: "step head."

Folio: The number of each page.

Fudge box: A morticed space on the front page in which type is inserted after the page has been stereotyped.

Galley: A metal tray used to contain type after it has been set.

Halftone: A printing plate made from photographic copy and consisting of minute dots.

Handout: A publicity release.

HTK or **HTC:** Means "head to come," the copy having been sent to the composing room before the head was written.

Jump: That part of a front page story continued to an inside page.

Kill: Direction to the printer on a proofsheet to eliminate the matter indicated.

Lead (pronounced led): A thin strip of blank metal, usually two points in thickness. To "lead out" means to put these spaces between lines of type that have been set "solid."

Make over: To change the arrangement of type and cuts in a page of type and to cast a new stereotype plate of the page.

Masthead: The standing heading on the editorial page that contains certain information about the newspaper, such as the name of the publisher, the subscription rate, and so forth.

Overhead: A story sent by telegraph instead of by the leased wires.

Overset: Type that has been set for a specific issue of the newspaper in excess of the space available for it.

Pick up: Direction to the printer to add to the relevant story certain matter that is already in type.

Precede: Short or fairly short matter that is put above a news story and below the headline.

Release: The time stated by the news source for publication of an advance item; for example, "For release Tuesday, Sept. 1 at 6:00 P.M." (For both radio and newspaper.)

Replate: To make over a page and stereotype it.

Revise: Noun. A second proofsheet taken to check whether matter corrected on the original proofsheet was corrected as directed.

Rim: The outside edge of a "horseshoe" shaped copy desk at which the copy-readers sit. (See "slot.")

Rule: A typehigh strip of metal for printing a continuous line.

Sidebar: A news story relating to a main news story that is an elaboration of the main story.

Slot: The inside space of a "horseshoe" shaped copy desk at which the "dealer" or head copy-reader sits.

Slug: (1) Any line of type cast by a typecasting machine. (2) The label put on a news story by a copy-reader. (3) A blank spacing strip thicker than a lead.

Stet: "Let it stand." Direction to the printer in the margin of a piece of copy to set the matter even though it has been marked out. In a proofsheet, it means do not eliminate matter that has been marked out.

Stick: About two inches of type; the amount held in the composing stick.

Stringer: A part-time correspondent for a newspaper or news agency who is paid according to the amount of copy he supplies.

Subhead: A descriptive line in the body of the story to break up the solid-appearing type mass.

Take: The portion of a piece of copy to be set by the individual printer and later assembled with "takes" that other printers have set.

Time copy: Nonurgent news copy set in advance to run in early editions or as filler.

Turn rule: A direction to the printer, in connection with an insertion or add, to place at the bottom of the copy a rule that has been turned upside down so that its base (instead of its fine edge) will be visible to the printer when he assembles the parts of the story.

Typo: A typographical error.

Appendix II ···

STYLE GUIDE

CAPITALIZATION

CAPITALIZE:
1. All months and days of the week: April, Tuesday.
2. Titles of books, plays, songs, etc.: "The Man Who Came to Dinner."
3. Titles denoting rank, official position, or occupation when they precede the name: Major Edward Williams, Gov. Murray Wilson, Judge Thomas Martin (but Thomas Martin, judge of the Superior Court).
4. Names of associations, companies, leagues, courts, and other organizations: American Medical Association, American League, Boy Scouts of America, Circuit Court, University of California, Motor Sales Company.
5. Geographical names: the Missouri River, Lake Michigan, Gulf of Mexico.
6. Streets, avenues, buildings, theaters, hotels, etc.: Twenty-first Street, the Blackstone Hotel.
7. Names of religious denominations and words denoting the Deity.
8. Names of political parties.
9. Sections of the country, but not the points of the compass: the West, west.
10. Abbreviations of college degrees: M.A., Ph.D.
11. Names of holidays: Fourth of July, Thanksgiving.
12. Names of races: Negro.

DO NOT CAPITALIZE:
13. Abbreviations of time of day: a.m., p.m., but 12M.
14. Seasons of the year: spring.
15. Names of college classes: sophomore.
16. Points of the compass: west.
17. College degrees when spelled out: bachelor of arts.

239

18. Titles when they follow the name: Thomas Martin, judge of the Superior Court.
19. Names of offices in a list of officers: Samuel Starr, president.

ABBREVIATION

ABBREVIATE:

20. The following titles: Mr., Mrs., Dr., Sen., Rev., Dep. Dist. Atty., Supt., Gov., Lt. Gov., Gen., Adm., 1st Lt., Prof. (only before a full name).
21. Names of states when they follow names of cities: Milwaukee, Wis. (but not "United States").
22. St. and Ste.: St. Louis, Sault Ste. Marie.
23. Names of widely-known organizations and agencies of the government (without periods or spaces): YMCA, DAR, CIO, FCC.

Do Not Abbreviate:

24. Christian names, such as William, Charles.
25. Christmas (not Xmas).
26. Per cent.
27. Names of streets and avenues.

FIGURES

28. Spell out figures less than 10 except in a street number (2342 Market Street) and when the figures are in a series of related expressions (the inventory showed 26 rakes, 2 shovels, 32 spades, and 1 hoe).
29. Avoid unnecessary ciphers: 11 p.m., $9.
30. Spell out numbers when they begin a sentence: Twelve years ago, etc. (When the figure is a large one, use "exactly" or a similar term before the figures: Exactly 12,765 persons voted, etc.)
31. Do not use *st, nd, rd, th* in dates: February 4.
32. Spell out fractions used alone (one-third), but use figures when the fraction is part of a number: 8$\frac{1}{16}$.

THE DATE LINE

33. Capitalize and punctuate the date line this way:
PORTLAND, Ore., Feb. 11—Two men were killed, etc.

PUNCTUATION

34. Numbers of more than four figures should be pointed off with commas: 23,176.
35. Use a colon after a statement introducing a direct quotation of one or more paragraphs and begin a new paragraph for the quotation; also use a colon after "as follows."

36. Omit a period after "per cent" (except when "per cent" is the last word in the sentence).
37. Omit the commas between a man's name and "Jr." and "Sr."
38. Punctuate the score of a game this way: Yale 10, Harvard 7.
39. Do not use a comma in "4 feet 6 inches tall" and similar expressions.

TITLES

40. When a name is used in a story for the first time, give the full name (or initials) with the title. Thereafter do not repeat the full name (or initials) but precede it with a title or "Mr."
41. Use the actual name or titles: School of Law (not Law School), Southern Pacific Lines (not Southern Pacific Railroad).
42. Write the Rev. Milton Mowrer the first time the name is used; thereafter write it Mr. Mowrer.
43. For a clergyman with the D.D. degree, write the Rev. Dr. Milton Mowrer the first time the name is used; thereafter Dr. Mowrer.
44. When the clergyman is a Catholic, write the Rev. Edward Dunne the first time the name is used; thereafter write it Father Dunne.
45. For archbishops of the Catholic clergy, write The Most Rev. Michael Shaughnessy the first time the name is used; thereafter, Archbishop Shaughnessy.
46. Give the title professor only to faculty members who have a professorial rank.
47. Avoid long titles, such as Superintendent of Public Works Mason Brown. Write it: Mason Brown, superintendent of public works.

ADDRESSES

48. In the news story write an address: Miles Nash, 765 Prewitt Street; George Stanwick, Portland, Me.
49. Omit "of" and "at" before an address.

PREPARATION OF COPY

50. Put an end mark (#) at the end of a complete story.
51. Double space your copy and write on only one side of the sheet.

INDEX